THE
P L O T

began   Tues 10 Sept '13

Sat 7

THE
PLOT

A Biography of an
English Acre

MADELEINE
BUNTING

GRANTA

Granta Publications, 12 Addison Avenue, London W11 4QR

First published in Great Britain by Granta Books, 2009

Map 3 on page 108, War: Reproduced by permission
of Ordnance Survey on behalf of HMSO. © Crown Copyright 2009.
All rights reserved. Ordnance Survey licence 100049103.

Map 4 on page 172: A detail of the map of
The County of York Survey'd in MDCCXVII, VIII, IX and
MDCCLXX Engraved by Thomas Jefferys, Geographer to
His Majesty MDCCLXXI Published 25 March 1775 by Robert Sugar
& John Bennett at No 53 Fleet Street. Facsimile published
by Harry Margary, Lympne Castle, Kent 1973.

All photographs and illustrations by the author
except p. 32, Bunting family gathering, private collection,
p. 78, Buff ermine moth by kind permission of Marion Frith
and p. 128, My father, private collection.

Attempts were made to trace the original
of Thirkleby Hall's shooting book on p. 160, but failed.
The publishers will be happy to insert an appropriate
acknowledgement in future editions if
this omission can be rectified.

A CIP catalogue record for this book
is available from the British Library.

1 3 5 7 9 10 8 6 4 2

ISBN 978 1 84708 085 1

Typeset by M Rules
Printed and bound in the UK by
Cromwell Press Group, Trowbridge, Wiltshire

For Eleanor Emma, Luke Maurice
and Matthias Jude

Contents

Contents

List of illustrations

List of maps

Prologue

'Wisdom sits in places' –
a saying of the Western Apache

In London I own a small piece of land. It was laid out as a rectangle of garden by Edwardian property developers, building for the expanding numbers of white-collar workers in a city at the heart of a rapidly globalizing world. For a few years, along with my four brothers and sisters, I co-owned another plot of land, inherited from my father, on a grassy hillside overlooking the Vale of York on the edge of the North York moors.

The soil of the city is rich with its history; the broken pieces of china calling to mind hundreds of years of soups, stews, bread and ale consumed by the generations of human beings who have lived on this piece of land. Many of those pieces are broken into such small fragments that they offer only the most indistinct of references to the centuries from which they came. I dig and weed the soil as earlier generations of women and men have done on what were once the farms of a village called Hackney. The larger fragments are instantly recognizable: the blue Willow china hints at the Hackney of the first half of the twentieth century, a place of migration, economic depression and war. This Hackney soil reminds me of the transience of the

populations that move in and – usually as quickly as possible –
out again. I, like those of many other communities – Hug-
uenot, Jewish – am passing through.

That is not something I can say for the Plot in Yorkshire and
the Chapel my father, a sculptor, built there. This acre of land
is so full of intense memory that it will never let me pass
through. Each time I visit, it snags the heart so violently that
I'm left disorientated by the force of emotion. It's a landscape
peopled with images so clear and voices so loud that it shakes
my sense of reality. On one occasion, walking with my own
children down the track leading to the Plot, the thought that
my earlier selves were about to emerge – from around the
corner, from the forest on one side, jumping out of the bracken
in a game of hide-and-seek – was overpowering. With some
kind of inner eye (an eye that doesn't measure material reality)
I saw my ten-year-old self coming down to meet me on the
track which leads to the Chapel. She was complaining that she
was bored – yet another visit to this plot of land her parents
owned. She was restless for all the freedoms children don't
have to shape their own lives, so she dragged her feet and
curled her lip resentfully. Yet I know now that the sights,
sounds and smells of that walk were permeating her mind and
shaping her soul in ways that would last a lifetime.

This land has always been a place full of dread and fear for
me. It was a central piece of the mythology that sustained my
family, and it came to represent everything that failed. As a
child, this plot and everything my father built on it intimidated me; as an adult, it would oppress me with the weight of
disillusionment. For several decades now, it has haunted me as
a monument to failed dreams.

Jean-Paul Sartre once said that we belong to wherever we
have managed to carve our initials and return to watch those

initials age. Sartre's claim holds true for my father, only he did more than just carve initials, he built a chapel on this acre of North Yorkshire, and tended it his entire life. When we called him as adults, he would start his news with 'I've been up to the Chapel to cut the grass.' Ill-health crept up on him, undiagnosed and untreated, and he fretted about how to ensure that the Chapel survived him. He made appeals to various institutions but found no interest. Defeated, he didn't mention the Chapel in his will. As he lay dying, he kept repeating that he had left 'everything in a mess' – he couldn't even bring himself to clarify what he meant by 'everything'.

What I haven't been able to answer since I left the family home in a tiny village, Oswaldkirk, five miles from the Plot, is why for so many years I felt I lived in exile. For several decades, the few visits back, however painful, always felt like a homecoming. It's why I have delighted in places I found all over the world, from Peru to India, that reminded me, in however small, even absurd, a measure, of where I grew up, and in particular of the Chapel and its acre. I began to notice that wherever I went I was looking for memories of the North Yorkshire moors. It's why the sound of a glider – the noise of the engine cutting, the soft swish of the metal craft high in the sky – has always stopped me short in my tracks: it is the sound of the Plot, since the gliders from the club a mile away often flew overhead. I am instantly transported, with the swiftness that only a memory of sound or smell can achieve, back to the hot sunny afternoons spent at the Chapel as a child.

Isabel Allende writes of how she always yearns to return home and the minute she arrives, is desperate to leave. A similar ambivalence overwhelmed me in the middle of an interview researching this book, and it filled me with an absurd hilarity. It was as much as I could do to stop myself collapsing in giggles. The interview was with a National Farmers' Union official and he was explaining – with the condescension he regarded as appropriate for me, a woman and a Londoner – why shooting was so pleasurable on the hillside of the Plot: 'The steepness of the hillside means that the birds come straight up out of the trees, like a bat out of hell,' he commented. That had been me: a bat out of hell. At sixteen, I had fled North Yorkshire for Brighton, as different and as far away as I could get without leaving England. I travelled to Asia, Africa and Latin America, I lived in the States and I ended up in London, in neighbourhoods such as Brixton and then Hackney, that reminded me of places I had travelled to. I put North Yorkshire firmly behind me, with its entrenched snobberies of 'incomer', class and gender: I was out of there and on to other things. It was six years before I returned, and when I came back the visits were brief, and followed the same pattern: a thrill of anticipation at the signs for the M1 and 'The North', which reached a surge at Watford. Then the arrival: the mud-encrusted, narrow roads, the gaunt hedgerow trees and the deep sense of desolation. Even now I do not like visiting the Plot alone, but take my boisterous, irreverent children or cheerful, thoughtful friends. Each time I left North Yorkshire, there was a tearing sense of loss, and always a promise to myself that one day I would repair that loss, resolve the ambivalence – find either a way to say goodbye for good or a way to come and go with a lighter heart.

On one occasion, heading north to research this book, my eye fell on a news story about an unresolved murder; a torso of an African boy had been found in the Thames and, after several years of forensic research, they had been able to track down the region of Africa from which he had come. They had analysed the build-up of minerals in his bones, accumulated in minuscule quantities from the water he drank and the food he ate. It was powerful material evidence of how we are, literally, made by place. This sense of place is not just a product of imagination and memory, it is also physical; the elements of the land, its rocks, earth and water, are measured in our bones. It's hard, perhaps even impossible, to abandon our own geography of memory.

I began to wonder if this acre of land, so full of ghosts, could help me piece together a new way of understanding my father and the family's history. Perhaps, like the red thread Ariadne span for Theseus to guide him through the Minotaur's labyrinth, I could follow the stories of this Plot – both the ones my father told and new ones I could discover for myself – and find a better account of my father, a difficult, complex man, and the place. If wisdom 'sits in places', as the Native American Apache say, what wisdom did this place have to offer? At certain points in our lives, some questions become insistent. They are not new questions, only the most impor- tant. You first learn them as a child: who are your parents? Where is your home? Where do you belong? Perhaps the Plot could provide some answers, and help me understand how a place can shape a life. As a journalist, I write about the fraught politicization of these questions, but there are identities of place that are much more particular and emotional – and uni- versal: they are a crucial part of how we understand ourselves. Even in highly mobile, urban societies, when the relationship with place has often been stripped down to bare function – one lives near work, or where the schools are good, or the property is a good investment – there are plots of land we dream of and use as a repository of meaning and wisdom, and a place where we find company.

The personal investigation is what has brought me back to this particular acre, but it needs to sit within a bigger story of how others have also used this bit of land and the relationships across time that I have with them. I need an understanding of the teeming histories under my feet on the Plot. Because in England we are always walking over stories, over a soil rich with the blood, toil, tears and sweat of generations, beside walls in which each stone has been cut and put in place, and each hedgerow planted and pruned by calloused hands.

Dad loved to tell his guests the stories of the Plot, the ones he found and the ones he brought with him; I eavesdropped on the tales of the battles, the travellers, the faith and the heroes. Now it is my turn to dig out what I remember from my father, find out new stories and see if I can piece together the plot. I'll use a right to roam across many types of knowledge, and at times I'll need to lean on other people's plots to help explain my own. Can I discover the Plot for myself, and in doing so find the difficult man who was my father, and finally lay all the ghosts to rest? And if I can, then perhaps so can you, on your plot.

BERGEN

OSLO

STAVENGER

NORWAY

THE
NORTH
SEA

ABERDEEN

SCOTLAND

EDINBURGH

DENMARK

SCOTCH
CORNER

NORTH YORK MOORS

ENGLAND

YORK

HULL

BREMEN

GERMANY

DALES

AMSTERDAM

NETHERLANDS

LONDON

BELGIUM

FRANCE

MAP 1
NORTHERN
EUROPE

MB

1

The middle of nowhere

There are over 32.7 million acres in England and this is the story of just one of those acres. So the first task is to take you there, to help you distinguish it from the many other millions of acres and their stories that are crowded into England, this small fragment of an island washed by the cold waters of the North Sea and the Atlantic. On the OL 26 Ordnance Survey map, the escarpment of the Hambleton Hills marking the western edge of the North York moors is accentuated by great curves and blocks of pale green to denote the woodland that cloaks the steep hillsides. At its south-west corner a promontory juts out over the surrounding wooded ravines before turning east. The higher land is scored by valleys, and it is just above one of these, where two tracks meet, where woodland and pasture abut, that there's a name, Scotch Corner, and a small black cross to mark the chapel my father built.

Or you could find a Google map of Oldstead, North Yorkshire, and, guided by the Hambleton Hills' rich curves of dark woodland on this wondrously forever-sunny day captured by satellite from space, allow the eye to follow the dark tree-lined track from Oldstead village up to a large bright triangle of pasture on the hill above. A few clicks on the cursor and, closer in, you can pick out the blurred outline of roofs tucked into the shadows of the surrounding trees. This is the Chapel, its pantiles pale pink against the surrounding trees, just visible from space.

Both these ways of finding the Plot still bear the characteristics of their origins as military technologies, the one to defend Britain from a French revolutionary army in 1791, the other a weapon of the Cold War. They will enable you to move across the land, to position yourself amongst millions of acres, and to find any one specific acre, however nondescript or obscure. They offer possibilities of speed and surveillance. They are about mobility and location, with an efficiency and accuracy that is very useful. They will get you to the Plot, but they offer only knowledge – of which our age has no shortage – not the understanding we need.

They will tell you nothing about how a place feels under your feet, how it smells or how the wind runs through your hair. Everything is flattened into two dimensions so that aerial dominance cannot reveal the shape of the land, how it curves, conceals and reveals, and how that reverberates in the muscles of your calves, the ache of your back and shoulders. They cannot convey how to live on this land, the nature of the soil and water and how to husband both to produce food, nor what to gather or hunt. They will offer no explanation for the scattering of farms and villages, the line of the roads or the shape of the fields, whose boundaries are the crackle glaze of the walkers' map. They can record features that people used to give meaning to this land – the burial mounds, the earthworks, the churches – but they can never explain those meanings. They describe only some of what's there, but give no explanation as to why.

These kinds of mapping say nothing of the people living

here, their relationships to places and other people, yet these are the kinds of knowledge some other cultures privilege in how they orientate themselves in a landscape. Some use memory maps dense with the narrative meaning that sustains human life. The Koyukon of north-west Alaska use stories to describe their landscape; 'narration as navigation', as Robert Macfarlane puts it, so that the land is 'filled with networks of paths, names and associations. People know every feature of the landscape in minute detail. The lakes, river bends, hills and creeks are named and imbued with personal and cultural meaning'. Narrative can be anchored to place, and a conversation can be a sequence of place names which serve to tell stories, provide moral guidance and encapsulate a rich repository of meanings. Eavesdrop on a family and such dialogues weave in and out of the conversation; any group of intimates with shared memories uses place to reference them. These are the maps needed to find the Plot.

An evening train from Newcastle to London is hurtling through the gloaming of a chilly April. Inside the casing of metal spinning along well-oiled rails there is the fug of many bodies, tea going cold in cardboard cups, biscuit crumbs. Beyond the glare of strip lighting is another world of dark outlines, which loom up, swallow us and then shrink as the train speeds past empty fields and the occasional lit window of a lonely farmhouse. Twenty minutes after we pull out of Darlington, the skyline to the east rises steeply to a plateau. For the next fifteen minutes, this great bulk of land heaped up on the horizon keeps pace with the train, a relatively even contour spooling as we speed south, brooding down on the lowland between us. I have had time to remember, time to scan the familiar outline, time to look out for the small, perfect reminder to take with me back to London: a glimpse of lumpy horse, more grey than white, cut into the escarpment. Kilburn's White Horse. A sip of tea and it has shot past, engulfed in the thickening dark. But the brief moment of recognition has taken me straight to the damp darkness as it gathers on the Plot, less than a mile from the White Horse; here, there's the occasional shrill shriek of a roosting pheasant, the plaintive cry of a lost lamb from across the fields and the wind stirring the trees. The Plot lies on this edge of the mass of rock that forms the North York moors, folded into the undulations once licked by glaciers.

I sit in the train hurtling south, but my imagination takes a walk up the track to the Plot. I know the track so well and have walked it in the dark before, so even in this fast-thickening dusk we wouldn't need a torch. We leave the cottages of the small village of Oldstead with their windows of cosy light, and head straight up into the forested hills, into the dark of the steep track. Trees overhang the path here and press tight in around you; later in the summer, the nettles spilling over the verge will sting the trailing hand. The only guide is my memory and the small patches of dark grey light overhead between the outstretched branches. Darkness produces its own palette of blacks and greys and the eyes strain to pick them out. They matter in night walking. Every sense is alert to catch the clues that orientate us: a breeze on the cheek, a shift in the degrees of darkness. Initially, the ground under- foot is even and the steep track draws you through a tunnel of greenery, bushes thick on both sides. Then the darkness thins and one senses the small fields opening out on both sides; there's a fresh whisper of wind coming down over the neigh- bouring valleys. Sound opens up the space above as the hoots of owls reverberate over the woods; at night they can reclaim this land as their domain without fear of human disturbance. Up here there are no roads, only a handful of remote, outlying farms. About halfway up it lightens, and on both sides of the track there is a break in the hedge. One can hear livestock stirring in the field, grazing, shitting and even, on occasion, a horse in night-time canter, its hooves thudding. Here the dim outlines of a magnificent ash tree are clearly discernible, its handsome grey trunk within arm's reach right by the track. Beyond, one can see the outline of a distant hill, while below, the small back road from Kilburn to Oldstead is periodically illuminated by the brief flare of headlights from a passing car. A handsome oak memorial bench has recently been erected here. Intriguingly, a neighbouring farmer and his wife told me that the horses they train are always agitated at this point on the track; over the years they've noticed how their horses start, and need to be calmed. Across in the field is a magnificent smoothly grassed hillock, ten feet high by fifteen feet; the Oldstead farmer and local historian Fred Banks told me it was an old lime-kiln, built up here to take advantage of the plentiful supplies of both limestone and timber. The carts would have had to reckon with the steep track down, laden with their precious load of lime with which to fertilize the fields.

But we press on – it's not the time to be pausing on the bench to admire the view. Now the track is rough, and there is one large worn boulder which can make even the most careful night-walker stumble. Staggering over the bumpy last section, which deters all motorists, one finally emerges at a wooden gate and the even turf of the Plot. The track continues, but here there is a dry stone wall and a low wooden fence. We have arrived in the middle of nowhere, and the dark heightens that sense of human emptiness. We are now surrounded by thousands, perhaps millions, of trees and their inhabitants: the crackle of twigs, the creaking of branches, the disembodied cries of unidentifiable animals. The sense of the busy, hidden lives of myriad creatures crowds around us.

Night brings a particular intensity to the Plot; the stories of this land press in on your imagination. And nothing is so compelling, so instantly familiar as the combination of smells that the night breathes: the invigorating freshness of pine trees, rotting bracken, sweet turf. The night is a time when in this crowded nation you can still find a measure of solitude. This was the plot my father first stumbled across as a sixteen-year-old boy on a school ramble. It was the remoteness that seduced him into returning, thirteen years later, to buy a fifty-year lease on the ruined farmhouse he had found there. Now, it is only in these dark moments of evening or night that one can recapture that sense of isolation which once defined this acre and thousands of its neighbours.

For many centuries there were a modest farmhouse and alehouse on the Plot at Scotch Corner. They were abandoned sometime in the early twentieth century when the Bulmers, the last owners, moved down into Oldstead. In the 1871 census, Richard Bulmer is listed as the head of the household at Scotch Corner; by 1881 Elisabeth Bulmer had taken his place, and by the next census in 1891 it was Henry Bulmer, presumably her son, who was the head of the household. They were described as farmers – not smallholders – so there would have been a number of sheep pasturing on the moors nearby, perhaps cows and pigs and certainly chickens. There would have been room for a vegetable garden, but probably no arable up here in the hills where the growing season was shortened by frosts and the steep hills made ploughing impracticable. The Bulmers appeared to have made some money on the side by brewing ale. Elisabeth is regarded locally as the last inhabitant of Scotch Corner. She left when already advanced in years to run the Black Swan public house in Oldstead. 'Alehouse' was perhaps too grand a term for what was probably the meagre business of brewing in an outhouse. Serving beer to passers-by – shepherds, the occasional farmer – in the kitchen would have been a useful sideline for a farmer's wife. This was the last vestige of Scotch Corner's centuries as a small inn on the Drovers' Road from Scotland. But brewing beer requires a good supply of water, and Scotch Corner perched up on the hillside had never had that to offer its inhabitants. In neigh-bouring Cockerdale, springs dot the narrow valley and feed into a buoyant stream, but Scotch Corner's inhabitants had to scramble down the hill and across a strip of land to the stream that rises in its neighbouring valley, Hell Hole. The local tradition is that the old Mrs Bulmer was gathering water by yoke and pail from the stream on a daily basis well into old age. After she left, the house and farm buildings fell into ruins, choked with briars until half a century later, a London school-boy arrived with a head already full of dreams.

If you chance on the Plot, the low one-storeyed building by the gate offers little interest. Metal shutters cover the windows. Pantiled, with rough stone walls, the back end of this building runs into a hillside covered with gorse and bracken. In front of it, the stone flags are now badly cracked, the paving uneven. We called this the Hut. Beyond is a grassy area surrounded by a low stone wall, thick with brilliant green moss. Twenty feet from the first building stands the Chapel. Built of the same materials of stone and pantiles, it is twice the height, an impos-ing block facing away from the gate, out into a line of cherry trees planted just beyond the boundary wall.

Wander across the grass and look at the Chapel and you realize that this is no ordinary farm building. The façade is almost forty feet in height, and there are two elaborately carved wooden doors. Above the lintel is a semicircular sculpture, a relief in apricot sandstone of Noah receiving the dove's sprig of olive. Noah's face is turned up, and his muscular arms reach out to greet this symbol of peace; his swirl of outstretched limbs and shoulders echoes the curves of his halo and the bird's wing. Noah may still look worried but it is a joyous image as the bird seems to offer the sprig directly to his mouth to taste. A couple of feet above Noah, in a rectangular niche, stands another stone sculpture about four feet high of a Madonna and Child. She is the pale grey of York stone, the same colour as the walls, and she's a hefty woman. Her son is a chubby, rounded football of a baby, all cheek and clenched fist. At either corner of the façade are buttresses ten foot high which jut out a foot or two. Once, they served as plinths for two herald angels, whose banners unfurled around their bodies.

Walk closer to the façade and the elaborate carvings of the doors can be seen through the clumsy wrought-iron security gate. A fluid patterning based on Celtic knotwork incorporates scenes from the Bible, such as Eve's creation from a rib of Adam, the temptation in the Garden of Eden and the Crucifixion. Carved into the bottom are the initials JB and the dates 1957–87. It was my father's tribute to the thirty years since he had first built the Chapel. Below the doors, on the threshold of the Chapel, lies his gravestone, inscribed with

JOHN JOSEPH BUNTING † SCULPTOR AND
ARTIST OF RYEDALE † BUILT THIS CHAPEL
1957 † DIED 19 NOVEMBER 2002 AGED 75

If you walk around the Chapel to the west side, you can see three small windows high up in the wall. Here there is also a stone bench built into the hillside, with a stone wall against which to lean. This was where my father liked to sit, and where family photos were taken. Now it's a dank, dark corner, facing into thick forest. High overhead, on the gable end of the roof, is a small metal cross.

The passer-by is bemused: who could possibly have lavished such care and attention on this remote structure? My father never put any signs up to indicate the nature of the place. In the early days he made a small, hand-painted wooden board – WAR MEMORIAL CHAPEL PLEASE RESPECT THE PREMISES – added his telephone number and propped it up *inside* the Hut. The intruder would only find this plea after they had broken in. The reticence was at odds with my father's interest in publicity; the Chapel was frequently featured in local newspapers and magazines and Dad kept every yellowed clipping. But for those adventurous enough to seek the place out, he was offering no more information. Those who stumbled unexpectedly across the place were puzzled. I used to bump into walkers who were delighted to find someone who could explain what the place was all about. More recently, my brother has put up a board which gives a brief account of the Chapel's history.

I haven't been in the Chapel or the Hut for years. So it is a child's memories that take me inside when I visit now. It was always very cold, the marrow-chilling cold of stone that never feels sunlight. In the Chapel, eyes had to adjust to the gloom because the only light came from the three small stained-glass windows high up on the west wall and from the open doors. My father, a devout Catholic, used to invite a priest to come and say Mass on Boxing Day or Easter Monday; I remember getting bored and being embarrassed by the family's tentative singing. The priest faced the altar and was often barely audible as he murmured prayers. I used to stare at the sculptures around me, and try to keep my bottom from going numb on the stone-flagged floor. I formed a very clear set of likes and dislikes about the sculptures my father had carved for his Chapel. There were two large crucifixes hanging on the walls; the one above the altar was a pale oak young man with his eyes ready to pop out of their sockets. He looked as if he was on a diving board and was going to jump on me. The eastern wall was dominated by a life-size Christ which my father had carved on a fellowship to Spain as a sculpture student. His head was framed in thick black hair and his painted face looked anguished; the richly varnished wood gleamed and the blood trickled down the torso and spilled over from the nails driven into the feet. This was the romantic, wronged Christ of my imagination.

Both these Christs were gloomily intimidating, so I averted my eyes, keeping them lowered on two dark-grey slate reliefs which stood on either side of the altar. Jesus revealing his glowing Sacred Heart was on one side, and the Virgin Mary on the other; the pleats of their clothing and features of their faces were outlined in gilt paint. I flinched from the exposed heart, a Catholic mystical image which suggested too much blood, but loved the way Mary's sash curved as it tumbled down her skirt.

Along the wall there was often a large wooden sculpture or two. As the family grew in size, there was no room for my father's life-size figures in our small cottage, so they were moved into the Chapel, where they towered over us children. One piece, six feet high, was called 'An Ape in Anger' and depicted a naked muscular man, his face, distorted with rage, turned upwards and his fists clenched. It gave me nightmares.

The only colour apart from the pale greys and creamy coffee of the Yorkshire stones came when a beam of late sunlight might occasionally fall through the stained-glass windows my father had made, and splashed rich reds and blues across the rough, unplastered walls and the stone floor, altar and benches. On the walls there were tablet inscriptions, dedications to men who had died in the Second World War whom I heard my father talking about with his friends. But he never explained to me why these people were important, and since they were men and they were dead, I had no reason to be interested.

What did pique my curiosity, however, was the effigy carved in York stone that lay, life-size, dominating the floor of the Chapel. His head lay at the altar, almost under the priest's robes, while the soles of his boots greeted one on arrival at the door. He was dressed in full battle fatigues and a paratrooper's helmet; his baggy trousers were tucked into his commando boots, and his thick-set arms lay across his body as if he were holding himself. At his neck was a checked kerchief, and around his waist ran a belt, its loops and pockets all detailed in stone. He lay, spread out across the floor on his rectangular plinth, leaving little space for the rest of us. For services there were two short benches for the adults, and children sat cross-legged on the floor beside this effigy. After Mass, when the Chapel was empty, I could come back and rub my finger around the treads on the soles of his boots, poke it into the indentations of his neckscarf and collar. I did not think he looked friendly – his jaw was set with the head turned to one side on his stone bier – but the ordinary intimate detail of this dead man's uniform made him vivid. There always seemed the possibility that he could come alive, break from his stone, stand up to shake out the creases in his trousers and join us for lunch. I thought he would be a rather awkward guest, a little shy.

It is the carving of the young soldier's boots and neckscarf
that has stayed with me over the years, rather than those intimidating Christs. Dad entitled the work 'Soldier' and referred to
it as a memorial to the unknown warrior, but the proportions of
this stocky young man were those of my father. Michelangelo
carved his own corpse in his masterpiece, the 'Pietà', as one of
my father's art pupils, Antony Gormley, pointed out to me. My
father's knowledge of Michelangelo's work was such that he
would have known this, but he never acknowledged the parallel to anyone. He had built a chapel in the middle of nowhere,
and placed in the centre of it a stone carving of his own dead
body.

My mother never asked him why he had built a chapel. Early
in their marriage, as she waited for the babies to arrive and made
a home for the family in the draughty annexe of an old house
they rented, he disappeared on to the moors to build his chapel.
They were very short of money; the furniture for their family
home was made from old orange crates and in winter the snow
blew under the ill-fitting door across the stone kitchen floor,
but my father put all his meagre earnings from his new job as a
part-time art teacher into the cement and roof timbers needed
for this strange project. The family car was pressed into service
to ferry the water to the site for mixing the cement after the
nearby pond on the moor dried up. He had no knowledge or
experience of building, but he built simply, using the stones of
the old ruins. He worked alone until the walls had reached
shoulder height and a back injury forced him to find a retired
labourer to help. Together they raised the roof and fixed the
second-hand pantiles. During the winter when the weather was
too rough to work on the moors, my father carved blocks of York
stone for the sculptures he had planned. Within eighteen
months he had done five major carvings as well as built the

Chapel. Then he turned his attentions to another part of the ruins from which he rebuilt the large one-roomed Hut. In the same time, my mother had had three pregnancies – one miscarriage, one son and one daughter. They were following the strict division of labour on which my father insisted. He had his art, my mother had the family – her own artistic career he expected her to set aside. My mother did not challenge the extraordinary diversion of his energies and family resources into this plot of land: this was the intense young sculptor with huge ambitions whom she had married. She – and in due course us children – knew the Chapel was Dad's; his family were allowed there on sufferance. These things were not explained; all we knew was that it was sacred ground to him and we had to be on best behaviour – it did not belong to us. Even after he was dead, I still felt I was trespassing. On one visit, my children and their cousins, his grandchildren, found some old sheets of corrugated iron and gathered bracken to make a den; it looked like a lean-to from an African shanty town. To my eye, it was wonderfully irreverent; it was something I would never have dared do, and of course we tidied every trace away before we left.

As a child I much preferred the Hut to the sombre gloom of the Chapel. In its own way, its construction was as extraordinary as the building next door. Here my father whitewashed the rough walls and hung framed drawings of his travels in Spain and north Africa. He made two large windows, and covered the cement floor with red lino and hessian matting; he built a wooden platform – perhaps for a bed? – in the pitched roof, with a ladder to reach it. He found furniture cheap in farm sales and bought a wooden table, a handsome wooden chair, benches, a chest of drawers and shelves. He got my mother to make red checked curtains. He brought up hurricane lamps, a gas heater and a camping cooker. On a rack by the door he hung his tools – an old-fashioned scythe, wooden rakes and brooms. He had created a home for himself on the moors at the very moment that he was producing a large family five miles down the road in a small, sparsely furnished cottage. By the time I can remember, much of this equipment was dusty with disuse. The wooden platform was cluttered with unused rolls of hessian, the hurricane lamps and gas heater either no longer worked or nobody had tried to make them work for years. I never knew of anyone who stayed there, except occasionally a monk from Ampleforth. Dad had dreamed through his teens of becoming a hermit; he built the hermitage but could never bring himself to be the hermit. Instead the Hut became a place for family gatherings and celebratory meals. For a decade from the mid-seventies it became a place in which to do battle with the bees of a big wild hive which took up residence in the roof. Much to my father's fury, these squatters took over, scattering their dead deep across the floor, table and benches, spattering their honey business over the ceiling.

When I was a teenager, I sometimes accompanied my father up to the Chapel. He would get the broom out to sweep the Hut and the Chapel while I weeded outside. Never has sweeping a small space of floor been made into such a performance of huffing and puffing and clattering of dustpans: Dad had no appetite for domestic chores. Over the years, he made few changes. In the Chapel a plaque to Robert Nairac, a Catholic soldier shot in Northern Ireland in 1977, appeared sometime in the eighties; the slate relief sculptures were removed after they mysteriously toppled and broke (in the allocation of Dad's work after his death, I chose them, by then glued clumsily back together again). Otherwise the Plot was always the same: the buildings had the same dank mustiness, the ancient smell of stone, and there was the sound of impatient birdsong in the forest outside.

It always felt something of a guilty relief to leave. We would use the top track, heading on up the hill away from Oldstead. Just above the Chapel the track takes a corner where the gorse is thick, and it doubles back on itself so that as one finally comes out on the top of the hill one can look back over bilberry bushes, small rowan trees and silver birch to glimpse the pale red tiles of the Chapel. Over the top of the roof the Vale of York can be glimpsed, fields and hedgerows dimming to a swathe of pale blue stretching away to a horizon sixty miles away, well beyond York. Turning to head north, a long straight track runs along the edge of the coniferous plantation. It is pretty now with a scattering of purple heather and feathery grasses in summer, but I can still remember in the seventies the rawness of the Forestry Commission's new ditches, its new track and the relentless neatness of the trees planted in dead straight lines. Nature had been drilled into a utilitarian landscape in which there was no room for verges where bilberry bushes or native trees could thrive.

At the end of the plantation, there's a corner, marked by a single, lopsided Scots pine. I always loved the plaintive whistle of the wind playing in its branches as it bowled over from the high moors to this last southern reach of the upland. Here the Commission track gives way to a much older fragment of a Drovers' Road. It widens to a generous fifty feet, with verges rich in wild flowers between the old stone walls; underfoot the stone is pitted with hollows and puddles. On a clear winter day, the bordering fields of root crops foreground a view which extends over the moors into a blue distance where the land slips into the sea and skies at the coast, forty miles away. With the sky arching high overhead, the sharp clear light seems to bounce off the North Sea, opening up an undulating expanse of moor and ocean which reaches as far as the lands from which the waves of migration came to people these islands – the Angles, Saxons and Viking Danes. It's a continuum of light, land and sea which wraps this northern corner of the globe. Once this eastern portion of England rolled into Germany and Holland, before the continental mass split, and the view serves as commemoration of how the unbroken scape of snow and ice used to run from Oslo to the upper reaches of the North York moors. The boundaries of land and sea are still under negotiation after thousands of years as the coast restlessly shifts shape, crumbling and periodically sliding into the cold sea stained by the sediment to the colour of tea. A little further along the track and we have arrived back at the cars parked on the road.

The Plot sits in a landscape rich in drama of every kind – topographical, mythological and historical – from long before my family played out its small story on an acre here. To generations in the villages clustered at the foot of the Hambleton escarpment, these hills have loomed above them as a sheltering arm or forbidding presence, depending on disposition or weather. This is a fickle landscape, and the quantities of sky and horizon ensure that on no two days does it seem alike. The steep bare rock of Whitestone Cliff and Roulston Scar provide an awesome reminder of their glacial past when they reared up out of a sea of ice. Now, the only marine echo of those earlier histories is that the cliffs tempt fulmars forty miles inland from their usual coastal habitat to nest in their rocky crevices.

Geologists still speculate as to how the interconnecting valleys, hidden ravines, cliffs and sharply defined outlying hills were formed at the end of the last ice age, 10,000 years ago when water poured off the plateau of the North York moors, and the melting glaciers ground along the floor of what became the Vales of Mowbray and York. Channels of water found their way round crumbling rock masses to erode steep gullies, while glaciers gouged out the deep lake at Gormire and rounded the contours of earlier geological upheavals to create the intimate intricacies of hill and valley around the villages of Oldstead and Kilburn that stretch through Thirlby up to Boltby. From the sharp cliffs periodically tumble huge blocks of the oolitic limestone embedded with fossils which chart even more ancient histories of shallow seas teeming with life.

These empty, bleak Hambleton Hills were a place of local magic and myth. Three miles from the Plot, Gormire Lake, at the foot of the steeply wooded slopes of the escarpment, was fabled to have no bottom, so deep is the depression in the rock. No stream feeds it and only recent research has been able to dispel the mystery of its water supply by discovering underground springs. Only a small stream drains it, so the water sits very still. Down by its muddy shore there is often hardly a breath of wind in this eerie space enclosed in cliffs and thick woods; welcome shelter for coot, great crested grebe and mallard to raise their young, but curiously oppressive, holding you immobilized. The lake is folded into woods, and can only be seen from the top of Whitestone Cliff on the Hambleton Hills; on one bright January day the grey twigs glittered as they shivered in the wind, and the lake was a slick of shining silver in woods brushed faintly with purple. A sweep of green fields separates Lake Gormire from the almost conical Hood Hill, as high perhaps as one can imagine Gormire is deep. On that January day, the hill stood proud in a landscape flattened by low winter sunlight so that the fields looked silky, their contours scoured smooth by the glaciers as they inched along the escarpment edge thousands of years ago. The Ordnance

Survey map marks Fairy Parlour Cave close by the precipice above Gormire, and there are many legends about these places. According to one, St John chased the Devil over the cliff to plunge into the bottomless lake of Gormire and be drowned. In another, a goose penetrated the rocks around the stream which drains the lake and re-emerged at Kirkbymoorside, twelve miles away, stripped of all its feathers. Another legend claimed that the lake was made in an earthquake which swallowed up a sizeable town and that the tops of the houses and the chimneys can be detected through the clear water. Yet another story claims that a local knight tricked the Abbot of Rievaulx into lending him a white horse, but the horse would not obey commands and plunged over the cliff into Gormire. As the knight fell, he heard a cackle echoing behind and turned his head to see the abbot, transformed into the Devil.

Even more intriguing are the 'windypits'. One sits close to the Plot in the pasture that adjoins the Chapel, hidden in a cluster of gorse bushes. It's a small example of a curious geological formation found on the Hambleton Hills and in neighbouring Ryedale where the rock has slipped on the underlying clay; this is called 'cambering' or 'gulling' by geologists. There are eight major windypits in the area according to a 1949 survey, but the true figure is probably many times that. These deep fissures in the rock vary in size but many of them have side chambers and passageways, sometimes opening up a warren of small spaces deep underground, and several have been excavated to reveal prehistoric pieces of pottery, meat bones and human remains. For the farmer they are an irritant because livestock stumble and fall down the chasms and are trapped in a slow death of struggle, starvation and rot. Their name comes from a strange phenomenon whereby warm air rises from the fissure in winter in small jets or puffs of steamy vapour. The warm dampness encourages sweet grass, which exacerbates the danger to livestock, attracted by the grazing. Conversely, in summer the rush of air from the windypit is cooling. Sometimes the air moves with enough force to stir the bracken and grass around the opening. When a westerly is blowing on to the Hambleton escarpment, the windypit by the Plot reportedly blows with particular force: the wind finds its way through the cracks, layers and fissures in tons of rock for over a mile to finally escape, with the faintest of sighs and shadow of a whistle, out of this deep hole. I've yet to hear it – perhaps the days I've visited have been too still – but listen very carefully, I was told by one of the Plot's neighbours, and the earth whispers.

The drama of this hidden landscape has long been a matter of local comment. In the 1760s, Laurence Sterne, author of *Tristram Shandy*, was living in Shandy Hall, Coxwold, from where he looked out across the fields to the escarpment just over a mile away. A letter purported to be written by Sterne referred to the hills as 'a bold ridge . . . thick with wood and finely varied by jutting rocks and broken precipices: and these are so abrupt, that they now not only by their magnitude, but by the shade they cast, increase the solemnity of the place'. Nearly a century later, in 1852, Thomas Gill described in his guide-book *Vallis Eboracensis* a walk up the escarpment from the Oldstead–Kilburn road, which would have been very close to the Plot: 'every turn in the road as you ascend the rugged cliff, varies the picture, and presents new and more fascinating scenery. To the right is "Hell Hole"; and the tourist will be awe-struck with the wild and varied views, extending over sunless ravines, savage dells, barren crags and bold romantic rocks, that afford shelter and retreat for beasts of prey.' But Gill's promise to the tourist proved unfulfilled; by the time they arrived in significant

numbers in the late twentieth century, these hills had been car-
peted in coniferous plantations. The rocky ravines and the
sudden startling shifts of view as one looked up at the cliffs had
largely been concealed in a dense forest of trees.

No account of this landscape is complete without reference
to its near-constant companion, the wind. Up on the back of
England, open to the spaces of northern Europe and its cool
grey lights, the wind is a relentless presence which plaits the
branches of the tenacious hawthorn and fashions its trunk into
contortions. In winter the winds sweep in from the North Sea
with their smell of snow, bowling over this, the largest continuous area of moorland in England, slamming into the traveller.
This is a land where movement requires the constant bracing
of the body, the pitting of tensed muscle, into the wind. Even
the villages' names describe this weather: Cold Kirby up on the
Hambleton Hills is where we stayed on the night of my father's
funeral and found ourselves wrapped in a dense November
fog which obliterated all features of what lay around us. It is the
sound and force of the wind, as much as what the eye can per-
ceive, that shapes the experience of space up here on the hills.
Walking along the escarpment as it curves round above Boltby
and Thirlby or along the track heading down to the Plot, the
sound of the wind is constantly shifting; the land is sculpted in
sound. Each tree reverberates with a different pitch, each angle
of the cliff produces variation in the soughing of the wind: to
the keen-eared this could be a walk mapped by sound. The
distance walked is measured not just by tired calf muscles and
the soreness of soles, but in the strain of the back and neck, the
burning of ears, the whipping of eyes by strands of hair and,
long after, the nag of an aching ear.

This is a landscape that, when walked, returns you to your
own body – both its strength and unexpected vulnerabilities –

so perhaps it is not surprising that in describing the shape of the land, one resorts quickly to the language of the body. The curves and contours of the North York moors are likened to backs, shoulders, arms, hips, breasts: these are the only metaphors that can suggest both the durability and the age-worn nature of the rounded headlands, the saddles slung between low summits and the slope of moor slipping down into dale. It is not a youthful body but one marked with the imperfections of age: the moors are the earth's crust at its most ancient, millions of years in the making with nothing as raw or recent as a jagged ridge or a mountain peak. As the art critic Herbert Read, born near Nunnington a few miles from the Plot, loyally put it, 'Mountains I have no love for: for they are accidents of nature, masses thrown up in volcanic agony. But moors and fells are moulded by gentle forces, by rain, water and wind and are human in their contours and proportions, inducing affection rather than awe.' Watch the way a little child relates to their mother's body, the casual way in which they lean against it, push past, shelter in the curves and you glimpse how one comes to find comfort in the moors' monumental solidity: the curves and dips, the wrinkles and bulges which echo one's own. And this is why, up there on the moors, one feels one is standing on England's curved broad back, her bent shoulders in the distance: this is where one feels the weight of this island's age.

This is nowhere, and now you know where you have arrived. The Plot has not been inhabited for over a century and its nearest neighbours lie cross-country more than a mile away, but it is time to dispel the illusion that you are alone.

So, & in conclusion, my father's plot is to be found in a woman's body.

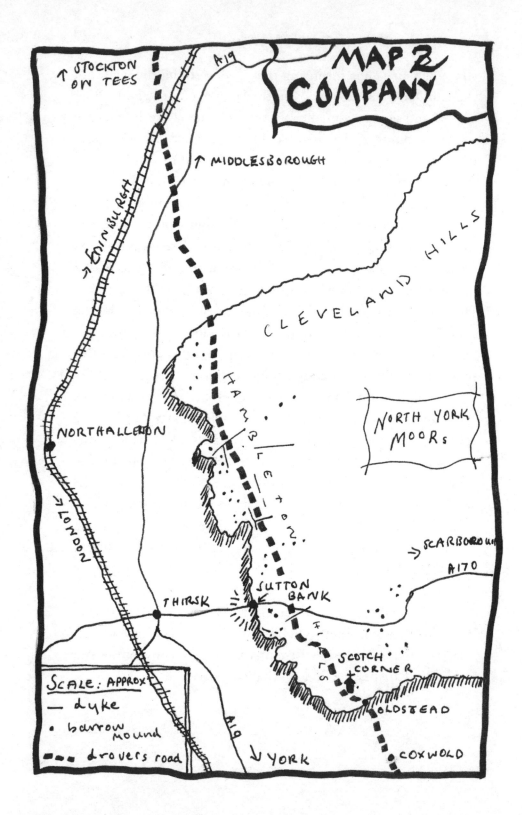

Part I: Company

Summer '72

2

Company past and present

My father loved company. It transformed him. It was when he smiled and laughed. He loved to play the raconteur, the historian, the art critic, the political analyst, and it was company that provided him with the audience he needed. He had many friends – almost all of them were men – and he faithfully maintained friendships which spanned his life. One of the most pleasurable memories I have of him was a lunch party he gave at the Plot, a decade before he died. It was a damp, dull day in late May, but in the Hut there was a vibrant conviviality. My father could be a good host. The big, Formica family kitchen table – around which the five of us children had once sharpened our combative, competitive wits – now beached up in this hut in the forest, was spread with a red and white checked tablecloth. There was plenty of wine, good cheese and bread and big bowls of salad. I remember lots of his friends, prosperous, tweed-dressed, good-natured and, above all, happy to listen. They regarded my father with a combination of indulgence and admiration. Their robust vehicles had navigated the track down with much less difficulty than my father's rusting, decrepit car; only their polished shoes and smart watches looked a little incongruous. This was a place where I'd only ever worn wellington boots and muddy anoraks. The dampness of the rough whitewashed walls of the Hut, the grey light from the open door, only provoked renewed warmth and good humour amongst the party. It was a reminder of what the Plot had taught us year after year: that gatherings in this isolated, remote place brought a very distinctive experience of companionship.

What makes that day memorable is that my father was at his happiest. A glass of wine in hand, leaning back in his chair, his short legs crossed, he recounted why he had built the Chapel, how he had been inspired by his travels to a hermitage in Algeria built by the French monk Charles de Foucauld. To my surprise, after several decades of my father's monologues running like indeterminate muzak in the background, for the first time I was fascinated. So was everyone else, and my father beamed as only he could beam – his whole face split by his broad smile, glowing with delight.

Company had always been a part, perhaps an unconscious one, of my father's plan for the Plot. He had chosen a remote acre but went to great lengths to build and furnish the Hut so that he could entertain guests there. We lived in a small stone cottage in Oswaldkirk, five miles away, but anyone who came to visit us was urged to make the pilgrimage over the hills to the Chapel. This was his one-man exhibition space, his gallery, his church and – a trifle eccentric – his place to entertain his guests. He listed in the autobiographical pamphlets that he wrote towards the end of his life the titled and important visitors and the dates when he had managed to entice them down the track into the middle of the forest. After his death, amongst the mounds of papers piled in the cupboards of his cottage were dozens of photographs of him at the Chapel:

clusters of unfamiliar faces, my father always in the centre. He kept boxes and boxes of them, still in their envelopes, sent by friends and acquaintances after their visits; they served in place of favourable reviews, providing the acknowledgement of him as an artist that turned out to be in short supply from elsewhere.

Back in the early days, when he was still brimming with self-confidence and hope, there was another kind of company he envisaged for the Plot: family. As he was building up the walls of the Chapel, my mother was growing bigger and bigger. Indeed she was so big that at five months everyone presumed her vast belly signified imminent labour. In a fit of ill-judged enthusiasm, they spent one night on the stone floor in the newly roofed Chapel – a particularly uncomfortable night, my mother remembers, as she shifted her bulk from one side to the other. In the next eight years, my mother produced five children, two boys and three girls. My father's overriding requirement of this kind of company was quantity; he loved the idea of big families. He held up the tallies of other families – ten, eleven, twelve – as models against which we as a modest five had failed. Meriting particular admiration was the family of a Spanish friend of my mother's which, regular as clockwork, had a new baby to show in every Christmas card for sixteen years. He was tribal in his admiration for sheer numbers, but his interest in the small children produced or the relationships required to bring up these broods was negligible.

Given such quantities, the Plot was the only stage big enough to host the whole tribe of the extended family. This is where we had the family gatherings, with Mass first, fidgeting and cold, and then mothers busily laying out lunch in the Hut while fathers stood about the bonfire. We children had the run of the place, shrieking with exhilaration at the space and the company. A photograph taken by my mother captures vividly one of these epic gatherings with two of my father's siblings' families. We were a total of eighteen, twelve children aged between a few months and fourteen years, and six adults. Everyone is smiling, except an aunt anxious at her misbehaving son – and my father. He sits at the centre, the adult brother, the paterfamilias, his shoulders hunched, hands on his knees, combative, his irritation barely concealed as he stares into my mother's camera. It's a sunny day with the thick long grass of late summer, but he's not happy. Such company never seemed to make him happy; small children at close quarters irritated him. Perhaps not surprisingly, I found no photographs of our family gatherings at the Chapel in his boxes or photo albums; it was a vision of company with which he had grown disillusioned. He wanted an audience, and the unruly brood – the older boys clambered up on to the high wall next to the Hut, the girls talked too much and laughed much too much – had no time for that. But we were beneficiaries of the vision he had once had, the combination of weather, the wild, picnics, bonfires and laughter. In my aunt's tribal photograph, I look happy – and proud; every child wants to believe their family is special, and as I sat on the ledge above my father, my bare feet dangling, this was not a matter simply of belief but, to my mind, unassailable fact. Who else had a father who had built a chapel on the moors and had led his people into the wilderness to feast on its riches?

I hear the reverberations of those tribal gatherings most times I return to the Plot. Several of the cousins have themselves returned to visit with their own offspring, now numbering thirty-two at the last count, only my father dead, and one cousin prematurely so. Big families are still begetting their own big families. The numbers my father so liked have provided brief, noisy interruptions in the uninhabited stillness that has enfolded the Plot for more than a century. I like the idea that our raucous assemblies in the early 1970s, the smell of smoke, the feel of bare feet on wet grass, echoed the Plot's earlier histories before it was abandoned. My father had brought friends, family and his collection of heroes – military, artistic and spiritual – to keep him company in the woods. But he had also found great solace in the company of the dead; it was for him a community across time which proved as entertaining, informative and shrewd as any he met in his life.

I camped with my family one August night a few years ago; we pitched tents, built a small fire, cooked sausages and watched the stars come out after a day of sweaty heat. From the track we could see the orange glow of the city of York and lights mapping the towns of Thirsk and Northallerton in contrast to the soft blackness all around us. I couldn't sleep; I lay awake listening to the noises of the forest and the soft stirring of the breeze in the pines. It seemed to me that there were plenty of other kinds of company to be had at the Plot if one was inclined to acknowledge them. As I lay there in the dark, I realized that the Plot was crowded with a caravan of ill-assorted characters accumulated over the centuries, of hunters, monks, warriors, farmers and shepherds. The stories I had heard my father telling guests came back to me. By digging out their histories, and discovering the use and meanings past generations had made of this acre of land, what more could I learn of my father, the company he liked to keep and his Plot?

When my father was building the Chapel, he would leave the car and walk across Oldstead Moor to where the Forestry Commission was ploughing the moorland to plant conifers, and he would fill his pockets with the worked flints and arrow-heads that had come to the surface. He had stumbled across 'an almost forgotten past', in the words of the Victorian antiquarian who had energetically dug these moors a century before. When my father rubbed the soil off the flints between his calloused fingers, he was feeling the weight and shaft of the blade much as it would have been felt by another craftsman thousands of years before. The era of such casual flint-gathering came to a close with the foresting of the area and the increasing use of tractors; the newly turned soil was too far beneath him for the tractor driver to spot them. But my father arrived in time to find these treasures and he kept them all his life. He was no local historian or archaeologist patiently accumulating small detail; he liked the big sweep of history, the grand narra-tive, and he liked the company of its protagonists on his Plot. He anchored his own thinking on death, memorial and remem-brance in that of earlier times; above all, he admired continuity.

Just as the view of the Vale of York comes into sight at the brow of the hill, the track makes an elbow corner down to the levelled ground of the Plot. It's a curious detour to make around a patch of rough ground dotted with hillocks of grass, heather and bilberry bushes, and my father always maintained that the track was skirting an Iron Age burial mound. As a child I remember the mound as more clearly defined, standing proud of the land, its height further magnified by the tall willow herb that bloomed in late summer. There's little sign now of any kind of mound among the rough ground, and when I took an archaeologist back to the spot he was dubious and I doubted my own memories. But this rough corner still merits a mark on the archaeological survey maps of both the Forestry Commission and the North York Moors National Park, coming under an all-purpose label of 'spoil heap'. The National Park's archaeologist, Graham Lee, agreed that it could have been a Bronze Age round barrow which has become indistinct after Forestry ploughing; the 1891 and 1912 maps indicate it, forty to forty-three feet in diameter, more clearly. With no quarry workings nearby, my father insisted he was right and stoutly stood by his claim that it was a burial mound, perfectly situated on the brow of the hill to provide a vantage point over the treetops of the wooded slope to see the Vale of York below, and at the same time greet the traveller coming up the steep hill on to the moors.

This possible burial mound on the Plot could have been linked to similar mounds strung along the escarpment of the Hambleton Hills to the north. Stand amongst the bilberry bushes – their berries sweet and tiny, their juice a deep red like pricks of blood on the finger – on the Plot's burial mound and face north: ahead of you, according to the Ordnance Survey, lie seventeen mounds dotting the escarpment (many more according to the closer reading of the archaeological survey) before finally reaching the northern edge of the moor, fourteen miles away. There are other scorings in and monuments on the land: huge earthworks whose scale, made without the use even of iron tools, let alone machinery, is daunting. This is a landscape which has been laboured and marked with huge ambition and determination. Now all we have are the grassed bumps and indentations over which to speculate, and they taunt us with the limitations of our knowledge.

Perhaps this escarpment of the Hambleton Hills acquired a particular significance as a border territory, the boundary between moorland and lowland. It could have been a place for burial, for celebration and ritual because we know from analysis of pollen in the soil of these mounds that flowering plants were placed on them as wreaths or bouquets. Perhaps it was

also a place for gathering and trading livestock; a valuable
pasture in summer when the lowlanders were still laboriously
clearing the trees and draining the marshy soils below. It's hard
not to assume that this imposing line of hills looming above
the plain would have held great significance, and that meanings were read into the exhilarating spaces it revealed. It is in
their qualities of light and sound, in the blue line of the far
horizons, that one tries to imagine the experience of the people
who arrived here after the ice sheets had retreated, and began
with their flint tools and fire to clear patches of the dense forest
that covered the moors when the earth warmed. Between the
Late Mesolithic period and the Early Bronze Age, 7–4,000
years ago, they made clearings in the oak, alder, hazel and birch
forests that covered the high ground, and hunted the wild
animals for food. They left scatters of flint on many parts of
the moors and at several points along the Hambleton Hills,
including Scawton and Oldstead Moors near the Plot, where
my father used to fill his pockets. The Scawton Moor flints
are known for their various types of 'leaf-heads', which are
very finely pressure-flaked and thin almost to the point of
transparency.

It is thought that the remains of the dead were buried in
mounds as early peoples began to settle on the land, marking a
shift from earlier nomadic patterns; these mounds were an
expression – or a cause – of their territoriality. The oldest
barrow on the Hambleton Hills is probably early Neolithic,
dating from around 3500 BCE, at Kepwick, six miles north of
the Plot. It's a long barrow and the trenches of the Victorian
diggers are still evident. But most of these Hambleton mounds
date from the early Bronze Age, between 2500 and 1500 BCE;
when plotted on the map of the North York moors, they follow
the line of the watersheds from one dale to the next. Perhaps

they staked out the use of land, a practice described in Genesis when Jacob and Laban marked the division of grazing lands with a heap of stones and a stone pillar and celebrated their agreement with a ritual meal. Several of these burial mounds stand at the head of tracks, or close to where old tracks come up the escarpment from the lower farmland. They mark a pattern of land use that has lasted centuries; in many cases, present-day township boundaries still follow the lines of the round barrows across the moors.

The concentration of burial mounds along the Hambleton Hills could also be no more than historical accident. Mounds were also built on lowland areas but there, where the soils are fertile and the population density has been heavier, they have been ploughed out or built over in the last thousand years. It is only on the relatively empty high ground of the moors and the escarpment that we can still read these ancient histories. The process of attrition has speeded up in the last century: one burial mound has been lost on average every day in the UK since the Second World War, mostly to ploughing. Surrounded by the plenty of this legacy – there are 1,000 burial mounds in north-east Yorkshire alone and many thousands more across the UK – we've become indifferent. These mounds represent a vast scale of effort on the part of generations who dug count-less tons of earth, dragged and assembled rocks and timber platforms, and created monumental ritual landscapes. If such effort had all been assembled in the one place, into one giant complex of earth construction, it would draw our admiration. But scattered across the landscape, now usually crumbled to a few feet in height, the mounds cause little curiosity except amongst the most devoted archaeologists.

Yet for two and half millennia, up to Saxon times, these markings in the land were used and reused for burials, for rituals and for boundaries, until the Church launched a thousand years of licensed neglect and piecemeal obliteration. The barrows were vilified as places of illegitimacy and subversion; they were home to hobgoblins, the Yorkshire moorland communities believed until well into the nineteenth century. These capricious characters emerged at night to cause nuisance or provide assistance to the farmers, according to Canon Atkinson in his detailed diary, *Forty Years in a Moorland Parish*, recording his life on the North Yorkshire moors in the second half of the nineteenth century. Barrows were portrayed to God-fearing folk as a frightening, hostile imposition on the land. For the brave, they became places for plunder.

What began in medieval times as an occasional hunt for treasure became a dedicated curiosity in the nineteenth century as hundreds of mounds were ripped open by a new breed of barrow diggers, and those on the Hambleton Hills were no exception. Collections of ancient objects, even if little understood, had become a respectable accoutrement of the drawing room. Compared with barrow-digging further south in places such as Wessex, the North Yorkshire moors offered meagre pickings for the trophy hunters. In one survey of 200 round barrows which had been excavated at different times in the last 150 years, most contained only pieces of pottery and cremated bones, from which archaeologists have deduced that these moors had witnessed a more egalitarian society than further south.

The absence of gold and jewels did not deter the likes of Thomas Kendall who, in the middle decades of the nineteenth century, gathered the biggest collection of prehistoric remains ever made in North Yorkshire; he assembled 135 pottery vessels, 27 urns, 26 axe-hammers and at least 26 stone and flint axes from mounds in the county. There are no notes as to where the objects were found or how the burial mounds he excavated were constructed. Such collections prompted growing concern, and by 1866 there was a backlash against these souvenir hunters: diggers were accused of 'desecrating these time hallowed monuments for no better purpose than the indulgence of a craving acquisitiveness and the adornment of glass cases with ill-understood relics to be paraded for the empty admiration of those who may descend to flatter the equally vain and ignorant collector', in the words of one critic, who summed up the depredations as the 'ill conducted pillage of idle curiosity'.

The Church had stamped out the rural traditions around burial mounds, dismissing them as remnants of a pagan past, but it was the Church, and in particular a dedicated cleric in northern England, that was instrumental in the emergence of a new academic discipline, archaeology. The Victorian imagination had been fired by the discovery of an earth vastly older than the Bible suggested. This prompted a thirst for knowledge of how human beings had developed, and a need to understand the process of historical change, and that in turn inspired a race to dig. The busiest diggers in North Yorkshire were clerics: the men with the education, leisure and social connections to get access to the land.

One of the most celebrated barrow diggers of the nineteenth century was a Canon William Greenwell from Durham, who spent over half a century digging – much of it in North Yorkshire. Several burial mounds on the Hambleton Hills were subjected to the enthusiasm of Canon William and his crew of labourers. It is not entirely fanciful to imagine that the beginning of the destruction of the barrow on the Plot was the work of Greenwell – he left such scanty notes that it is hard to calculate which mounds he excavated – and my father always maintained that it had been excavated in Victorian times. One

mound on which he did leave details was Kepwick Long
Barrow, six miles north of the Plot up Hambleton Street, where
he found the remains of five bodies and two flint flakes. His
trenches are still visible. Greenwell is sometimes referred to as
the father of modern archaeology; at one time Augustus Pitt
Rivers himself was his 'enthusiastic pupil'. His collecting
through the second half of the nineteenth century was voracious. He dispensed with his church duties cursorily (he used
to boast that he had a pile of fifty-two sermons, one for each
week of the year; once he had used one he put it to the bottom
of the pile, in a process of recycling which lasted over half a
century). He was fond of declaring that he had not been to
church for fifty years without being well paid for it. Freed from
onerous clerical duties, he pursued his wide range of interests,
from barrow-digging to cataloguing medieval manuscripts,
angling and collecting Greek coins, Bronze Age implements,
flints and Anglo Saxon carving. (His most enduring claim to
fame was the trout-fishing fly he invented and which is still in
use, the Greenwell Glory.)

Greenwell and his contemporaries dug as if a race were on.
The canon claimed he had dug over 400 burial mounds in fifty
years of digging, including an unknown number on the
Hambleton Hills. His great rival on the North Yorkshire moors,
the diarist Canon Atkinson, boasted of managing four a day on
occasion, and probably excavated around eighty to a hundred
in his lifetime. Given this pace, it is hardly surprising that their
methods were rough and ready: Greenwell described his standard technique as digging a trench from south to north through
the centre of the mound. Atkinson's technique was to cut
straight down from the top. As Atkinson admits, the method
did lead to occasional mishaps: 'my spade suddenly passed
through no less than four thicknesses of "Ancient British"

pottery. To say that I was vexed, annoyed, discomfited at such apparent proof of my reckless rather than unconsidered working, would be to convey a wrong impression, for I knew I had been working as carefully and watchfully as usual . . .'

Many of the barrows Greenwell dug on the Hambleton Hills had already been disturbed, and he complained bitterly that they had been ransacked 'by persons indeed of better education, but who have thought that enough was gained if they found an urn to occupy a vacant place in the entrance hall or a jet necklace or a flint arrow-point for the lady of the house to show, with other trifles, to her guests requiring amusement'. Greenwell may have still had some of the characteristics of such trophy hunters, but his methods were a considerable advance. For the most part, he carefully removed delicate objects and subsequently arranged for detailed drawings or lithographs of them. An article in the *York Gazette* of 1910 on his excavations on the Hambleton Hills reported that 'on discovering a cinerary urn in this mound [he] was so elated with his find and so fearful lest it should be injured on transit that although he had a horse and cart at his disposal, he carried his precious treasure in his own arms to the foot of the steep Sutton Bank for fear that the jolting of the cart might break the urn'.

But he did not always record where he found his treasures. His masterwork, a daunting 750 pages entitled *British Barrows*, published in 1877, went to unprecedented lengths to record his activities and was a milestone in the development of archaeology, but didn't include maps. Even his contemporaries were exasperated; his great rival, the East Yorkshire grain trader J. R. Mortimer, who dug many barrows in the Yorkshire Wolds over the same time period, complained: 'It seems a great pity that . . . barrow diggings are not better conducted and the examination made with far greater care and labour than what we read in the newspaper details of Yorkshire diggings.'

The rivalry of Mortimer and Greenwell was driven by the importance of the task they were both undertaking. These barrow diggers were using the burial mounds of north-east Yorkshire much as children might use a sandpit; arguing and playing with the contents to make stories. The mounds of the Hambleton Hills, even perhaps the mound on the Plot, assumed a modest part in a generation's search for histories to fill the bewildering vacuum of deep time. Thanks to the likes of Greenwell, the North York moors have ever since been a place understood to be ancient, somewhere that could reveal old histories, and bring the visitor back to their past. Digging enabled 'some knowledge to be acquired', wrote Canon Atkinson, who declared himself to be trying 'not unsuccessfully to decipher a partly obliterated page of history'. Greenwell wrote at the end of his life, 'nor can I look back to any part of my life with less regret or greater satisfaction than that which has been passed in an endeavour to revive, in however faint a form it may be, the almost forgotten past'.

Rather like their contemporaries in remote regions of the world, these men were explorers, but their field of enquiry was the past. Greenwell's passion was to organize; all his interests were about cataloguing, ordering and labelling. He organized the chaotic library of manuscripts of Durham Cathedral, publishing volumes of medieval records. It was the same impulse that fired his fascination in craniology, as he lined up his skull collection to speculate about how races 'improved' and to demonstrate theories of 'racial progress'. Both Greenwell and Mortimer were absorbed by questions of whether races had been replaced by invasions and migrations or had gradually developed. They were intrigued by the developing three ages system, of Stone, Bronze and Iron, a way of breaking up the past into more manageable sections, and labelling it according to the progress of technology. As geology was establishing a chronology of rock formation, as Darwin was publishing *On the Origin of Species*, Greenwell, Atkinson and Mortimer were furiously digging in Yorkshire, hoping to chart a comparable schema for the island's human history.

The Victorians were living through disorientating change and discovery. Their cities were proliferating rapidly, their wealth and global economic power was unprecedented, and at the same time their sense of the order of the universe was being assaulted by scientific discovery. Barrow-digging expressed a deep desire to find in the land a story of identity, a trajectory of history that could offer insight into their own age and how it had come about. In the time of Greenwell, history had become immeasurably longer – the earth was not 4,000 years old but 4 billion – and the species' characteristics were not hand-crafted by God but dynamic and thus unfinished. The moors of north-east Yorkshire offered Greenwell and his contemporaries a library of an evolving humanity. The very emptiness of the moors gave these possible pasts ample space to expand in the imagination of the passers-by.

Fortunately for Greenwell, this study of the past also proved very profitable. Having built up extensive collections through assiduous trading and canny purchases, he was able to sell them for substantial sums. He sold his coin collection for £11,000 to an American and the 'Greenwell Collection', with its large numbers of Bronze Age weapons and implements, was bought by the American collector J. Pierpont Morgan for £10,000 and donated to the British Museum in 1908. Even for an ardent collector such as Greenwell (he resumed collecting immediately after the sales) the temptation of such sums was irresistible, and he was able to use the proceeds to buy back the family estates, which had been lost in a legal battle when he was a boy.

What proved of less interest to the Victorian barrow diggers were the earthworks built after the mounds. They were equally impressive constructions but they offered no promise of treasure or collectible objects. Along six miles of the Hambleton escarpment lie fragments of a system of ditches and dykes which date from about 1000 BCE. It is known as the Cleave Dyke System, and its most southern fragment is less than a mile from the Plot. Several stretches run parallel to the escarpment, whilst at right-angles to these there are four dykes running west–east for a few yards to the head of river valleys. In many places the dykes have been ploughed out, or they disappear into brambles and thick bracken. It is only near the stand of trees that marks Sneck Yate that one can grasp what might once have been its scale. Known as Hesketh Dyke, it stands 5.6 feet high and 46.6 feet wide, with ditches on either side 3 feet deep and 20 feet wide – a ridge of earth heaped up and stretching across the field. It's the size of this earthwork that catches the imagination; something was important enough to warrant the back-breaking labour of digging and moving the stony earth whose contours are now softened with grasses and wild flowers. The system would have taken blisters, wooden spades and the sweat of dozens of men over many years to build: a labour that was all the more expensive because it had to be diverted from the struggle for survival of growing and hunting food. The Cleave Dyke System is the tantalizingly elusive monument to the labour of generations.

The Cleave Dyke links up many of the round barrows. For years there has been debate about what defensive purpose it might have served, but now the weight of opinion has swung conclusively behind the idea that the dykes were a system of territorial boundaries, subsequent to that of the round barrows but intended for a similar function and often aligned with them. The dykes continued the natural contours of river valleys to demarcate 'estates' which contained all the elements needed for mixed farming – upland grazing, arable land on the lower hills and meadows in the dales with access to river water. Once they had been dug into the ground, these boundaries solidified, and were used in medieval times (and since) as township boundaries. The barrows and the dykes define this hilltop area around the Plot as a place of abutting interests where boundaries warranted expensive investments of time and labour to marcate. That effort was perhaps particularly necessary because by the time of the Romans – and possibly even earlier – it had become a place of passage. In a country still thick with forest, and criss-crossed with rivers and streams, with only small places of cleared land which were intensively farmed and settled, the passage offered by this escarpment of upland moor was one of England's vital transport arteries for over a thousand years.

3

Passing through

It's quiet on the Plot. Attentive listening is required to catch
the small stirrings of leaf, branch, bush or blade of grass. It is
never silent – no English acre ever can be; it is replete with the
murmurings of other livelihoods which we are too busy to
notice, let alone learn to identify. The most distinctive sound
of the Plot is the soughing of the pines, strangely mournful but
soothing, quite unlike how wind plays on any other tree.
Perched on this hillside, cocooned in thick forest, this is a vantage point from which to feel the busy-ness of daily life: on the
plain below, the train hurtles north to Scotland and the steady
stream of traffic plies between Teesside and Leeds. But this is
an acre that is sitting out this century's innings, as it did the
last. The gorse bloom their deep yellow and perfume the air
with delicate traces of tropical coconut and vanilla. In summer,
the willow herb shoot deep-pink spears up, their individual
buds slowly unfurling from bottom to tip in a staged display
which lasts weeks. The heather and bilberry flourish on the
edge of the forest.

Yet the little-used feel of this Plot is a relatively new experience. The straggle of walkers who now come down the track

and across the acre are the last remnants of a steady procession of human feet over two millennia, possibly longer. The Plot sits on the main route running fourteen miles along the western edge of the Yorkshire moors. As this track dips down off the moor, it crosses the Plot. Thousands of feet and hundreds of thousands of hooves have travelled this way along one of the oldest roads across the moors. This is one of the Plot's strongest claims on history, and it gave my father, a keen walker, great satisfaction. He had made his mark smack in the middle of a site crucial to the ancient history of northern Britain, of Celtic saints, Scottish clansmen and battling kings. It was as vivid and as meaningful to him as the news he heard on his ancient wireless.

The track is known as Hambleton Street, a reference to its use by the Romans, but also as the Hambleton Drovers' Road and even Via Regalis or the King's Way. Some argue that it was a trade route originating in Mesolithic or Neolithic times, because the higher ground along the escarpment is relatively level and well drained, providing ease of passage on this broad track across common land. By the Middle Ages travellers used Hambleton Street to avoid the manorial dues exacted by landlords in the valleys below to cross land, ford rivers and graze animals. The wide verges of Hambleton Street offered good grazing for livestock. Animals, news, money, technology, goods, ideas and armies all passed along it at some time or another. The Plot was not out of the way then, but a staging post on a crucial route across the North York moors and south to York and beyond.

The track offered relatively safe passage across an area of England that inspired great fear. The moors were regarded as a wilderness, a place of wild animals and lawlessness. In the seventh century, St Bede noted that the holy man St Cedd chose a site (now the village of Lastingham) in the middle of the North York moors that was 'amongst high and remote hills, more suitable for the dens of robbers or haunts of wild beasts than for men'. The moors were the last place in England where wolves roamed and, as late as the seventeenth century, the animals were still a source of worry. The moors' reputation had not improved by the eighteenth century; Daniel Defoe, charting his journey around Britain between 1724 and 1726, described the Hambleton Hill escarpment as 'black, ill looking, desolate moors', and kept away. In 1794 J. Tuke gloomily referred to the Yorkshire moors in his *General View of the Agriculture of the North Riding of Yorkshire* as a 'wild and extensive tract of mountains' and stated that 'the great altitude of these moors renders the climate extremely cold and bleak which will always be a bar to their improvement'.

Defoe's use of the adjective 'black' to describe the moors was not unusual. Heather moorland is more accurately grey or brown in winter, but black indicates the fear the moors inspired. The highest point on the Hambleton Hills, a bracing day's ten-mile walk along the Street due north of the Plot, is called Black Hambleton.

Journeys across this land were therefore anxious affairs. Getting lost, stuck, robbed, cold, hungry, thirsty: these were all real risks. The moors were a place of threat, and a trial to cross, with few markers in the undulating landscape by which to orientate oneself and no shelter from the icy winds and sheets of rain that could tear in from the North Sea with a sharp Arctic edge of cold. There were days when thick white fog lay heavily, shrouding all distinguishing points of the path in its chilly dampness, and a straggler could quickly lose all sight and sound of their party in the muffled quiet. The roads were never good: where the peat was thin it washed away, leaving deeply pitted rock, whilst boggy peatland was churned into a quagmire under the weight of cattle or carts.

Arthur Young, the famous agricultural writer, was just one of many thousands who used this route to travel across the moors. One can imagine his chaise tipping, almost losing an axle perhaps, at the rounded six-foot boulder that breaks through the surface on the track just below the Plot; the horses dragging the chaise, snorting with the effort, up the hill from Oldstead's inn where they might have passed the night before attempting the steep ascent to the moors. He went on to describe his experience in 1771, in particular his descent on the northern edge of the moors in Cleveland, with horror:

> You are obliged to cross the moors they call Black
> Hambleton, over which the road runs in narrow hollows
> that admits a south country chaise with some difficulty,
> that I reckon this part of the journey was made at the
> hazard of my neck. The going down into Cleveland is
> beyond all description, terrible, you go through such
> steep, rough, narrow rock precipices, that I would
> sincerely advise you to go a hundred miles to escape it.

A perilous crossing of an intimidating wilderness: this is the frame in which to consider the grassy track that now crosses the Plot. If you were heading south to York, the Plot is the point at which the tired traveller finally, after fourteen miles of bleak moorland, begins to drop down out of the wind. Here there is some pasture and a narrow levelling of the land on the hillside before the track drops steeply to the undulating countryside below. It was an obvious point for rest; the arduous task of crossing the moor was accomplished, the view was now clear ahead over the Vale of York. The grey bulk of the towers of York Minster is already visible in the distance, only another twenty-odd miles away, and within reach of a day's hard walking. This is one of the most important characteristics of the Plot: its history has been bound up with rest, a pause in the journey; it has been a place of relief for centuries. It offered protection from the wind's ceaseless buffeting and a place where the eye is comforted by the lush greens of pasture after the barren upland. For a traveller coming up the hill from Oldstead, perhaps this was where they straightened the back to ponder the view before cresting the hill and braving the moors.

When Young risked his neck on the steep ascent to the plot, the track was in its heyday as a drovers' road. The drovers were bringing cattle and sheep from the Scottish uplands down to England. Some were to be fattened on English pastures, some were for the market in York, some went on as far as London's meat markets. Such was the popularity of the Plot with these Scottish drovers that, according to one local interpretation, they bequeathed it the name Scotch or Scots Corner by which it is marked on the Ordnance Survey. It was a trade that began in medieval times, and as the security on the perilous English–Scottish border improved and cattle-thieving declined in subsequent centuries, it swelled to significant proportions before the advent of the railways made the long journey with plodding cattle uneconomic.

As you sit in the quiet of the Plot now, imagine that for half a millennium livestock made their way across this land, wearing down the stones of the track at the corner to make the slight depression. Perhaps the animals were let out to pasture in the field opposite, while the drovers took an ale at the farmhouse. Some local histories have it that at this time the farmhouse was a hostelry for the drovers. The yard, now grassed over, would have been loud with the bellowing of cattle, the bleating of sheep and the curses of the drovers. Underfoot it would have been thick with mud and shit,

churned by hundreds of hooves. There would have been dogs
scavenging for scraps; the drovers sometimes sent their dogs
back alone, to retrace the journey unassisted, fed along the
way by innkeepers who would recoup the payment on the
drover's next visit. The shelter and comfort of a moorland
inn was the focus of intense appreciation. The pleasure of
the banked-turf fire, the tankard of ale and a slice of cold
meat were celebrated by travellers. The Chequers Inn, on
the drovers' road above Osmotherley at Slapestones Ford, was
famed for a turf fire which was said to have burned continu-
ously for 200 years.

The roughness of these Scottish drovers was much remarked
upon; they were variously described as thick-set, hirsute men,
shaggy, unkempt, wild and fond of their drink. Many of them
bore the characteristics of their origins as cattle raiders: they
were at a remove from settled society, beyond the intimidating
reach of local patronage, and beyond the sanction that would
enforce local norms. They had a rare freedom and independence. Charles I was horrified to discover they did not observe
the Sabbath, and brought in a law specifically requiring drovers
to do so. While their boisterous drinking sometimes made
them feared, they brought news and even occasionally letters,
as well as good custom, to remote inns.

Such was the economic importance of the drovers that suc-
cessive attempts were made to regularize and bring them
under control. A licensing system was introduced in Tudor
times requiring signatures from three justices of the peace, and
the stringent application process required that the drover be a
married householder of at least thirty years of age. The licence
lasted a year and the enormous sum of £5 was charged as a
fine for any contravention of the order. The authorities noted
with horror that the licensing system prompted a flood of

unsuitable applications: 'such a great number of persons seeking only to live easily and to leave their honest labour, have and do daily seek to be allowed and licensed . . . being most unfit and unmeet for those purposes'.

It was a life that offered few comforts, however. In the early eighteenth century the Scottish drovers were described as 'bare-kneed and bare-headed, though many of them were old men'. In time, the kilt of plaid wool gave way to homespun tweeds, but the feel of wet wool against the skin was an experience that lasted centuries. They carried a modest diet of oatmeal and some onions which were mixed with ewe's milk, or blood bled from the cattle to make a black pudding. A ram's horn filled with whisky was used 'regularly but sparingly'. The Scotch Corner's hostelry would have been thick with the smell of damp wool, peat smoke, onion and cowshit. The simplicity of their life and the roughness of their manners masked the skill required of them and the complexity of their work. One licence granted in the County of Westmoreland described their profession as 'the art and mystery of a drover'. The skill lay in matching the herd to the road for the best possible profit at market. Drive the cattle too fast and they arrived in poor condition and earned a lower price; drive them too slowly and they arrived at market late. The drover needed to know every mile of the way – where there was grazing, where it was possible to overnight the herd, where to stop for rest days. The Scottish drovers took a cut from the farmers for the livestock they took to market. The risks of cattle raids and disease were high but so also was the opportunity of making considerable profits. And they must have done so, given how the Tudor authorities grumbled at the deluge of applicants. Some two hundred years later, Walter Scott's grandfather, a drover, was reckoned to have built up a tidy fortune.

Drovers returning from York or London were likely to be carrying large sums of money and could be easy prey for bandits. The quarter sessions in both Thirsk and Northallerton, the courts nearest to the Hambleton Hills, recorded major robberies: in 1692, a drover was robbed of £144, whilst in 1726 Will Wood was robbed of 124 guineas and two half-broads in gold. In both cases, in a rough-and-ready form of justice, the villages where the burglaries took place were ordered to repay the money. Even as late as the mid-eighteenth century, the drovers were suffering big losses from cattle raiders – the law had a precarious hold on northern England's remoter parts – and in 1747 stolen cattle were valued at the staggering sum of £37,000. Recognition of the drovers' vulnerability earned them special exemptions which allowed them to continue carrying guns, swords and pistols despite the Disarming Acts of 1716 and 1748.

Part of what made the drovers so vulnerable to highwaymen was that theirs was such a slow business. Cattle managed ten to twelve miles a day and were therefore an easy target for a bandit on horseback. R. L. Stevenson's hero, in his short story 'St Ives', escaped with two drovers: 'a continued sound of munching and the crying of a great quantity of moor birds accompanied our progress which the deliberate pace and perennial appetite of the cattle rendered wearisomely slow'. In his novel *The Two Drovers* Walter Scott acknowledged that droving was a 'tedious, laborious and responsible office'. Cattle carry their huge bulk with effort, and little accelerates their placid docility, whether admonishments or a stick on the rump; they don't have the edgy skittishness of sheep, which prompts them to trot smartly at the sight of a sheepdog. The Scottish Lowlands to York was a journey of perhaps three weeks with rest days, the journey on to London another month or more.

It was so slow that the drovers took to knitting stockings as they walked behind their beasts, according to early reports. It's a poignant detail; these big, hairy men with their wild manners having the deftness of finger to knit as they walked. It describes an age when idle hands were regarded as a luxury; an age when every spare interstice of the day was gainfully employed to swell the household income.

But the knitting must never distract the drover from his primary task. The Irish were famous for their droving skills and how they encouraged the cattle to 'go sweetly along a road'. It required considerable skill to handle a large herd. If riled, cattle can become dangerous so the skilled drover has to coax the beasts on gently. The ideal was 'two or three deep, the same thickness all along, streaming away like a flock of wild geese', recommended *Field and Fern* in 1865. It was easier to manoeuvre on a wider track and the cattle appreciated the broad verges for grazing. The most easily identifiable characteristic of an old drovers' road is its breadth between two good boundaries of wall or hedge to prevent the cattle from escaping into neighbouring fields. Stretches of the drovers' road into the outskirts of York are still recognizable by the width of the verges, which are now sometimes used by travellers. Likewise, up on the moors Hambleton Street is in many parts still recognizably a drovers' road because of its generous breadth, the stony path spread out over fifty feet with broad grass verges.

One of the greatest expenses for the drover was that the cattle's feet had to be shod to protect them from deteriorating on the stone tracks. Because the hooves were cloven, each head of cattle required eight shoes. All the main stops on the drovers' routes would have had a blacksmith. Shoeing an ox was no easy task: the beast cannot raise one foot at a time (as a horse does to be shod), so it must either be lifted in a brace or thrown on the ground; manoeuvring a large animal would have been heavy and difficult work.

Many thousands of cattle followed the main droving routes from Scotland to England every year. In 1662, 18,574 cattle passed through Carlisle alone; by the 1700s it was estimated that the figure was 30,000 a year and by the end of the century it had risen to 100,000 using the half-dozen interconnecting drovers' roads to southern England. The trade epitomized one of the most enduring features of the British agricultural economy: livestock are bred in upland areas which cannot be used for crops, and are then moved down into the rich pastures of the lowlands for fattening. It has proved an efficient use of land for centuries, both generating an upland economy and maximizing the value of pasture on the lowland. Scotland and Wales were able to breed cattle but not to fatten them in sufficient quantities for the English market, so they drove them to pastures in England. As the towns and cities of southern England grew, the demand for meat rose. This cattle trade was one of the elements that underpinned England's industrialization and London's expanding role in global trade. The cattle that plodded along Hambleton Street and grazed at Scotch Corner ended up on the dinner plates of London's and Birmingham's bankers and industrialists. They also ended up, salted, in barrels to feed a hungry army and navy. For most of the eighteenth century Britain was at war – with Spain, Austria, America and above all with France – and that meant the demands on Scotland to keep producing its cattle steadily increased.

It's a fair assumption that the most vibrant period of the Plot's history was this half-millennium when the bellows of cattle echoed off the escarpment cliffs at night; when the blacksmith's hammer might be heard late into the evening to accommodate the needs of a client arriving late; when the drinking and singing of the drovers might have been heard a mile away down the hill by the villagers of Oldstead in their beds. What if a herd arrived as another was already settled for the night; imagine the cacophony of cursing, the corralling of reluctant beasts to keep the herds separated. The noise and smells of these boisterous men would fill the air: the anticipation of markets and good money to be made, now finally within sight; the relief of having left at last the wild remoteness of the north – the Borders, the Cheviots and the Yorkshire moors. From now on, their path was across a gentler land.

It was a path that, many weeks later, perhaps even after a period of fattening in Norfolk pastures, led the cattle into markets in London, not far from where I now sit in Hackney. Their route into the city makes uncanny family connections, pleasing links from place to place, from story to story, from plot to plot. Eleven miles north of London, the small market town of Barnet was a major fixture on the drovers' route, attracting thousands of the Scottish dealers. It became a suburb of London in the twentieth century, and it was where my father was born in 1927 and from where he made the journey in reverse, north from London to Yorkshire. In the eighteenth century Barnet had yet to arrive at its genteel future and was the biggest livestock market before Smithfield, attracting traders from across Europe and even as far away as Russia, from where Don Cossacks came to inspect the horses.

The main drovers' routes into London merged at the Angel, Islington: one branch came down from the north through Highgate along the Holloway Road, the other from the west along the Marylebone Road. From Angel, it was a short journey down St John Street to Smithfield, the biggest meat market in the country. Just north of the nearby City Road were fields where the drovers could rest the cattle before market, an area just south of where I now write. It was a difficult, noisy business, herding cattle through streets crowded with traffic, and perhaps this was the hardest part of the long journey, requiring skill to ensure no beast strayed or panicked – goring of passing pedestrians was not unknown. Nearly 70,000 animals passed through these London streets every week in the mid-nineteenth century and most of them on just two days. Such was the demand on Smithfield that other markets opened up to try and attract the drovers. There was one in Islington, another in Whitechapel, and a market opened briefly in 1836, occupying fifteen acres on St Paul's Road, also in Islington. The junction is marked by a handsome, now redundant church, designed by the architect Charles Barry who went on to design the Houses of Parliament. It's a ten-minute bike ride away from where I live. The church would have loomed over the fields full of bellowing cattle for a while, but the market was unlicensed and it was closed down.

The connections are distant now, buried under tarmac, streets of terraced housing and blocks of flats. The idea of cattle being driven along the traffic-clogged Holloway Road and St Paul's Road seems fanciful enough without imagining how these streets were the last stage of a journey to London for cattle and their drovers that could have brought them along Hambleton Street and across the Plot at Scotch Corner.

The railways finished off the droving trade. But Scotch Corner fell silent even earlier, when in the eighteenth century someone thought to make some money by instituting a toll on the Drovers' Road less than a mile up the track from Scotch Corner on Shaw's Moor. Tolls were the bane of the drover, because they not only increased his costs but were also time-consuming. Cattle had to go through the tollgates one at a time so they could be counted and the toll calculated. It was a laborious business which both slowed progress and made the cattle agitated. The toll at Scotch Corner, named Shaw's Gate, proved a mistake, prompting the development of a new track which bypassed the tollgate and headed straight down the bank. Scotch Corner lost its regular trade, although some element of its function as a hostelry lingered on. The tollgate was later dismantled, but the damage had been done and there were now other ways down the escarpment into Oldstead. Freed from the tramp of hundreds of hooves, the track became overgrown, retaining few traces of the bustle that the drovers had brought to the Plot.

4

A limited kind of company

It was February on the North Yorkshire moors, and the cold pressed clammy against the skin, whilst visibility was down to a few yards. We had walked up through the fields in the shelter of drystone walls, but on reaching the moor they ended, and we only had the stone track to guide us. A route that had seemed straightforward from the map now became shrouded in uncertainty as the whiteness of fog closed around us. It muffled the sound of our feet scuffing the stones of the track, it swallowed up the dale that lay below us and confronted us with a wall of white.

The plan had been to leave one path and join up with another a few hundred yards across the heather, but the thickness of the fog made even such a small distance without the security of a track daunting. The children were exhilarated by this wet, white world and were running around, shrieking with delight. I counted and recounted them, anxious that no small person should go astray running just that bit too far and disappearing in the fog. To try and find the path we needed, we formed a chain, each person within sight of the next, to survey the blurred outlines of the heather ahead for the track.

I sat down, only the ground seemed certain in this obscurity, and someone needed to stay put within sight of the walls that would take us back down into the dale. Beside me stood the baby-pack where my ten-month-old was wedged in a thick wad of clothing, his face cherry red, sleeping contentedly. Disembodied voices came and went in the whiteness: shouts to offer directions, or reports, interspersed with bursts of laughter. Occasionally I could make out the dim form of a body.

But we were not alone. I heard the grazing first, the distinctive sound of sharp teeth cutting the midwinter offering of a wind-blasted clump of grass, the odd shoot of younger heather. Then, through the sharp cold, that penetrating smell of sheep which pervades every corner of the moors. It's a mixture of droppings and the thick oiliness of wet wool which clings to a good tweed or a ewe's cheese, and is concentrated in its most pungent form in the medicinal lanolin cream. Staring hard into the mists, it was just possible to pick out the unkempt, shaggy forms. Their heads were down, stolidly grazing, undeterred by their unexpected visitors. Once the initial issue of whether we had brought fodder had been resolved, these sheep showed no more interest in us, and we, of course, showed little interest in them. Wherever you are on the Yorkshire moors, you will never be entirely alone; chances are that within a few feet there will be a sheep.

This was the kind of company Dad had little time for. He wanted them there, chomping away on the grass, but they were scenery. They had no epic story to tell; he liked his history on the grand scale, with battles, ideals, redemption, the collapse of civilizations and the like. In comparison, the steady continuity of sheep was too humdrum, too modest in its ambition, to occupy his thoughts. His attitude changed slightly when he became friendly with a prosperous local farmer late in life. He suddenly discovered that the world of sheep-dealing had its own unexpected glamour: pockets stuffed with more cash than Dad earned in a year, wads in discreet backhanders to seal deals at huge markets in different parts of northern England and Scotland. He travelled there in fast cars and drank heavily with his new-found friend, a massive overbearing man whose every utterance was at foghorn volume. He recounted his adventures, breathless with boyish excitement, on the phone.

But sheep meant more than money to me. As a child I fell asleep on summer nights in our cottage in Oswaldkirk soothed by the sound of the sheep in the fields across the road, and I woke to their early-morning bleating. It was always the sound of home. I watched them from my bedroom window, and whenever and wherever we walked they were our constant companions. We observed them give birth to small bloody bundles in the fields on chilly April expeditions, and we passed them sheltering in the shade of a tree, panting in the heat of a hot summer's day. I remember one winter morning, my grandmother was visiting and she had also been watching the sheep from her bedroom window in the cottage. She came down to breakfast in a state of great alarm. 'They're all dead! They're all dead!' she exclaimed, pointing to the hill opposite. 'I've been watching them and they haven't moved. They are all standing there dead.' We tried to reassure her that dead sheep don't stand, but she wasn't having any of it – she came from north London – so my younger brother and I put on wellingtons and overcoats and trekked across the fields to the hill and ran around flapping our arms among the flock to ensure that she, safe in the warmth back home, could see them moving.

On the North York moors, sheep comfortably outnumber every living creature with a population of 295,633 – just over eleven sheep for every man, woman and child resident in the area in 2006. More than any other creature they have created the character and shape of the moors; their grazing ensures the wide open views do not give way to scrub, and eventually woodland. It is the sheep, in well managed quantities, whose grazing keeps the heather low and leads to the new growth that is stimulated by their saliva as they work away like hundreds of thousands of conscientious park keepers to ensure that resplendent August show of even purple spread.

The moor is scored by their incessant efforts to survive and prosper in an unpropitious habitat. The sheep tracks criss-cross the heather, mapping the moor with paths that lead nowhere, take you in circles and get you lost. They don't follow human purpose but snake off across the hillside in search of grazing, water or shelter. The sheep wear the moor bald in the lee of a hill or wall, or around the roots of a hawthorn where they gather to shelter and ruminate. Lie down to rest on a hot summer's day and it is the sheep, along with the sweetness of heather and grass, that provide the distinctive combination of smells which defines the moor. It is a place where the elements are exposed: the shit, the minerals and the sharp astringent vegetation slowly rotting to peat. This land is their habitat and the hefting – mothers introducing their lambs to a particular area of the moor – ties them to a place for a lifetime. We are only ever visitors, whilst this is where the sheep live their short lives through all the variations of day and night, weather and season.

Walking on the drovers' track along the escarpment of the Hambleton Hills, on Black Hambleton and over Arden Great Moor, sheep are one's best company. Their ancestors have grazed these areas for centuries, and have worn deep tracks up to the escarpment such as at Sneck Yate Bank, where the track connects the villages below with the commonland pasture.

Many of the fields up here on the escarpment were once moor and have now been ploughed, but sheep are often still the beneficiaries; the grazing has been improved and many of the root crops grown are used to supplement their winter diet. The latter provide that rotting-vegetable smell, much like stale school dinners, that lingers over the land on damp November days. The nearest farm to the Plot, Cam Farm, runs a large flock. Sheep were probably kept on the Plot itself for much of the last millennium; there are ruins of old pens in the forestry below the Chapel. The drovers' track from Oldstead up on to the moor would have been used to drive flocks up from the villages to the grazing on Shaw's Moor, and bring them down again for lambing. This is a land determined by the needs of sheep, both for pasture and for passage. Initially, it was a few small flocks as part of mixed farming, but since the arrival of the Cistercian monasteries in the twelfth century, sheep have been the main form of farming across the moors. It is sheep that have been the most constant form of company on the Plot for over 800 years.

But this is a very particular kind of company. Sheep spend nine to eleven hours every day grazing and another eight to ten ruminating, usually at night, to extract the thin nutritional value of their diet. Over the course of their lives of seven or eight years these upland breeds can eat 100 times their own weight; their teeth tell their age, worn down by the relentless work required of them. Sheep's lives are characterized by an industrious single-mindedness; they have no time to waste, unlike that other long-time domesticated companion of human beings, cattle, who are curious creatures, only too happy to be distracted as they fix their huge, languid eyes on your progress through their field. While humans have had an intimacy with cattle – the physical proximity of milking and the necessity for winter shelter ensured a close relationship – and individual cows have often earned their own nicknames, there is little love lost between humans and sheep. They are remarkably self-sufficient animals, surviving in the harshest of environments where not even red deer can thrive. They require very little human care: apart from the lambing season, sheep are the least labour-intensive of any form of agriculture. In the UK, one shepherd can now look after 1,000 sheep; in New Zealand, the figure rises to 2,500–3,000.

Only up close can you get a sheep's attention, and it is only sustained when there is hope of fodder; the eyes stare back unflinching, the brilliant golds of the irises offsetting the astonishing black rectangular pupils. The prominent eyeballs are able to scan a field of vision of up to 306 degrees without the head moving. We cannot be deluded that any part of this encounter is about affection or loyalty on either part. The sheep that met us on the moor that February day were indifferent to our predicament – there was no gesture or expression that even the most resourceful interpretation could take for communication – but they were still company; their placid stolidity was a reassuring sign of familiarity and continuity.

Most people do not much like sheep. They are derided as timid, stupid, and even their sociability and tendency to stick together are regarded with contempt: 'sheep' is a term of abuse for the unthinking herd. Such is our disregard that one word covers both singular and plural. The sheep's expression of blank disdain would seem to indicate that those feelings are reciprocated. This has always been a relationship of clear-eyed mutual self-interest; human beings have protected and ensured fodder for sheep, and thus facilitated the multiplication of their genes to the current billion-strong population worldwide, while we have used every part of the sheep to meet our own needs.

To some evolutionary theorists, it is a moot point as to whether humans domesticated sheep or vice versa.

David Sullivan, a shepherd for fifty years, has immense respect for sheep and believes he has learned a lot from his lonely work in their company: 'They are beautiful animals. You can learn so much about people and yourself from them. They're not stupid, they're very intelligent. They can recognize faces – of both sheep and people – and remember them for years.' And he adds thoughtfully, 'I sometimes think that if they all ganged up on me, they would catch me out.'

His small cottage is lined with sheep memorabilia; there are china sheep on the shelves and a Victorian print of a flock hangs on the wall. 'I love sheep,' Sullivan says simply, despite the fact that his choice of career has led to a life of very hard work and has nearly bankrupted him three times.

When I ask why he loves them, he replies: 'Because they need me.'

But there is nothing sentimental in Sullivan's recognition of mutual need. He is brisk on that score: 'It is a completely natural process that sheep end up in the butcher's. We've grown separated from our food source. What matters is that the sheep are treated properly and slaughtered humanely.'

A sheep farmer regards his flock with a combination of carefully calculated self-interest and solicitude. He (and it is usually a he) will go to considerable lengths to help a lambing ewe, often working late into the night or early in the morning in miserable weather, even getting up at intervals through the night like a new mother to feed lambs that have been abandoned. He will talk admiringly of a breed for its good 'mothering', and hill breeds are particularly prized for their maternal skills. The use of anthropomorphic terms acknowledge the proximity of these mammals to human beings – their female reproductive organs are the closest to humans' of any other creature – and yet these attributes are exploited for commercial gain. The ewes are expected to produce at least one lamb, and preferably two, every year. The valiant efforts of hill sheep to protect and rear their young are part of why they are bred, and yet every year, when the ewes and lambs are separated at six months, this drive to mother is brutally thwarted. The lambs are loaded into lorries to the auction market for fattening; the anguished bleating that attends the event dispels any illusion that this is anything but deeply traumatic. Yet as a shepherd would also add, within a few days the ewes are grazing as phlegmatically as ever.

As with family, strong relationships are not always about affection so much as long-standing ties, and there is no animal with whom human history is more tightly bound than the sheep. The fortunes of ovine and human have been linked for nearly 9,000 years, and at many points over that timespan human societies have been dependent on sheep for their survival, just as sheep have been dependent on humans. This is the oldest and most continuous co-dependency between domesticated animal and human. The sheep is the one animal that has been used to meet every human need. Only when the full list is compiled does the extent of this become apparent. Meat, now the most significant product, was the least important until very recently.

From the beginning, sheep offered protein, and both blood and milk were extracted from the animal. Homer's *Odyssey*, around 1000 BCE, described a black pudding made from sheep's blood. Sheep's milk is particularly rich in fat and has been used across Europe to make some of its most famous cheeses, from ricotta and Roquefort to halloumi and, originally, Wensleydale.

Sheep provided wool, which was used for felt, clothing and oil, while their fat – tallow – offered the main source of lighting. As late as the nineteenth century, the demand for tallow was so great that the fat of a sheep was worth twice as much as the meat. Wax was rare and tallow candles offered the only refuge against the dark for centuries: in homes and churches, light would always have been accompanied by the distinctive, pungent smell of sheep. People would also have smelled of it – tallow was used in soap and sheep fat was rubbed on to sores to help them heal. Lanolin, extracted from wool, was used as the basis for ointments for skin conditions. Such was the respect for the curative properties of sheep products that these feature in many healing traditions across the world. Just the smell of sheep was thought sufficient to cure whooping cough and tuberculosis. One treatment for the former was to roll a child in the dew of a sheepfold while another was to wrap the patient in a freshly removed sheepskin.

Sheep bones have been used to make music; the Roman word for pipe, *tibia*, is now used for one of the leg bones in all vertebrates. One such pipe made from a sheep tibia was found in an Iron Age barrow on Malham Moor in the Yorkshire Dales. A bag of skin from the sheep was often attached to this pipe to make a type of musical instrument found in cultures all over the world, but most famous now as Scottish bagpipes. Sheepskin was used to make drums as early as ancient Egypt. It was used for writing too: the skin, once stripped of wool, stretched and dried, made parchment.

Sheep dung, as a fertilizer, ranked third after wool and milk – and above meat – in importance in medieval England. Dung was also used in the scouring of wool, removing its natural oils as part of the refinement process for making yarn. It was even used for fuel. Sheep gut was used for slings, bags, even violin strings, while the hides were used to make ropes, whips and footwear; oiled skins were used until relatively recently by North Sea fishermen.

Finally, the horn was used for cups, handles, spoons, lantern windows, tent pegs, combs and shoehorns. In sum, sheep met the need for food and clothing, for music and writing, for light, for tools, rituals and weapons, and for healing.

The Bible reflects the central and enduring the relationship between human and sheep in Middle Eastern and European cultures. Sheep are one of the most striking continuities running through both the Old and the New Testaments; the metaphors of lamb and shepherd used in the Bible have proved resonant over several millennia. Abraham sacrificed a ram in place of his son Isaac, and this theme is picked up again in the New Testament, where the Paschal Lamb is the dominant metaphor of Christ's sacrifice in the crucifixion. 'Lamb of God, you take away the sins of the world, have mercy on us,' runs the Catholic Mass. The single lamb becomes the symbol of innocence and powerlessness, portrayed in many paintings through history. Alongside this theme of sacrifice is an equally important theme of God as the shepherd. David the psalmist was a shepherd and sang 'The Lord is my shepherd', a hymn of cosmic consolation. God, as shepherd attentive to the needs of his flock, leads them to 'pastures green' and to water to 'revive their drooping spirits'. God as lamb, God as shepherd; God as sacrificial victim, God as protector. The contradictions of the relationship between sheep and human – do we protect them or exploit them? – have been played out in these sacred texts, used to offer spiritual insight into compassion and sacrifice in the relationship between God and his people.

Arguably, the humble sheep has done more to determine the course of human history in western Europe than any other animal. It was one of the most widely traded commodities of the European medieval economy and it was woollen exports that drew Britain, a damp island off the continent's northern coast, into the long-distance networks of trade with Italian merchants and the weavers of Flanders. Medieval Britain was quite literally built by the wealth generated by wool. It paid for monasteries, parish churches, cathedrals, wars and even the enormous ransom of a king, Richard the Lionheart. Wool and its manufacturing were at the core of the English economy for several centuries; as late as the seventeenth century, wool made up two-thirds of British exports. The Lord Chancellor's official seat in the House of Lords is still a woolsack; the second most important political office in the land, his power rested on wool.

Sheep have been our most constant source of company, and the evidence of that company is in the tracks left through our language, place names and surnames. We talk of being 'on tenterhooks', a reference to how woven wool had to be stretched; we 'give it a whirl' from the whorl or weight used in spinning; we can be 'dyed in the wool'; and we talk of 'heirlooms', harking back to the most valuable household possession as a source of income that passed from family to family. Across England, one of the most common words associated with place, dating back to Saxon times, is 'sheep' or 'sceap' – 'skip', 'ship', 'shap' or 'shep' – from which we get Skipton, Shipley and Sheppey. Countless English surnames derive from sheep and their care, such as Shepherd, Shearer, Lamb, Hoggart, Tucker and Hogg; others come from the wool trade, such as Draper, Dyer, Fuller, Webster, Weaver and Walker. Sheep and their products mapped places and people.

Having been the basis of the medieval economy, sheep played a key role in the development of capitalism. Shares are still referred to as 'stock', and one of the basic institutions of capitalism is still called a 'limited stock company'. Karl Marx awarded sheep a central place in the development of the instruments of capital formation: it was the capital accumulated by livestock – in particular sheep – farming that was reinvested to achieve the agricultural improvements of the seventeenth and eighteenth centuries. Wool played a crucial role in Britain's industrial revolution in West Yorkshire – the destination of much of the wool produced on the North Yorkshire moors. Other parts of the country in the seventeenth century had larger woollen manufacturing centres, such as those around Exeter and Norwich, but West Yorkshire had a great number of small, independent clothiers who depended on weaving to supplement income from farming on the poor-quality land of the Pennines. These innovators could rely on plentiful supplies of wool, and the Pennines' soft water was needed for the manufacturing process. Furthermore, the water running off the moors was steeply graded and could be used to power mills. It was with Yorkshire wool that Britain developed industrialization of textiles; the skills and machinery were later transferred to cotton and brought into being the textile industry of Lancashire and West Yorkshire.

Britain exported its success story across the world. It was sheep that made the Antipodean British empire profitable. Britain still holds an important position as supplier of breeding stock to the Antipodes. Charles Darwin was fascinated by the knowledge of sheep breeders, whose expertise had accumulated over centuries by the time he began his studies on evolution. Dolly the Sheep, the first cloned mammal, was a British (Scottish) invention, reflecting a tradition of genetic manipulation going back centuries. There is hardly a branch of British political, social or cultural life that has not been affected by sheep; they feature in every art gallery and in many a novel. This long, sprawling history is now working through an igno- minious chapter towards what some fear might even be its end, particularly for hill farmers. After a millennium as one of the world's great sheep-rearing nations, Britain is dropping fast down the ranking, currently sixth after China, India, Australia, New Zealand and Argentina. On upland like the North York moors, sheep have been the only form of viable farming over the last half-century, propped up by subsidies, but as the latter have been cut back farmers are selling their flocks and the future holds great uncertainty. Could new anxieties about global food supplies lead to a revival of sheep-farming, or will it continue to shrink as ageing farmers retire and their offspring look elsewhere for a better and more secure income? The foot- and-mouth outbreak of 2001 was an eerie indicator of what that future may hold; the fields were empty and silent, the land strangely still.

5

A quiet metropolis

After two days of rain we walk along the track to the Chapel with the sound of the skylarks hovering over the fields. The wind has dropped, and there is a thick, moisture-laden fug. Dropping down to the Plot on the track we lose the small breeze, sheltered by the trees. Around the Chapel, midges cluster in the dank shade and I get bitten all over my neck, hands and face. We slap them away, and jiggle, sandwich in hand, unable to sit. It is a brief picnic. We head on down the track to the pub at Oldstead to heal the bites with a pint of Black Sheep.

My mood lifts when we stop by Shandy Hall, the home of Laurence Sterne, in Coxwold. The sun is now shining, and we wander through the enchanting garden which looks across the valley to the wooded hills of the escarpment and the Plot. Just visible against their dark bulk are the ruins of Byland Abbey.

'Moths,' enthuses the curator Patrick Wildgust when I explain how I'm writing about the company I can find on the Plot. His answer brings me up short. Moths were not the kind of company I had ever noticed on the acre. In London,

I wage perennial low-intensity warfare on moths, which select my best-quality clothes to feast on. 'What about the moths on the Plot? We could do a moth record there,' insists Wildgust.

I am tempted to ask why.

Seven months later, I received an email from Wildgust. I was in the office on a noisy London street; outside dirty windows, there was a clutter of buildings as far as the eye could see. Wildgust told me that on the evening of 8 August he took three colleagues, the Yorkshire Moth Recorder, a lepidopterist and an ecologist, up the Drovers' Road to the Chapel, and they trapped, identified and released thirty species in three hours. They matched up species with food-plants and habitats, and found that the ancient woodland plants along the track supported a rich diversity of moths.

Wildgust helpfully listed the names – both the Latin and the vernacular, with their codes so that I could find their images on the internet. From my keyboard in London, I could glimpse the company that visits the Chapel unre-marked-upon. It is a population that knows the plot more intimately, and has been a more persistent presence over millennia, than human beings. It takes a computer to introduce me to company I've been unwittingly visiting for forty-four years.

The vernacular names entranced me: Garden Grass-veneer; Grass Emerald; Small Fan-footed Wave; Riband Wave; Red Twin-spot Carpet; Purple Bar; Small Phoenix; Dark Marbled Carpet; Green Carpet; July Highflyer; Small Rivulet; Clouded Border; Brimstone Moth; Peppered Moth; Lesser Swallow Prominent; Yellow-tail; Dingy Footman; Lesser Broad-bordered Yellow Underwing; True Lover's

Knot; Antler Moth; Small Angle Shades; Dark Arches; Small Dotted Buff.

Here was not only a glimpse of the crowds I had ignored on the Plot, but also a history of human curiosity, a reflection of human endeavour and preoccupations – carpets, footmen, lovers and shapes – as cryptic and elusive as the species they named, captured in a system of categorization.

Wildgust's enthusiasm for moths is appealing. This is a species that does not offer human beings any kind of performance – no song or scent or aesthetic pleasure, given that the subtle beauty of their varied markings is hard to see in the dark. To view the exquisite grey frosting and lacework of their wings requires patience and persistence. This company, teeming at dusk in the thick grass verges and sleeping out the days, is perfectly camouflaged as twigs. Busying about short lives with purpose and energy, the moths were a sharp reminder of how the Plot is a small metropolis.

This was another kind of company my father did not care for. He fought a small, albeit ineffectual, battle with the wildlife of the Plot. He stamped down the molehills; he sprayed those bees that took up residence in the Hut and eventually killed the wild hive. But there was worse.

It was a sultry day, grey but heavy with late-summer heat. There were several of us children and we'd accompanied Dad up to the Chapel to cut the grass. My parents' marriage was collapsing in a welter of despair and fury, and we children were all sucked into the drama as terrified witnesses, confidants or desperate arbiters, summoning family conferences to stave off the horror of the family falling apart. Perhaps he badgered us into weeding or trimming the grass by the walls.

For as long as I could remember we had shared this piece

of land with a family of adders. As small children we accompanied each other cautiously down the path to a spot in the bank which always caught the sun. Here, above the wall, on a smooth bed of pine needles, an adder would usually be coiled, lazily absorbing the heat of the sun. His dramatic patterning rippled over the folds of reptilian skin, the brilliant tawny yellow scales glinting in the sun. We thrilled at the possibility of danger, we delighted in our bravery, and we always tiptoed away as quietly as we had arrived. *The* adder had a definite article, like the Chapel, the Hut and the track, such was its centrality in our lives. Once, when a monk borrowed the Hut for a fortnight's retreat, he reported that the adder came to bask on the stone doorstep, effectively trapping him inside. But the monk was unperturbed; he seemed to understand, as we did, that we shared this Plot with another family whose discreet comings and goings we only glimpsed and who, during the long periods we were not there, reclaimed the run (if one can use such a word of snakes) of the place.

But on this particular August afternoon the adder was not in its usual place; it was on a section of the track at the entrance to the Plot where the turf is smooth, and has a slightly hollow ring when stamped. Our dog, Fan, got agitated. For a brief moment there was fear, a need to protect, but it passed and the dog was on the lead. We could have walked quickly away, but my father had a spade and he raised it. The snake, electrified by the danger, was transformed from the sleepy sunbather of our acquaintance and launched into a spellbinding performance. Its body was flexed, its head a foot off the ground, its tongue flashing in and out, hissing with fury. The dog was in near-apoplexy as it tugged furiously on the lead. And my father – were his eyes round and popping as they always were when angry? – brought the spade down on the writhing body. Again and again and again. I watched, horrified yet unwittingly fascinated. Finally it lay limp, pathetic, no more than a piece of waste to be tossed into the undergrowth; a beautiful, dignified creature whose species had happily coexisted with us for two decades was dead.

6

The view

If my father had had to name the single characteristic of North Yorkshire that he most loved, it would have been the views. The walks he took us on were always over hilltops and moorland; they were always about big skies and wide-open vistas. I had to grow up before I could see what he loved so much. He would sit squeezed into his little car, careering along the country roads: 'Look, look! Marvellous,' he would instruct. It was one of the very few things he wanted to teach me. Even as an adult I was admonished to look at the view (as if I hadn't learned) with a combination of boastful one-upmanship and profound pity for me as an urban dweller, boxed into straight lines and deprived of horizons. What he was really saying was, What riches can you possibly find anywhere to compare with this? It was one of the few things on which I think he was probably completely right.

It must have been the view from Scotch Corner's ruins that first struck the sixteen-year-old on a ramble through the woods to Gormire Lake on a June day in 1944, and ensured that he did not forget the Plot. It looked out across the Vale of York towards the city and its minster, twenty miles away, and stretched well beyond to a horizon in south Yorkshire. Thirteen years after his first visit he returned, and signed the lease on the land; he mixed the mortar and hauled the roof timbers into place; and when his Chapel was finished he built a stone bench cut into the bank from which to contemplate the view.

But the view was to prove a fickle companion: even while he was building the Chapel, the Forestry Commission's heavy machinery must have been audible as it ploughed the moor for coniferous plantations. The stone bench was where, instead, he would watch the sapling trees edging up slowly, year by year, hemming in the curious stillness that has enclosed the Plot ever since. He lost his view. Now the Chapel faces a thick wall of conifers, screened by a row of cherry trees thirsty for light, planted by a stricken forester's conscience. You have to leave the Chapel and stand up on the drovers' track above the Plot to catch a glimpse, elbowed by trees, of the view that my father first discovered as a teenager. By the uneven ground of the burial mound there, the eye catches the sight of the towers of the Ferrybridge power station on the horizon, sixty miles to the south near Selby. To the right, the escarpment curves round above the neighbouring valley of Cockerdale, coming to a wooded point. On your left, forestry now conceals how the escarpment doubles back into Hell Hole. Leaving the Chapel behind and heading back to the road, you find yourself crossing Shaw's and Oldstead Moors, a bald land of huge fields which roll away to the line of forestry plantations. Beyond the drystone walls in the distance the moors lie to the north and east in layered outlines of rounded ridges: these were the views that accompanied my father's weekly visits.

My father had fallen for the Plot because of its view and its remoteness. It very quickly lost both; never did he imagine that the view from the Hambleton Hills would bring quite so much company. He had found a forgotten corner of England where farmers worked meagre soils on an explosed upland; a bleak, inaccessible place to live where the few scattered farmhouses hunkered down behind copses as protection from the wind. Over the last half-century, it has become a place visited by hundreds of thousands of people every year. Nine million people annually visit the North York moors, and a good proportion of them arrive by climbing Sutton Bank on the A170, just over a mile from the Plot. People drive from all over northern England, thinking nothing of travelling sixty miles down from Newcastle or fifty up from Doncaster to enjoy Sutton Bank's view. One tourist website makes the wonderful claim that 'one can see for ever' from Sutton Bank on a clear day. It feels like that: a great spread of land and sky which stretches from the edge of the steep escarpment. Walking here is the nearest one can get to flying while keeping one's feet on the ground. From each point, the expansive views roll out towards distant horizons. There are no abrupt disruptions to snag attention, little detail near at hand to grab focus, so the eye wanders, gliding over moor, dale and vale, providing a deeply satisfying exercise of the tiny muscles that work our vision. It means that later in the evening, in the warmth of a pub, there are not so much memorable details of the experience but sensations of space, shape and contour. The very sparseness comes as a relief to eyes weary of the hyperactive stimulation of cityscapes.

A care-home worker from Hull told me one rainy day in May that it was her second visit within a week; she loved the view. She said walking along the edge of the escarpment made her feel on top of the world. It was the view that gave

her a sense of getting away from it all, of perspective. 'It
recharges my batteries,' she said, her thin face tense with the
anxieties of her life in Hull, 'I can get in touch, get that connected feeling.' A father and his adult son were pulling on
waterproofs and bracing themselves for the cold rain outside;
they came every weekend from Middlesborough (a sixty-mile
round trip) to walk. Why? I asked; 'Because we like it,' they
replied, but felt no need to offer any further explanation as
they headed off on to the rain-sodden, wind-blasted escarpment, the rain dripping from their hoods, the swishing of
their waterproof trousers set to accompany them all day.
Sutton Bank and the Hambleton Hills is now on one of
England's most popular long-distance paths, called the
Cleveland Way; it follows many parts of the Drovers' Road.
Its decline from the mid-1800s turns out to have been a brief
lonely interlude of a century, and the Drovers' Road is now
rarely without a group of dogged walkers with backpacks and
stout boots. On one occasion, as a brilliant August sun blazed
out of a blue sky and the white clouds scudded alongside us,
the atmosphere was that of a carnival along the narrow path
between the bilberry bushes on the escarpment edge at
Roulston Scar, as we were hailed by couples who had driven
down from Durham for the view, the exhilaration reverberating in their loud laughter.

    For this largely urban audience, views must be accessible
by car and happily lend themselves to the camera. That get-
away-from-it-all experience must be easy to find, so they are
signposted as 'viewpoints' – perhaps helpfully with the
symbol of a camera – and marked on the map with a semicircular spray of blue dashes. Thus directed, the crowds
arrive, so lay-bys or car parks need to be built, and pedestrian
crossings are arranged to ensure that the appeal of the view

does not cause traffic accidents. At Sutton Bank they have built a visitor centre with a pricey car park and a café to facilitate visiting the view, as a stop-off point on one of the main routes from the industrial areas of southern and west Yorkshire through the North York Moors National Park to the coast.

My father hated the company of tourists. He called them grockles; from behind his wheel in the car, he would pour contempt on them in a running commentary on their motoring skills – slow, uncertain of directions, they were '*dawdling*', he complained, as if this were a crime – and he went on to launch a scathing critique of their clothing, facial hair and footwear: he was particularly suspicious of anyone with a beard or sandals. Not even on the Plot could he get away: you can hear the steady hum of motor traffic going up Sutton Bank accompanied by the intermittent roar of motobikes a mile away through the forest. The backfiring of vehicles on the one-in-three gradient up the escarpment ricochets around these valleys. The cross-country motorbikes can suddenly erupt from a corner on the forest tracks, brilliant with fluorescent stripes and zig-zags; the riders in psychedelic suits charge their machines up the muddy lanes, farting and roaring, the rock and turf reverberating beneath your feet. Or a group of mountain bikers hurtles down the track, red-faced, caked in mud, panting with exhilaration, forcing you to the verge. Overhead, the gliders from the club a mile away are loosed from the aero-tow, which tugs them up into the sky on a long metal cable, as its old engine splutters. The Plot is on a popular walk and one is never alone there for long. There are often campers on Bank Holidays – scouts, outward bounders or some such – in the woods across the valley and their shouts drift up the hillside. All around the Plot there is the pressing noise of activity,

Nat
Porlock

exercise and recreation. The solitude my father sought in a remote hillside was lost and the view he found drew far more company than he could ever have imagined.

The walkers stroll past the Chapel, peering over the stone-wall windbreak into the grassy clearing, some curious enough to push open the small wicket gate and walk in. I like the way the walkers use the Plot. The indifference of some, who show little interest in the nondescript stone buildings, is particularly impressive to me. Such is the modesty of the Chapel and the Hut, many presume they are just farm buildings or a forestry warden's hut. There are moments when the isolation of the place confers a peculiar brief conviviality, like the time we met a woman in late middle age from South Yorkshire up for a day's walk with a friend. Within minutes she had confided much of her life story – of never having married, of being still a virgin, she declared with peals of laughter reverberating around the forest – as well as that of her younger friend's broken marriage.

Equally admirable to my mind is the sense of entitlement of the group of walkers who once opened the gate, calmly picked their way through the picnic we had spread on the ground outside the Hut, and approached the Chapel. Such was their familiarity with the place that they assumed it belonged to them every bit as much as it did to us. After a while they settled themselves quietly on a wall nearby and opened up their picnic. Initially open-mouthed at what would have outraged my father's sense of proprietorship, I checked myself; I have subsequently realized that no one can really own, in any conventional sense, such an orphaned place. It belongs to many strangers: those who regularly walk their dogs up there and the walkers on day-trips from cities many miles away who return every year.

Several years ago, as we drove the car full of our camping kit down the track, we passed some walkers, and when they subsequently arrived at the Plot they told us they had been worried that our car indicated that the place they regularly visited had been made into a weekend retreat. The walkers who come frequently have created their own understandings of this place, like the couple whom we once met who said they returned annually on their anniversary.

'Nowt but bloody views,' complained a Yorkshireman mending a roof in Ampleforth, commenting on his county. Views are a tourist taste. Sutton Bank now perfectly fits the point made by landscape historian Trevor Rowley that 'large areas of rural England . . . are seen by millions and trodden on by hardly anyone at all. There are huge tracts of countryside emptier now than they have been for thousands of years.' The walkers follow the routes that offer dramatic views, but the land over which they look has never been so empty. The path from Oldstead to Kilburn, for example, was once the route for generations of schoolchildren going to and from school, and for worshippers attending church and chapel in Kilburn. It is now only used by the occasional walker; on the times I have walked it, I have met other people once.

The company of tourists is restless. In 1950 the English travelled on average five miles a day and this has multiplied six times in fifty years to an average of thirty miles a day. In the sixties, as car ownership expanded, 'going for a drive across the moors' became no longer a journey with purpose but a pleasure in itself. The moors are particularly well suited to motoring: the big panoramic views are exhilarating at speed because they fit into a windscreen; these are views that you have time to see because there are no mountains to crane your head at or dramatic ravines to frustratingly glimpse. You can bowl along the A170 – surely one of the most beautiful roads in England – with moors, hills, forests, stately homes and ruined castles spread all about you. The motorbikers love these roads.

When I fall into conversation with bikers gathered at the marketplace in Thirsk, there's a couple who have come over from Pontefract and Doncaster and are heading out to Whitby – a round trip of 250 miles. It's an average mileage for their outings, which see them criss-cross the north of England every weekend. They boast of doing 140 mph on a clear stretch, but closer to 70 or 80 over the moors. Their view is not limited by the car window, it is all around them. They like the thrill of danger, of recklessness and of nomadic move-ment, but it brings little loyalty to place, and even less intimacy.

We see more landscapes than ever, but most of them are a blur, glimpsed at speed. We gain a sense of the length and breadth of England, and with that this island has shrunk. We have acquisitive eyes filling visual catalogues with new images; we can compare and contrast across countries and continents. Yet the more we see, the less the vast majority of us understand what we are seeing, or know it in the way that previous generations who worked the land could claim. How did the eye come to assume such dominance in experiencing the land?

The word 'landscape' originated in Anglo-Saxon and was used to denote a small patch of cultivated ground, but it slipped back into common usage in the eighteenth century with a new meaning in which it had to meet demanding requirements. It had to have 'prospect' and 'perspective' so that the eye could sweep over aesthetically satisfying contours and find circular movement from horizon to foreground. Detail was irrelevant, and so also was what lay beneath the surface; the visual appearance was everything. Geographer Denis Cosgrove argues that this emphasis on the view in the eighteenth century was a response to capitalism and urbanization: 'landscape is an idea which undermines the collective use of land. It is locked into an individualist way of seeing . . . It is a way of seeing which separates subject and object, giving lordship to the eye of the single observer. In this, the landscape idea either denies collective experience . . . or mystifies it in an appeal to transcendental qualities of a particular area.' The views that were singled out for praise in the eighteenth century, Cosgrove explains, were those where one did not end up 'gazing upon other people, whether workers or tourists'. The view from Sutton Bank fits Cosgrove's definition: looking out from the escarpment, one's perspective is uninterrupted by fellow tourists, and the distance to the farmland below is such that there is no risk of spotting the Eastern Europeans who pick potatoes in the area. The parallel lines of pylons that march in tandem the length of the Hambleton Hills are far enough away to fade and the steam clouds of Ferrybridge, one of England's biggest producers of carbon, can with a little effort be ignored on the horizon.

An understanding that the panoramic view symbolizes 'egotistical domination' runs back to biblical times, argues historian Simon Schama, citing Satan's temptation of Jesus in the desert, when he took him to 'an exceedingly high mountain' and 'showed him all the kingdoms of the world and their splendour', offering it all to Christ if he would worship the Devil. The eye that skims the surface, surveying the land from an ego-centred viewpoint, and that sets up an active viewer and a passive land, is known as the 'western gaze' in landscape studies. It is a perspective that privileges control, writes anthropologist Barbara Bender, and she points out how it has become central in describing how we think: our relationship with land spills over into the understanding of our imagination. So you have 'a point of view' or a 'field' of study; you 'chart new territories', 'ground' your knowledge and 'break new ground'. The view (and the turns of phrase it has prompted) disregards the agency of other people.

Fields and woods are not considered the creations of human activity but aesthetic shapes and colours, and the view takes scant notice of the forms of life invisible to the naked eye, let alone those beneath the surface: the worms, woodlice, ants, beetles, flies; the great wriggling, heaving quantities of life working the land for their own survival. The privileging of the visible brings its own political priorities: the coniferous plantations provoked outrage when they were planted, whereas nitrate pollution barely reaches beyond the wallcharts of expert environmentalists. The viewer today has been schooled into passivity, so that the primary task is contemplation of the land. The tourist from urban West Yorkshire admiring the view at Sutton Bank is the culmination of nearly 300 years of cultural dispossession designed to control imaginative and physical access to land, and with that, the crucial questions of who the land belongs to – and who belongs on the land. The story of how this happened can be traced through various places, all within a few miles of the Plot.

The most enduring formulation of landscape has proved to be the eighteenth-century concept of the picturesque: satisfying landscapes were those that could provide a pleasing composition of foreground and distance, preferably with a ruin or rugged tree trunk to add interest. Looking at a view was a process of composing pictures. The fashion for the picturesque came at the peak of the bitterly contested enclosure movement, when millions of English acres, in particular common land, were split up into rectangles and squares using the straight lines and regular corners of new surveying techniques. The strips of the open field, which ensured a distribution of differing grades of land, was amalgamated into larger fields for the sole use of their owner. Across the country, 200,000 miles of hedgerow were planted between 1750 and 1850, transforming a swathe of land across central England from the southern limits of the North Yorkshire moors down to Wiltshire.

Along the top of the Hambleton Hills the land was parcelled into large rectangular fields in the nineteenth century; only the old names indicate its history as 'town' pasture for the local villages. Enclosure deprived people of access to common land not just for grazing, but also for kindling, peat turfs and quarry stone. The latter was particularly important to the surrounding villages, as the quantities of old spoil heaps and quarry workings scattered along the Hambleton Hills show. The consolidation of landholdings created a landless and newly impoverished workforce; they often had no option but to leave the land to find work in the fast-growing industrial cities. Britain was the first – and the most ruthless – of all European countries to force people off the land. It took a century of energetic forgetting of the history of contested enclosure and its brutal depopulation of rural England for people to come to love the chequered patchwork landscape, hedged in hawthorn, that it created.

What the advocates of the picturesque sought were landscapes with no traces of enclosure or industrialization: the

Lake District was discovered as a landscape that appeared
'natural'. Devotees complained that the Yorkshire moors were
dull; they lacked the drama of the Lakes or even the Dales.
The view from the Hambleton Hills did not meet the
requirements of the age; there was no point of immediate
interest in the foreground, no quaint ruins within sight. But
for the eighteenth-century tourist the arduous journey up
Sutton Bank could be rewarded, a few miles further on, by
exactly the right kind of view at the Rievaulx Terrace (providing, of course, that they could get permission to visit from
the landowners, the Duncombe family). Here, nature had
been improved to meet the aesthetic requirements of the
picturesque. In this area of North Yorkshire, the picturesque
was never natural, it had to be constructed, and Thomas
Duncombe spared no expense. A broad grassy terrace was
built in the 1750s above the valley of Rievaulx; walking
along the terrace, one glimpses through gaps cleared in the
woods the ruins of Rievaulx's monastery. Arthur Young
described his enchantment in *A Six Months' Tour of the North
of England*:

> You look through a waving break in the shrubby wood,
> which grows upon the edge of the precipice, down
> immediately come upon a large ruined abbey, in the
> midst, to appearance, of a small but beautiful valley;
> scattered trees appearing among the ruins in a stile [*sic*]
> too elegantly picturesque to admit description. It is a
> casual glance at a little paradise which seems as it were
> in another region.

On either end of the terrace, exquisite temples were constructed; in one, ceilings were painted with copies of works

seen in Roman palaces on the Grand Tour, and visitors were expected to sit around the walls for their cup of tea (a new luxury) while pondering this ostentatious model of taste and cosmopolitan experience in the midst of the Yorkshire countryside. Alexander Pope had announced that 'all gardening is landscape painting', and the Rievaulx Terrace was one of the boldest attempts of that age to illustrate his point; the aim was to bring to life the paintings of Claude Lorraine on the Yorkshire moors. Rievaulx was 'unique, perhaps the most spectacularly beautiful . . . landscape conception of the eighteenth century', claims the landscape historian Christopher Hussey. It was a model of how to entertain company in a remote place; did my father ever recognize his Plot as a very modest imitation?

The creation of such designed landscapes depended on the skills of surveying, mapping and fortification developed for the expanding British trade empire (rather as Teflon was a by-product of the Cold War space race). It was expensive, but the newly arrived Duncombe family had a fortune from their recent past in City banking, and they used their landscaping projects to demonstrate that despite their mercantile origins they had all the taste required for their new landed status: it took twenty men a day just to hand-scythe the grass of the terraces. Rievaulx also made an important political statement: the ruins were a reminder of 'Gothic tyranny' and 'corruption and superstition justly overthrown' whilst, in contrast, the classical temples represented the Enlightenment. Thomas Duncombe was a Hanoverian Whig and 'his opposition to the Jacobites could have provided a motive for memorializing the ruins', observes one landscape historian. This was one eighteenth-century interpretation of the Yorkshire landscape, expensive, ostentatious, and designed to illustrate status and political ambition. The picturesque was never simply about beauty.   *eg Halswell - Som*

William Wordsworth and his Romantic interpretation of nature and how we are to look at it proved even more influential. He took landscape out of the eighteenth-century picturesque frame that made it contained and static. Above all, he walked this landscape. It was not just something to look at but also to feel with one's body. He got footsore, tired and thirsty. His legacy is metaphorically in the backpack of every walker, and sits on the dashboard of the cars parked at Sutton Bank: how the English tourist sees and experiences the land owes much to Wordsworth. By the late eighteenth century a new road had been built up the escarpment at the Bank, cutting into the steep rock face and taking sharp hairpin bends to finally open up direct access to the moors beyond. It was part of an improvement of roads in the second half of the century which fuelled a new fashion for travelling to discover the English landscape. On 15 July 1802, a few years after the Sutton Bank road's construction, Wordsworth and his sister Dorothy walked the new road on their way from Thirsk to Helmsley via Rievaulx, a good fifteen miles. As they walked up the escarpment, Dorothy described how glad they were to come upon a stream, they were so thirsty. 'The view was hazy, and we could see nothing from the top of the hill but an indistinct wide-spreading country, full of trees, but the buildings, towns and houses were lost,' she wrote in her journal. A few months later, on 4 October, the day of William's marriage near Scarborough, they returned by the same route to Grasmere in the Lake District. William, his new wife Mary and Dorothy reached the top of Sutton Bank just after sunset. Despite the dusk, they did not want for a view, wrote Dorothy:

Far far off us, in the western sky, we saw shapes of castles, ruins among the groves, a great spreading wood, rocks and single trees, a minster with its tower unusually distinct, minarets in another quarter, and a round Grecian Temple also; the colours of the sky of a bright grey, and the forms of a sober grey. As we descended the hill, there was no distinct view, but of a great space.

William wrote a few lines of poetry to mark the occasion: 'Composed October 4th, 1802, after a journey over the Hambleton Hills, on a day memorable to me – the day of my marriage. The horizon commanded by those hills is most magnificent.'

> *Dark and more dark the shades of evening fell;*
> *The wished-for point was reached – but at an hour*
> *When little could be gained from that rich dower*
> *O prospect, whereof many thousands tell.*
> *Yet did the glowing west with marvellous power*
> *Salute us: there stood the Indian citadel,*
> *Temple of Greece, and minster with its tower*
> *Substantially expressed – a place for bell*
> *Or clock to toll from! Many a tempting isle,*
> *With groves that never were imagined, lay*
> *'Mid seas how steadfast! Objects all for the eye*
> *Of silent rapture; but we felt the while*
> *We should forget them; they are of the sky,*
> *And from our earthly memory fade away.*

Wordsworth had invested in this view from Sutton Bank the Romantic drama with which, 200 years later, we still interpret it. The view was now a thing of splendour and awe, charged with significance to human beings. It is to the Wordsworths and their muddy boots on that day in the twilight of 1802, that we can trace the exponential growth of twentieth-century tourists following the same route up the Sutton Bank switchbacks. It was he who urged them to find places that would give them experiences that would benefit their souls. His idea was revolutionary because it entailed the perception that beauty could lie in space and distance, that one could enjoy the great bowl of sky over the Hambleton Hills, a panorama of clouds forming and breaking up as they eased their way over England, linking up oceans from the Atlantic to the North Sea. He promoted the idea that human beings could come to love rather than fear the enormity of nature, and find ease in the humility by which such scale shrank human egotism. These are Romantic ideas which flourished in the twentieth century, facilitated by a string of inventions, from Gore-Tex to cross-country motorbikes, that reduce the fatigue, wet and cold. Walking the Hambleton Hills and the moors became an exhilarating aesthetic experience rather than a dice with death.

Within a few decades of Wordsworth's evening walk over Sutton Bank, another man came to the Hambleton Hills to make use of the view. A mile east along the escarpment from the Plot is a stone tower perched on a spur of the hills, which was built in 1837 as an observatory. Like my father's Chapel, it seems Mount Snever Observatory was a kind of retreat, a place where its owner could withdraw to contemplate the heavens. This stone tower sits on a platform of stone, six feet high, so that visitors would have had to bring their own ladders with them; a clever way to deter the idly curious. It was built by an owner of Oldstead Hall, a successful industrialist from West Yorkshire of whom little is known except the dedication on a plaque high up on the tower: JOHN WORMALD, IN THE FIRST YEAR OF THE REIGN OF QUEEN VICTORIA CAUSED THIS OBSERVATORY TO BE ERECTED. Above the door on the south side, facing out over the Vale of York, another plaque offers a verse from Alexander Pope, with a few modifications to commemorate the coronation:

Here hills and waving groves a scene display
And part admit and part exclude the day
See rich industry smiling on the plain
And peace and plenty tell Victoria reigns
Happy the man who to these shades retires
Whom Nature charms and whom the muse inspires
Who wandering thoughtful in this silent wood
Attends the duties of the wise and good
To observe a mean, be to himself a friend
To follow Nature and regard his end.

There is a small path through the woods to the tower, but the trees have grown up to obscure the view, and it is not much visited now. In sharp contrast, twenty years after Wormald built a monument to his private passion, another man also decided to use the view: the White Horse, cut into the hillside high above the village of Kilburn, has become a symbol of its county, and a landmark on the main north–south routes that run across the Vales of York and Mowbray from York to Darlington and Newcastle. It's an equivalent of the Angel of the North, made long before such things could have been called art. When the *Daily Express* wanted to capture a quintessential picture of England in the summer of 2006, it printed a large photo of the White Horse of Kilburn beyond the red poppies of the wheatfields and green woodland. There are few days in the year without at least a handful of people wandering over this patch of hillside, inspecting the whitened scree amongst the heather.

Thomas Taylor, whose idea it was in 1857 to make the White Horse, would have been delighted. Born in Kilburn, he left to make his fortune in London and, having achieved something of his ambition, he wrote to the Kilburn schoolmaster with a plan to cut a horse on the hillside. Taylor headed the subscription list with a donation of £1, just under a quarter of the total funds required. He never explained why the scheme had taken his fancy other than to say that he had seen the white horses cut in Berkshire and Wiltshire, and he added that he thought Kilburn's should be as large as possible. It seems he wanted a landmark to put the village on the map. A horse was most appropriate given the Hambleton Hills' association with racing since the Vikings. One of England's finest natural racecourses, Hambleton was second only to Newmarket in the eighteenth century, and is still used for training racehorses.

There are sixty-seven figures carved into hillsides across Britain; most of them are in southern England, in the natural white of the chalk rock on the downs of Berkshire, Wiltshire and Dorset. Apart from the Uffington Horse in Oxfordshire, which probably dates from the late Bronze Age or early Iron Age (1400–600 BCE), many of these figures represent a curious fashion of the late eighteenth and nineteenth centuries. Kilburn's White Horse, the largest in land surface area, is the only such figure in northern England.

Taylor emigrated shortly after conceiving the plan, and the task of creating the horse fell to the schoolmaster, John Hodgson; a collection was made to cover the cost and volun-

teers offered their labour for free. One schoolboy even wrote
a poem describing the event as the village labourers cleared
and cut the hillside. The White Horse has tested the ingenuity of generations of Kilburn folk: it was a project born from
a culture preoccupied with the look of the land, and Taylor
had never paused to consider the suitability of the Hills'
contours or the type of rock for this venture. It has proved a
struggle to keep the horse white, involving applications of
limewash, and paint, and there have even been desperate
(and unfeasible) plans for a concrete or plastic surface.
Furthermore, the only place big enough on the escarpment
was a patch between two deep gullies where the bottom of
the site ran on to unstable sandy subsoil and bare rock. A
figure couldn't be carved on to this type of surface, only
painted with limewash, and it was going to be vulnerable to
erosion.

Hodgson struggled to fit a recognizable horse on to the hill
and found that, after several redrafts, the legs had to be fore-
shortened and the tail squashed. Over the last century and a
half Kilburn has had to grapple with how to keep the horse
looking like a horse. The paint has a habit of spreading down
the rock, making the creature look more like a giraffe; at one
point, enthusiastic renovation turned the animal into something resembling a rhinoceros. There were bitter complaints
at the time of Edward VII's coronation, when a celebratory
tidy-up managed to ensure that Kilburn could no longer see a
head to the horse. But any deficit in the reality has been
compensated for by the postcards that became a stock-in-
trade of the surrounding area, and postcard manufacturers
did their bit by touching up their photos with judicious dabs
of white.

If what Thomas Taylor wanted was to put the tiny little

village of Kilburn on the map, he succeeded. Tucked into the folds of the wooded hills, Kilburn was a small agricultural village which was likely to be bypassed by the great changes of the nineteenth century. But this was a way to be noticed, to catch even the attention of passengers on the passing trains, fifteen miles away. More and more city dwellers were experiencing the countryside from a train window, and a white figure in the landscape was a way to define your locality in the railway age. It was an early use of marketing, and with the arrival of paid holidays, and the new hobbies of walking and visiting the countryside, tourists from cities such as Leeds and Bradford came out on the railway to Coxwold and walked up onto the Hambleton Hills to visit the White Horse and admire the view. Kilburn farms found a new source of much-needed income, offering bed and breakfast.

Both the observatory and the White Horse are within a mile of my father's Chapel as the crow flies, and the three monuments show how human beings use a view to make memorials on the landscape and for what purposes – coronations, war memorial, local identity. One was built to stretch the capacities of the human eye into space, another was built to attract the human eye and gain fame and recognition. It turned out that my father had had more in common with these other monument builders than he might have realized; the White Horse, the Observatory and the Chapel were all initiated by individuals who either came from, or lived, elsewhere in cities such as Leeds and London. These city folk were building tributes to a land they loved, they were articulating an expression of belonging and identity. They were indulging their romanticization of a landscape, born out of their own experience of industrialization and urbanization.

All three were designed as, or have become, symbols of patriotism.

There is one more view to be had. In 1934 the Yorkshire Gliding Club was founded on a level area of ground on the cliffs of Roulston Scar beside the White Horse. The position of the club, looking out over the Vale of York towards the Dales, offers a superb 'ridge lift', thermals and 'cracking wave' from the Pennines, I'm told in the club's canteen among the steaming cups of tea and fish and chips. I'm quickly lost as veteran pilots talk of how the temperature of the land interacts with the wind to provide the tools a glider needs. The vast sky that the Wordsworths eulogized is read as a kitbox for movement through three-dimensional space. The famous view is subjected to a whole new perspective. I brace myself: it's time to go up in a glider.

It's a May bank-holiday weekend; my trip was planned months in advance as a good time of year for gliding (though the website promised gliding seven days a week, 364 days a year – weather permitting – at Yorkshire Gliding Club). I book in weeks ahead but it sounds as if I couldn't have left it any later, such is the demand for flights; an efficient female voice offers me one of her last slots. I feel very fortunate.

But I've forgotten the Yorkshire weather, and when we arrive it is threatening rain, the cloud is low and it is as chilly as January. The cheery voice at Yorkshire Gliding Club is brisk: 'Absolutely no question of any gliding.' It sounds like she's already said it several times to other callers. We put waterproofs on protesting children and head for the hills to gorge ourselves on the views. The wind is edged with salt as it streams off the moors and rips into us at Sneck Yate, where the Drovers' Road abuts the ancient earthwork of Hesketh

Dyke on the top of the Hambleton escarpment. 'It's a wind too lazy to go round us', as they say in Yorkshire. We scramble over the dyke there before heading on to burial mounds further along the escarpment; our ears burn and the children's cheeks are whipped pink. The sheep are huddled miserably in the lee of a wall. The rain is only visible as a shiver of light as it scuttles over the escarpment. The rain has settled in, but, as the young lad on the till at the Co-op in Helmsley told us one night when facing a bicycle ride home in teeming rain, 'It's only watter, it can't get further than the skin.'

We walk along a boundary between two sets of sound, on one side the roaring of the sycamore and beech trees and the whining moan of the firs jostled by the wind, and on the other, fifty feet below us in the shelter of the land, birdsong in the forest stillness. Beyond the old quarry cliffs, the fir trees on this part of the escarpment have been pollarded by the wind. They've been bent at right-angles, their branches brutally snapped, but still they thrive, undaunted, thick with pine needles. And there lies the view: the fields below us are the colour of creamy jade with the new summer grass; the light is pearl as the thin mists shift across the landscape, allowing occasionally a shaft of dim sunlight to gleam through the thick grey cloud and briefly illuminate the pale green of a particular field. It is mesmerizing to follow these moments of light as they come and go over a land criss-crossed with the lines of dark hedgerows and punctuated by the rounded shapes of single trees.

We drop down off the escarpment along a track which leads us through the midday dusk of a Sitka spruce plantation. It's an impenetrable brown thicket of branch and twig, so we are forced to march along a corridor lit only dimly by intermittent patches of white sky between the overhanging branches above us. It makes us feel like ants caught in a deep-pile carpet. Wherever there's a gap in the trees, the undergrowth swells with a green so brilliant it scratches a retina attuned to the brown gloom. On the edge of the track, the Sitka sprouts new needles like soft, fat, bright green caterpillars dripping from its twigs. Finally we emerge from the plantation, bleary-eyed, onto fields where the sheen of the silvery wind-blown grass is like the billowing of unfurled silk.

The gliding will have to wait. At least I've been in good company.

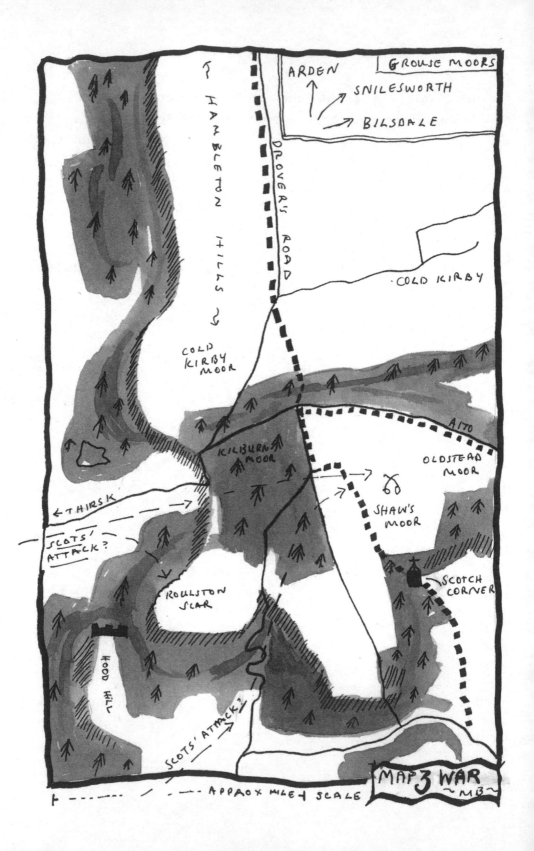

Part II: War

7

Medieval tales

Dad was lying in a bed in an overheated ward in York. His neglected body had finally caught up with him, the undiagnosed heart and kidney condition that was to puzzle doctors was already making him confused. He was tetchy, complaining of armed policemen in the hospital and terrible food. We dismissed (wrongly as it turned out) the former as the ramblings of an agitated mind, and brought in delicacies to tempt his weakening appetite. He dismissed the latter as incubating salmonella. When he said he was bored I brought in poetry books, which he likewise dismissed; boredom was to prove his greatest trial in the last weeks of his life. Death is so boring, he complained as he lay there waiting, and there seemed no fitting rejoinder. *Yes, you're right, watching you die is boring*, or *No, watching you die is not boring, in fact it is rather interesting*. Neither sounded quite right. We had reached stalemate.

For some relief, we found the keys to the Chapel in his cottage. I'd never dared touch them before, and they jangled heavy in my pocket. I fingered the cold metal of the fob. Now I had it in my own hands I could look more closely at it: the polished-steel blunt-pointed part of a Second World War bomb which he had found on the moors many decades before. It was a strange, discomforting thing to finger, to feel the smooth craftsmanship and the design of this object made to kill; it represented the frantic pressure of the munitions industry, the thousands of women crowded onto hastily assembled production lines churning out the weapons that would destroy their counterparts across the water. It was not something I would have chosen as an everyday object to furnish my life with. But as we drove to the Chapel with the key clanking in my pocket, and the petulance of a bedridden father reverberating in my head, his choice of talisman seemed of a piece with the man and the place.

We parked the car in a lane in Oldstead, and pulled out a chair so that I could sit and feed two-month-old Matthias on the verge – to the astonishment of a passing farmer. Then we climbed up the track to visit the Chapel. That was the first time I visited without Dad's dominating presence. There had been heavy rain, and the thick growth of late summer was drenched. Bracken and branches were bowed with the weight of water; the sun broke through occasionally, bringing a welcome warmth to the dampness of the path through the wood. The air was fresh and clean, invigorating after the closeness of the hospital ward. What weighed on my mind was not his irritability, which I had spent a childhood developing strategies to avoid or attempt to convert into approval, but the sense that he was diminishing before my eyes. The powerful father who had projected himself in so many roles – seer, great artist, overpowering presence in the family – was shrinking to humbler proportions. Already the world seemed a slightly more spacious place, and there was a sense of relief. At the same time, this dying man revealed glimpses of a vulnerability that I found astonishing. Like the smile that greeted my arrival on the ward,

full of frank pleasure at seeing me. Like the moment of softness when he nicknamed his new grandson Jumbo on account
of his appetite and steady growth, and commented with wistful
envy on the simple contentment of the sleeping baby. He
knew he was facing one of life's greatest challenges, death. It
was this unfamiliar man I thought about as we picked our way
through the sopping grass and arrived at the Chapel.

Matthias was hungry again so we unlocked the Hut and I sat
down on the sagging old sofa to feed him. The sofa had been
abandoned here after the family home was dismantled in the
wake of my parents' separation. It used to be the television
room sofa, and its lumps and bumps were shaped by our view-
ing of all those terrifying episodes of *Dr Who* and hundreds of
Blue Peters. With Matt's precious head tucked into the crook of
my arm, and feeling the pleasure of being able so easily to sat-
isfy his hunger, I looked out of the door to the crumbled old
stone wall, and the hawthorn bush that had sprung up – a precursor of many more, I suspected, if this land was left to go its
own way. A rose on the end of a long arc of unpruned stem was
hanging over the doorway, trembling in the breeze; it was
yellow tinged with orange, a fat, old-fashioned head of velvet
petals and intense scent. It glowed against the sombre shadows
of the stone and the encircling woods. And for the first time, in
the space that he was already leaving vacant, I asked myself
why. Why had he ever built this War Memorial Chapel? Why
had it been something that he could never really share with his
family? What private story did it explain? The key fob beside
me on the sofa seemed to offer a clue to unravelling a story that
began long before I was born.

War leaves little material evidence of its impact and certainly nothing in proportion to the devastation it causes.
Periods of peaceful economic growth throw up elaborate

churches, grand stately homes, copses, hedges, parkland, magnificent barns, clusters of cottages, but war leaves only the occasional ruin, the inexplicable hollows and mounds of an old battlefield. In the twentieth century, some of this absent history rose to the surface; my father's bomb part emerged when the Forestry Commission ploughed the moors. (More recently the invention of the metal detector has harvested another crop of war memorabilia: pieces of chain mail, and buckles.) Several times war has affected the Plot. My father talked of the Bronze Age burial mound as that of a warrior: did he have any evidence or was it part of his recognition that this had always been a land shaped by war, and that he simply layered his own war on to the histories of earlier ones?

The most devastating war of all was William the Conqueror's suppression of the north. It was the winter of 1069, three years after the Norman invasion, and William's earlier attempts to impose his authority in the north had failed; he returned, determined to deal out such harsh punishment that the region could pose no further threat to him. The rebels broke up into small groups and, adopting classic guerrilla tactics, scattered into some of the area's most remote and inhospitable places. Some sought refuge in the then isolated Lower Tees valley, which lies to the north of the Yorkshire moors, now the industrial urban sprawl of Teesside. The Conqueror divided his army up into small units and pursued the rebels into the marshes and hills, ravaging the countryside as he went. Villages went up in flames, peasants were slaughtered indiscriminately, crops and tools were burned and cattle captured. His intention was that the land should not be able to support either rebels or invading Danes for years to come. It's an atrocity that has lingered in the memories and language of those living on the Yorkshire moors for nearly a thousand years. He used the Hambleton Drovers'

Road on his way south, and the history was so infamous that even the road that bore him would from then onwards be named in his memory as the Regalis Via, King's Highway. On his way south from Teesside to York, King William was caught in a snowstorm on one of the bleakest part of the North Yorkshire moors, the Cleveland Hills, as he headed towards the Hambleton Drovers' Road. He and his army were lost and stumbled around, unsure of their bearings, and his cursing was such that the saying passed into local custom in Bilsdale that 'he cusses like Billy Norman'.

Such was the ferocity of William's attack on the north that its impact lasted for decades. Half the villages of the North Riding and over a third of those in the East and West Ridings were wholly or partially destroyed; the ensuing famine is estimated to have killed 100,000. The county was left a wilderness. 'For at least nine years, no attempt was made at tilling the ground,' writes Simeon of Durham, 'between York and Durham every town stood uninhabited: their streets became lurking places for robbers and wild beasts.' The monastic chronicler William of Malmesbury wrote that 'even a generation later the passing traveller beheld with sorrow the ruins of famous towns, with their lofty towers rising above forsaken dwellings, the fields lying untilled and tenantless, the rivers flowing idly through the wilderness'. There were reports of survivors being reduced to cannibalism, cracking open the skulls of the dead so that the brains could be sucked out. Famine was followed by plague. A survey in the area seventy years later found little record of pasture, fisheries, livestock or salt pans. It was not until the 1130s and the Cistercians' arrival in the region that the work of reconstruction began. Some historians claim that the devastation was the cause of economic inequality between north and south until the late Middle Ages.

By the spring of 1070, William had largely achieved his object, and resistance was reduced to a few bandit groups. The harrying of the north was a turning point in his strategy to rule England, and it earned him the reputation of a being a 'stern and violent man'. He resolved that he would no longer tolerate English nobles and they would be replaced by his Norman, French or Flemish allies. One of those followers was Roger de Mowbray, who was given the manor of Thirsk which included the acre of the Plot. His family was to dominate the area for the next 400 years, bequeathing its name to the broad swathe of land between the moors and the Dales that is still known as the Vale of Mowbray. Eight miles to the north-east of the Plot, at Helmsley, another Norman follower, Walter L'Espec, began building his castle, and sixteen miles away, another Norman castle was also built at Pickering. The suppression of the north was to be maintained by a French-speaking army of occupation, which would keep the peace through a network of forts. In total, 400 castles were built across the Normans' new kingdom over the next thirty years. Many were temporary constructions of timber, and only eighty were rebuilt in stone; most followed the pattern of an earthen motte or mound topped by a defensive area called a bailey and surrounded by earth ramparts. The Normans were much influenced by the tradition in France and the Rhineland of seeking out high hills in uninhabited places to build their castles.

This history lends credence to the claim that a mile and a half from the Plot, a Norman motte-and-bailey castle was built on the top of Hood Hill. That there are the remains of medieval fortifications is not in dispute, but their date is; Graham Lee, the North York Moors National Park's archaeology officer, has surveyed them, and believes they are Norman. Hood Hill makes the perfect defensive position. The hill stands proud of the Hambleton escarpment, but this is only evident from the north. It looks down on a deep valley known as Happy Valley, whose name is probably derived from the old dialect verb *hap*, meaning to hide or cover, explained the local historian Fred Banks. From some vantage points, Hood Hill melds into the escarpment so that its defensive capabilities are well concealed. Reaching the summit requires a steep scramble up wooded slopes. The castle played a significant role in the twelfth century in protecting the surrounding farmland from raids by bandits from further north; there is a record from Henry II's reign of the King sending 300 soldiers to Hood Castle to rout a band who approached along the aptly named Thief's Highway, which runs along the base of Happy Valley.

It was another August day in which rain had crashed relentlessly out of sodden skies, finally easing in the late afternoon, leaving the air still, broken only by the occasional smattering of raindrops. There was every reason not to attempt the climb up Hood Hill: we had a car journey ahead of us that evening, the ground was drenched, and as Fred Banks – with whom I had spent the afternoon discussing medieval ploughing patterns – pointed out with a wry smile, we were not going to see much of the fortifications beneath the midsummer vegetation. Nevertheless we set off at a brisk pace along a path that ran under the White Horse and then under the steep rise of Sutton Bank. On the other side of the path, in pasture dotted with clumps of reeds, the deer of a venison farm stared dumbly, their coats heavy and dark with water. Branches of ash heavy with bunches of blackened seeds splashed sudden showers on our faces and shoulders. There was a gap in the clouds, and the sun burst suddenly through, setting a million raindrops to sparkle; the leaves glistened, the mud gleamed and the

puddles bore bright reflections of sunlight. As the path led
into the gloom of the coniferous forest, the pale brown mud
sucked at our boots, and a soft shimmer of sunlight penetrated
the tree cover to touch the green of the ferns. The path known
as the Thief's Highway narrowed, and the contours rose on
either side of this ravine known as Happy Valley; on the one
side stood Hood Hill and on the other the looming cliffs of
Roulston Scar. As we turned to climb Hood Hill, the sun
disappeared and the forest breathed a damp mist which hung
in white wisps. We came to the edge of the plantation and,
unsure of our path, took our bearings from a patch of sky, heading up towards it, over a barbed-wire fence and straight up
through sopping bracken. It was steep and we grabbed at stalks
to pull ourselves up. Abruptly, we came out of the bracken onto
the rounded ridge of a hill covered in the pale-gold grasses of
late summer. Their seeded heads were impossibly delicate,
and scattered amongst them were pale blue harebells, trembling with the weight of droplets of rain. It was an exquisitely
woven carpet flung over this hilltop, which sat like an island in
the thick green of forest. In a matter of minutes we had gone
from the drama of the tall pines to the brave modesty of these
small grasses and flowers bobbing in the breeze of their
exposed position.

But it was the view that took the breath away – the view that
probably brought those Normans to this summit. To one side,
across the tops of the pines and the steep ravine, was the rock-
face of Roulston Scar, almost orange in the intermittent evening
sun. This was the best vantage point from which to see the scale
of the vertiginous drop of several hundred feet of bare rock into
woodland. The Hambleton Hills stretched away to the east,
thick with the woods that conceal the Plot and its neighbouring
valleys. To the west lay Thirsk and, beyond it, against a skyline

of ragged grey cloud and sunlight, was the horizon of the Pennines and the Dales where William the Conqueror placed another of his castles at Richmond. To the south we could just see the tip of the stone ruins of Byland Abbey beyond Oldstead and the village of Kilburn spread in its gentle dip. Curtains of grey rain drifted across the land, illuminated by shafts of sunshine which turned fields from grey to green or ripe wheat-yellow as the light tumbled from the heavy sky.

We wandered among the brambles and bracken of the pitted summit surface, looking for evidence of the fortifications which had been reclaimed by the hill. We almost tripped over boulders where hawthorns crouched in the crevices. The only aspect of the fort that remained self-evident was its primary characteristic: we had a bird's-eye view in every direction, the perfect vantage point for an occupying force which trusted no one and suspected everyone. This was a castle built not as a demonstration of authority – it was too remote for that – but as a lookout post, alert to every unexpected, unfamiliar movement along the Drovers' Road or through the Vales of York and Mowbray. It was in the kind of country where the last rebels lurked; the names of Thief's Highway and Hood Hill (a 'hood' was an outlaw, as in Robin) indicate that its history as a refuge for the lawless lasted longer than William the Conqueror's suppression. For the foot soldiers serving the Normans, it would have been a bleak posting, the wind scurrying across the moors hitting their outcrop with full force, and the relative safety of York a long day's ride away. Perched up there, there was little on which to while away their time other than to watch the birds that nest on Roulston Scar wheeling in the air around them.

A hundred and fifty-two years later, the Plot did not merely offer passage to pillaging kings and their armies, it became the

battlefield itself. Some attribute the name of Scotch Corner not
to the drovers but to a great Scottish victory at the Battle of
Byland, and they suggest that the Plot's neighbouring valley,
Hell Hole, earned its name for the massacre it witnessed in the
battle. Names offer their own cryptic record of a place's salient
history, even if it has not featured prominently in the history
books. The Battle of Byland warrants only a few lines in many
accounts of the period, yet some historians argue that it was a
key moment in medieval history and in the development of
two nations, England and Scotland. It rivals the more famous
Battle of Bannockburn as a crushing humiliation of Edward II
at the hands of the great Scottish national hero, Robert the
Bruce.

By 1322, Edward II's conflict with one of his most powerful
noblemen, Thomas of Lancaster, had finally reached resolu-
tion with the latter's execution for treason, and Edward could
belatedly turn his attention to the far more troublesome issue
of Bruce's persistent raids across the border into northern
England since the Battle of Bannockburn seven years earlier.
Edward had repeatedly refused to recognize Bruce as King of
Scotland and make peace, so Bruce had used the raids to put
pressure on England and to gather wealth for the rebuilding of
his war-ravaged kingdom. Edward, with the generous finan-
cial assistance of many northern monasteries which were
anxious to see an end to the threat of raiding Scots, led an
army of 20,000 men north. But rather than meet this army in
a battle, Bruce retreated into the Highlands, instructing his
men to leave nothing on the ground that could provide an
army with food or forage. The Scots destroyed their own land:
roofs were ripped off, crops trampled, bridges destroyed and
streams contaminated with corpses. The English army found
itself marching into a territory which offered only hunger and

disease. Meanwhile Bruce swung round south, avoiding Edward and taking a raiding party deep into Lancashire, pillaging towns as far south as Preston in the hope of drawing Edward back from Scotland. But Edward decided, disastrously, to split his forces, sending his one competent military leader, Sir Andrew Harclay, south while he remained in Scotland; when Harclay protested, he was summarily dismissed. Edward settled into the ruins of Holyrood with Queen Isabella in a near-deserted Edinburgh, but there was little food to be had. Supply ships, belatedly ordered from England, were hijacked by the Scottish and ended up providing food and weapons for the enemy.

The English army were forced to eat their own horses; they were now afflicted by 'divers fevers and agues'; dysentery, hunger and driving rain contributed to bitter demoralization. Maddened by their humiliation, on 2 September they set fire to Holyrood Abbey, and Edward ordered the indiscriminate slaughter of those inhabitants of Edinburgh who had not fled: 5,000 men, women and children were murdered. The retreating army continued their blood-crazed savagery at Melrose Abbey on the borders, where they crucified the abbot on the abbey doors; they tortured and then slaughtered his fellow monks. As the English limped south, disease-ridden and starving, they were harried by groups of Scots. Bruce followed at a distance, biding his time, well aware that each day's march reduced the English numbers further.

At Barnard Castle, Edward heard that Bruce had a force at Carlisle and called his men to meet him on 'Blackehamour' – probably Black Hambleton – on the Cleveland Hills for a muster; at this point he probably had only a small escort with him, but still believed Bruce's force was no more than a raiding party. While his forces gathered, Edward continued south to

Rievaulx to enjoy the comforts of a rich monastery. His soldiers travelled along the Hambleton Drovers' Road and arrived at Scawton and Shaw's Moor, just above the Plot, four miles from Rievaulx.

Bruce, knowing the depleted state of the English army from his scouts, decided to drive home his full advantage. He gathered his whole army together – perhaps 4,000-strong – and in one of the most remarkable marches of the medieval period moved them up the Eden valley through the Aire Gap to Northallerton, a march of 100 miles in eight days. He now had the King of England only fifteen miles away to the east. The disparity between the two forces was evident: on the one hand, the Scots were hardened and well practised in mobile warfare, whilst on the other, the remnants of the English army were bewildered by their failure to engage Bruce in battle and exhausted by their long march north and south again. The Scots were led by an inspirational leader and a brilliant tactician, the English by a discredited king who had spent much of the previous few years squabbling with his courtly favourites. Some medieval chroniclers put the English army at hundreds of thousands, and the *Chronicle of Lanercost*, which provides the most detailed account of this period of Anglo-Scottish history, suggests with characteristic medieval exaggeration over 60,000, but recent analysis puts the English force at no more than 1,000. They were outnumbered by the Scots.

This exhausted, battered army was probably camped on Shaw's Moor. This is where the Drovers' Road follows the track down to the Plot, running across an area of former upland heath now largely given over to fields of root crops. There is little protection from the wind and rain off the high moors in the distance; the soldiers huddled on this plateau and exposed to a particularly wet autumn must have looked longingly at the Drovers' Road stretching away towards the south with their hopes of safety and home.

On 14 October Bruce moved his men from Northallerton and arrived at the foot of the Hambleton Hills; the *Chronicle of Lanercost* wrote that he 'marched into England to Blackmoor (whither he had never gone before nor laid waste those parts, because of their difficulty of access) having learned for a certainty from his scouts that the King of England was there'. Edward sent his nephew, John of Brittany, to oppose Bruce on the ridge of the Hambleton Hills. Some have suggested that the English took up position on Roulston Scar, but it seems more plausible that they were either just to the north, along the escarpment at Sutton Bank, the area where the A170 now does a series of dramatic hairpin bends to climb the steep ascent. Alternatively, they could have been to the east of Roulston, on Shaw's Moor with the Scots gathered below. That would have put the Plot right at the centre of this great medieval battle.

When Bruce arrived, he decided on a frontal attack and, under the cover of the smoke from many small fires, a party of Highlanders moved round to the east of the English position to attack them from their flank. Some reports claim the Highlanders scaled the ridge; others maintain the Scots headed up a narrow wooded gully of which there are three in the area: the one now used by Low Town Bank Road or the valleys of Hell Hole and Cockerdale which lie either side of the Plot.

The English were fending off the frontal attack, throwing stones down the incline, when they realized a second attack was coming from behind. According to one report, the English cavalry wheeled around to head down the gully to repel the Highlanders, but its narrowness gave them little room for manoeuvre and they ended up charging their horses into

Scottish spears and staves. Finding themselves attacked from both sides, the English were routed and the Scots charged through the encampments on Shaw's Moor.

Meanwhile, according to the *Chronicle of Lanercost* (an account which is particularly unflattering to the English) Edward was feasting in Rievaulx Abbey on 'two swanis roastit, divers fowls, Salmonys and other fishis with divers pies of meat and fruitis and sweetmeats. A Tun of Claret wine and a keg of burgundy wine with the best abbey ale.' It was not a meal he had time to finish. With his soldiers dying, dead or in flight, the way to Rievaulx lay open, and the King was within tantalizing reach of Robert the Bruce, only four miles away. To capture the English King would have enabled Bruce to force terms and exact a hefty ransom, and he sent on a party of cavalry. But by the narrowest of margins Edward eluded their grasp, and left Rievaulx with only a handful of knights to protect him. After a few miles, at the village of Nunnington (where my father lived for the last fifteen years of his life), the Scots lost the English party in the dark and the King raced on to Pickering, where he changed horses and continued across the wolds to Bridlington.

His plans to take a ship to London were thwarted by the stranglehold that the Scots had on the port of Hull and Edward was forced to head back to York. Such was his precipitous departure from Rievaulx that Edward left a vast quantity of royal plate and the Royal Seal behind – the latter Bruce graciously returned to him, but not so the treasure. According to the *Meaux Chronicle* the 'Scots entered the aforesaid monasteries of Rievaulx and Byland with violence, put on the clothes of the religious without reverence and all the goods of the monastery, vestments for divine service, consecrated chalices, books and all the sacred ornaments of the altar they carried away with them'. The Scots may have plundered but they did not take the lives of the monks nor murder the abbots as their English opponents had done.

The Scots remained in Yorkshire for more than a month, and only returned home when the rain got heavy. There was no attempt to force them back across the border; it was the longest time they had spent in England. Contemporary chroniclers were scathing about Edward II's cowardly retreat, describing him as 'ever chicken hearted and luckless in war'. Sir Thomas Gray remarked that 'after Byland, the Scots were so fierce and their chiefs so daring, and the English so cowed, that it was no otherwise between them than as a hare before greyhounds.'

This was a battle in the heart of Edward II's English kingdom, and it was an ignominious humiliation in which the King lost an army, a huge quantity of treasure and the Royal Seal, and abandoned his queen. He had a perilously narrow escape across the Yorkshire wolds, and in saving his own skin, he left his army to be killed or taken hostage. The monasteries and subjects of northern England were left unprotected from the vengeance of a victorious Scottish army, intent on dealing out some measure of the brutality recently inflicted on its own land. There is a strong case to make that the Battle of Byland marked Bruce's greatest success. It demonstrated English royal ineptitude and inadequacy, and the savage consequences.

A year later Edward reluctantly signed a thirteen-year truce with Scotland and two years after Byland, the Pope recognized Bruce as King – a vital step towards his ambition for an independent, sovereign Scotland. Five years after Byland, Edward II was deposed, and negotiations finally began on a treaty recognizing Scotland as a nation which was duly signed in 1328. The peace was not to last but it was a pivotal chapter in the development of the medieval Scottish nation. It's for this reason that Scottish nationalists now remember Byland as energetically as English historians have forgotten it. For Scottish nationalists, the battle has taken on new life on the internet, as a deeply satisfying chapter in the history of English incompetence and superior Scottish skill. Scotch Corner is thus elevated to a war cemetery. One detailed account claims that 960 Scots lie buried in the ground just below the Plot, and that you can hear 'the spectral pipes play their sad refrain for the dead; and just possibly the echoes of a voice singing in Gaidlig, the Columban hymn for the dead'. Or possibly not. In the same account, a mass grave of nearly 8,000 Englishmen is identified just below the cliffs of Roulston Scar. The precision of the total buried appears impressive, but ultimately it cannot be justified. The numbers reflect the inflations of medieval chroniclers, and it is hard to be exact about the positioning of the graves when there is such uncertainty over where this battle took place. Besides, it is unlikely that anyone can organize mass graves after a medieval battle in a countryside that has been ransacked. The victors may have had time to bury their dead, but the English did not. Both soldiers and local inhabitants were too pressed in saving their own lives from the marauding Scots, who after the Battle of Byland raided through much of the surrounding countryside. The bodies would have more likely rotted where they fell on the moor. But much like the medieval scribes centuries before them, these internet chronicles serve their purpose, elaborating new myths to fit current political strategy, and anchoring them for credibility in a specific place.

Scotch Corner has been made into a place of pilgrimage for those rallying to the cause of Scottish nationalism: I suspect my father would have had a wry appreciation for such a use of the Plot and indulgence towards a country that he fondly idealized through much of his life – when Yorkshire became crowded, he dreamed of escaping to the Hebrides. The nationalist internet chronicles even see significance in the Celtic knotwork my father carved on the doors of his war memorial chapel, citing such detail as appropriate to the place's Scottish memories. Dad may not have had much sympathy for their politics, but perhaps he would have recognized that they were resuming a task that he had taken up, many decades before, of creating new meanings for this acre of land.

After my father died, my brothers found an extraordinary amount of paperwork in the cupboards of his small cottage. He did not seem ever to have thrown out a letter, card or envelope; Christmas and birthday cards spilled out of cardboard boxes, postcards poured in a thick slick across the floor. One file, strangely, was bursting with the empty envelopes of every letter he had ever sent my mother, another box held the letters, cards – even sweet wrappers with scribbled notes – of their six-year courtship. In the midst of these papers they found a history of the name 'Bunting', which claimed that one of the earliest references to the surname is the records of the Court of Sessions in 1326, when two brothers, Alexander and Henry Bunting, were convicted of a murder in a street brawl. In the subsequent trial, the King intervened and pardoned them on account of their exceptional bravery in a battle with the Scots. It could have been the Battle of Byland. My younger brother had just chosen a name with no precedent in the known family history for his first child. Alexander Bunting is likely to be the only person in our extended family to bear the name 'Bunting' into the twenty-first century; it was an uncanny linking of names and places across nearly seven centuries.

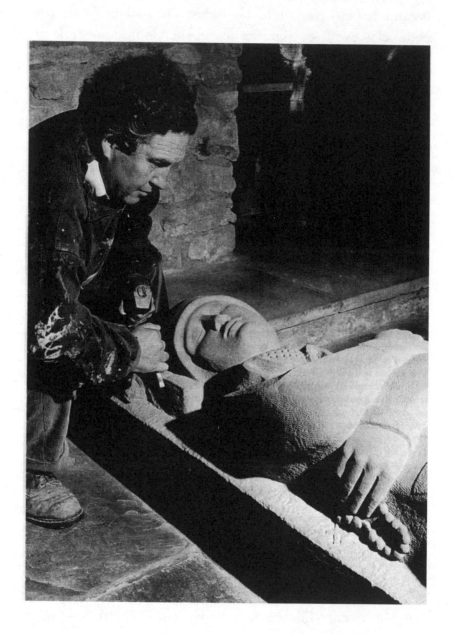

8

A land fit for heroes

My father talked about the Battle of Byland, but I do not remember him talking about the day he first found the Plot as a sixteen-year-old. After he died, I found the date in one of his autobiographical pamphlets. It was 6 June 1944 – D-Day.

It was also the day every boy at Ampleforth was expected to make his own way by foot or bicycle to the school's annual summer picnic at Gormire Lake, eight miles away. My father, and perhaps some friends, must have taken an unusual route, scrambling along the hillside above the ruins of Byland Abbey, to arrive at the abandoned farmhouse at Scotch Corner. The Plot was about halfway to the lake, so perhaps they paused there. There would not have been much to see. Mrs Bulmer had left half a century before and in the intervening decades the roofs had given way, the walls had collapsed and brambles had grown up among the old sties and sheep pens. It was not much different from other ruins scattered across the moors. But it had the view, and something made the teenager remember the spot. When he came to compile the list of key dates in the building of his chapel, this is where he started: 6 June 1944. The plot of land had inspired a schoolboy ambition.

D-Day had been four years in the planning. My father noted the incongruous juxtaposition of a schoolboy outing and the event of huge historical weight in his history of the Chapel: '1944 Goremire Day – D-Day – Visit Scotch Corner first time. Hear of invasion.' He and his friends would all have known older boys or former pupils, and some would have had brothers, who had embarked ships to cross the Channel and fight in Normandy. They would have started the day with prayers, and perhaps a devout boy like my father fingered a rosary in his pocket for much of that day. It would have been strange to enter into the usual schoolboy japes associated with this picnic, knowing that at every moment hundreds of thousands of young men, only separated from them by the slimmest of age margins, were walking up the Normandy beaches into the deafening roar of German guns. A few years older and they would have been the ones seasick and shivering from the Channel sea spray in the landing-craft, rather than rambling across the Yorkshire hills. It could not have been far from my father's mind that, with his seventeenth birthday only a few weeks away, it was little more than a year before he would be called up. The invasion was one he expected to be joining before too long; the waiting and training were almost over. It had fallen to his generation to be sacrificed. Adulthood for the age group born in the late 1920s was synonymous with conscription and war. These were young men brought up to face the probability of short lives.

Intense emotions, one imagines, on a historic day, and for my father they were pinned to a specific place. The view the boys contemplated from the Plot was England at its most peaceful and pastoral, and it must have seemed to those teenagers painfully precious. In part, my father was respond-ing to a wartime propaganda effort which used the images of ancient England as symbols around which to rally the nation. The English countryside was idealized as a 'patriotic utopia', as cultural theorist Patrick Wright phrases it. It had become a place of redemption, where it was possible to find the humanity that was absent from the killing machines in skies above the cities of Europe. For a boy who had watched the bombing raids on London from his bedroom window in Barnet, the pastoral landscape of North Yorkshire was a place of sanctuary. These powerful cultural currents of patri-otism were focused on the ruins of Scotch Corner: this was his 'patriotic utopia'. He had arrived at a particular place on a particular day, and the intersection of space and time gave this acre a significance for my father that lasted his lifetime.

These connections to the Plot were only deepened when the war ended, three months short of my father's eighteenth birthday, in May 1945. This age cohort reached adulthood to discover with the arrival of peace that they had all their lives to live. Peace prompted relief but also guilt: what chance of the calendar had saved them, while so many, a few years older, had died or experienced terrifying ordeals? How had these eighteen-year-olds won their reprieve, or had they rather cheated their fate? Rare among men in the middle decades of the twentieth century, my father did not have direct experience of war. Onto this plot of land he projected a survivor's guilt; he lived in the shadow of other men's sto-ries of war and their deaths, and had a powerful sense of debt to thousands of men who had had the short lives he himself had expected. My father never talked of this, but the stiff prose in the autobiographical pamphlet spoke loudly: 'For my part I have repaid some of the 50 years interest on a debt that cannot be repaid. Let the chapel at Sutton Bank act as security for that debt.' He carved the corpse which could have been his, and laid it in the chapel on the moors, a down-payment for a life he had never expected to live.

He dedicated his war memorial chapel in particular to three men, all of whom had been at Ampleforth. They were older than him and he neither knew, nor to my knowledge ever met, any of them. It was only when I traced their obituaries that I discovered what they had had in common – all three had shown artistic promise. Michael Fenwick was killed in Kowloon in 1941 at the age of twenty-one, but before he joined up he was a brilliant Oxford Classics student and poet. Michael Allmand was killed in Burma on 23 June 1944, aged twenty, and was posthumously awarded the highest military honour, the Victoria Cross, for his bravery. He also had been at Oxford, where he had founded and edited a literary review known as *Wind and Rain*. The third, Hugh Dormer, was a talented writer and diarist, and was killed six weeks after the 1944 Gormire Day picnic in a tank battle in Normandy at the age of twenty-seven. My father carved simple stone inscriptions with the names and dates for all three men and mounted them on the walls of his new chapel. The only addition he made in the following four decades was a plaque commemorating Robert Nairac, another Ampleforth pupil, killed in Northern Ireland in 1977.

The most significant of the four men to my father was Hugh Dormer, and his interest bordered on obsession at various points. My long-suffering mother had to put up with a trip to retrace one of Dormer's missions in occupied Europe for SOE, the Special Operations Executive, on my parents' first holiday alone together after years of small children. When my mother finally left Dad, his fascination with Dormer became all-consuming as he took refuge from the collapse of his family in a past he thought he understood. It baffled me that when I phoned him from my new life as an adult, he wanted to talk about Dormer. He tracked down one of the men who had accompanied Dormer on one of his SOE missions, Charlie Birch, and persuaded him to return with him to France to retrace the route they had taken. He made Dormer the object of three different visits to France – and he was not someone who travelled abroad often. He wrote a study comparing Dormer's published diaries with the maps and landscape he had explored, and one of the booklets he wrote in his last years was entirely devoted to the man. After it arrived in the post as a Christmas present, it sat on a shelf unread. Only when researching this book did I finally read it, hoping to understand what Dormer had represented to my father.

Hugh Dormer was a few years ahead of my father at Ampleforth and he left before my father ever arrived. The offspring of one of England's oldest recusant families and deeply devout, he was Head Boy, got into Christ Church, Oxford, and was held up to pupils of my father's age as a role model of everything an Ampleforth education was intent on creating. He enlisted in 1939 and conducted two operations for SOE in Occupied France, for which he was awarded a DSO medal for bravery. In January 1944 he rejoined his tank regiment for the invasion of Normandy, spending some time training near Ampleforth and visiting the school when my father would have been there; Dormer noted in his posthumously published diaries that the boys were praying for him. His name may well have been in my father's mind as he came upon Scotch Corner in 1944. Six weeks later, Dormer was dead, buried at the side of a road in Normandy.

In 1947 Dormer's diaries were published, and were reprinted several times over the following decade. Ampleforth boys were urged to read them on their annual retreat, and a memorial to him was erected in the school library. By then, my father had left the school but he read the diaries. Dormer's combination of fervent Catholic faith and patriotism was regarded by Ampleforth as the perfect exemplar to offer its pupils. He was a symbol of everything Ampleforth understood about itself in the middle decades of the twentieth century. He was a very useful hero. The Benedictine school, with its roots in the traditions of Lancashire recusancy, had determined on an ambitious strategy to reintroduce Catholicism to the heart of the Engish establishment. Ampleforth was to be transformed from a modest provincial private school to a national public school for the Catholic élite. To do that it created its own mythology of Englishness, laying claim to direct descent from the Benedictines ejected from Westminster at the time of the dissolution of the monasteries. It prided itself on representing *English* Catholicism, in contrast to other Catholic institutions which owed their origins and influence to the Continent or to Ireland. It even claimed to be more English than the Church of England, tracing an unbroken spiritual lineage back through the recusant families to the earliest days of Christianity in England. It set itself against 400 years of anti-papist suspicion in a bid to convince England of the Englishness of Catholicism. From there, the next step was the conversion of England: an aim for which Ampleforth boys in the forties prayed every Sunday as they lustily sung such hymns as this:

Still in this land of ruins glows divine
The spirit kindled here in happier days
Still, Father, there are English hearts all thine
And English lips still left to sing thy praise.

Dormer resolved the centuries-old tension between Catholicism and English patriotism; in his diaries he described his efforts in SOE to liberate Catholic France and Belgium from Nazism, and he wrote of his religious idealism as he reconciled himself to the likelihood of dying for his country.

He was also a flamboyant character, idealistic, romantic and with a canny eye for dramatizing his war. On one level, his diaries read like a boys' own adventure story, on another they are an intense, if sometimes grandiose, meditation on self-sacrifice, Christianity and patriotism. They perfectly express the war my father spent his adolescence waiting for and dreaming of. It was the war he would have liked to fight – one of idealistic self-sacrifice, intense piety and daring adventure. To my father, certain passages must have offered the immediacy of a voice from beyond the grave; for example, in late 1943, Dormer tells how he was stationed at Duncombe Park, four miles from Ampleforth. He describes how they drove over to Ampleforth to dine in 'the silence of the monks' refectory and listened to the plain chant of Vespers and later to the carefree laughter of boys. I realized then better than ever how much I was fighting for.' My father knew he could have been one of the boys that Dormer heard.

Dormer was part of a particular connection between Catholicism and the armed forces which emerged at Ampleforth, focused on secret special forces. Dormer was not the only former pupil to be drawn to the secrecy and adventurousness of unconventional warfare. It is a history that my father found a compelling contrast to industrialized high-technology warfare – such as saturation bombing and nuclear war – that dominated the first half of the twentieth century, because of the way it connected to older traditions of warrior courage and skill. David Stirling, the founder of the SAS, was at Ampleforth a few years ahead of Dormer.

Another of the Chapel dedicatees, Robert Nairac, was a true successor in many ways to Dormer. He had considerable charisma and a taste for fast cars and falconry, and worked in military intelligence in Northern Ireland. Nairac's time under-cover in Northern Ireland in the seventies is still steeped in controversy; one SAS colleague concluded that 'no one seemed to know who his boss was, and he appeared to have been allowed to get out of control, deciding himself what tasks he would do.' The circumstances of his murder in a pub he was visiting alone in South Armagh are still strongly contested.

Nairac belongs to a tradition of militarism that celebrates the swashbuckling, unconventional soldier who breaks away from routine to achieve great glory in the manner of T. E. Lawrence (a man for whom my father never quite lost his schoolboy fascination). This tradition had resonances in Catholic recusant history, with its secrecy, hideaways and deception: the experience of the fugitive, of persecution and martyrdom were all references close at hand for Dormer. The latter referred to martyrdom at several points in his account of his escape through occupied France, and on several occasions it was only the urging of his comrades that secured his sur-vival: 'I had no wish to flee further but would have preferred to stand and face our pursuers.' Dormer's willingness to face death – a death that he described as preferable to the loss of honour – has echoes of a sixteenth-century Catholic priest on the run.

The object of Dormer's two expeditions behind the lines in occupied France was to blow up a shale oil factory in Burgundy. Dormer aborted the first operation after only a few days and lost several men before making a long and arduous escape back to England via Spain and Portugal. A few months later he was asked to make a second attempt on the same target, and this time he describes the explosions in his diaries, and concludes that the operation was very successful.

After these two SOE missions, he returned to his tank regiment in January 1944 and waited with a combination of dread and eager anticipation for D-Day:

> I am sending this book away tomorrow as I think the hour will strike in the next few days and my final journey will have begun. God knows no man ever set out more happily or gladly before – and lead where it may, I follow the path in ever-mounting spirits. God grant me the courage not to let the guardsmen down, knowing as I do how they count on me. I ask only that He do with my life as He wills – if I should be privileged to give it on the field of battle, then indeed would the cup be full. There are times when I feel the tide of happiness so mounting in my soul as though the flood-gates might burst and the frail body and its bonds break asunder. My soul is exhilarated like a bird that would sing for ever till its lungs burst. No man ever went out to meet his fate more joyfully than I.

Shortly after D-Day, Dormer arrived in France and drove through the detritus of burnt-out tanks to camp in a cornfield for several weeks awaiting action and watching the bombing of Caen. Finally the call came and he drove his tank into battle with a bunch of roses given by a French farmer 'as a memory and a fragrance of nicer things in all that unpleasantness. The scent of roses might help to perfume a little the smell of cordite and burning flesh.' A few days later, he was shot as he tried to escape after a tank battle.

My father identified not just with Dormer the adventurer killed in battle, but also with another side of this intense young man. Dormer had dreamed of becoming a hermit, perhaps on the west coast of Scotland. He regarded modernity as corrupt, and gloried in a profound pessimism in which he cast himself as the lonely visionary. The note written in 1943 and printed at the beginning of his diary expresses the combination of fierce idealism, egotism and doom on which my father built his own eccentric, contrary life:

> Again and again one gets that moment of intuition, that sudden vision of how the old world is falling into chaos around us. Ideas and principles that have never yet been challenged in the centuries are questioned for the first time by scientific unbelievers; the traditions of the army, the security of classes and the respect of man for his superiors, the values of religion, the sacredness of the family itself are all violated and derided. While everything that he has been brought up to believe in falls around him, man feels that he must strike out alone into the new future and seek for himself the unprecedented pattern of the adventure of his own life. There is no security or faith left anywhere save in the tower of his own mind, while the darkening storm rages outside louder and louder with ever increasing violence. All, all is being swept into ruin and dissolution as never before; the very pillars of the West are falling.

Dormer had not only lived the war my father would have wanted, but he understood the world much as my father did, and had created a heroism out of the catastrophes of his age. His hyperbole is understandable given his times, but my father lived off such sentiments, with increasing intensity, for another fifty-odd years. To anyone who would listen – and some who would prefer not to – Dad lamented the imminent end of the West, moral collapse and the end of civilization. Every international crisis prompted expansion of his gloomy prognostications to his captive audience, my mother. While he talked, she stitched elaborate patchwork quilts for her children, for their possible future marriages and grandchildren. She stitched through the Cold War of the fifties, the Bay of Pigs, the three-day week of 1974 and the oil crisis of 1973–4. It was an elegant act of domestic sabotage, sewing with a stubborn faith in the future while he relished the drama of his apocalyptic warnings.

In the midst of this feverishly imagined chaos, the one place that offered my father refuge and some stability was the Plot. In his wilder imaginings, perhaps he saw the family holed up there, eking out a living from the land after nuclear disaster had finally struck. Dad's pessimism placed us all on the edge of imminent calamity, and to a child it was terrifying. He projected onto the land his desire for stability and for escape – so I did likewise. The anxieties and fears that kept me rigid awake at night focused on land. My nightmares were always of perching precariously on the edges of cliffs and steep hillsides and being swept in landslides to the bottom. I was terrified by the idea that our old stone cottage at the bottom of a steep hillside might be knocked into a pile of rubble on to the road below by a colossal movement of the earth; it was a possibility my father frequently referred to (and which in part materialized under the house's subsequent owners). These anxieties were reinforced by the village where we had our annual summer holiday, on the North Yorkshire coast at Runswick Bay. The magnificent cliffs there are a regular drama of landslides of wet clay and crumbling rock; every year, the contour of the land changes. Land was fickle; it shifted shape.

My father's reiterations of doom were illustrated by the ruins we lived among in North Yorkshire. Now it is a celebrated tourist area, but before heritage had turned every old stone into a commercial opportunity, it was a landscape of ghosts. The ruins of great monasteries and castles were features of our daily lives, and they offered their own silent comment on how time had been called on a certain way of life. My school was housed in an old stately home, Duncombe Park in Helmsley, six miles from Scotch Corner, which was redolent of its more glorious past. The gilded drawing room echoed to the thump of ungainly attempts at ballet by little girls, whilst in the formal gardens the elaborate patterns of low box hedge made the perfect course for make-believe horse jumping. At playtime we rambled through woods and stumbled across collapsing follies and an abandoned conservatory overlooking tennis courts where the weeds were bursting through the surface. At lunch in the dining room, the enormous oil paintings of ladies swathed in lace and silk towered over us, surveying us with disdain as disrespectful, grubby trespassers, as we ate our boiled cabbage and compulsory cod-liver-oil capsules.

We lived on a land that shifted unsteadily under our feet and we moved in a landscape full of references to abruptly, often violently, terminated ways of life. The message was plain: not even the grandest of human ambitions is constant,

not even the most laborious effort secures permanence. Great
abbey churches, once international centres of spiritual and
temporal power, now hosted nothing more than weeds and
house-martins. The landscape seemed to justify Dormer's
assertion that 'All, all is being swept into ruin and dissolution
as never before.'

As the century wore on, it turned out that it was not just
land that crumbled and collapsed. My father's faith in
Dormer as the war hero foundered. M. R. D. Foot's history of
the SOE punctured the myth that Dormer's operation to
blow up the shale factory had been successful. Although
Dormer had claimed that his explosion led to a 'ball of fire
that rolled skywards', Foot discovered that in fact the operation hardly did any damage. Several lives were lost, many
French were put in great danger and nothing was achieved.
Charlie Birch, the sergeant who returned to France with my
father to retrace his SOE mission, referred to Dormer, his
commanding officer, in a curious phrase as 'dead as a door-
mat' and far too religious. He regarded Dormer as close to a
liability on their missions and had no time for his idealism
and thoughts of martyrdom. The two journeys my father
made with Birch to France forced him to reconsider both his
hero and the nature of military authority. The war had made
Birch a sceptic: in a later operation in Italy, he was dropped
behind enemy lines with a large container which he subsequently discovered held nothing more than a tree trunk. It
was a 'false mission' and it led Birch to conclude bitterly that
ordinary soldiers like him were 'expendable'. For his courage
and effort in the war – which included the retreat from
Dunkirk before he joined SOE – Birch was left with severe
disabilities for the rest of his life.

Pointless missions, expendable soldiers and lives lost or

damaged for very little gain: they formed a small, dispiriting tale of the Second World War. It was not the war my father had grown up believing in, and he struggled to salvage something from the wreckage: 'probably the example of Dormer and Birch, rather than the destruction they caused, was the most important factor of their missions in France', he concluded in his booklet on Dormer, but example of what, and for what purpose? He was confused, and in the last years of his life he finally stopped talking about Dormer. The loss contributed to his sense of disorientation; he was of a generation for whom heroes had always been a powerful emotional inspiration, and the Second World War was a heroic epic struggle which had overshadowed much of their lives. Dormer was his most important hero, but he had accumulated others: sailors, artists, politicians and writers. Intense admiration of the achievements of other men (and it was almost always men) had been part of the furniture of his life; they compensated for the limitations of his humdrum routine, lived in a cluster of small, quiet villages in the Yorkshire countryside. His heroes lived the lives he didn't have the opportunity, fortune or courage to live.

The modern tendency to dismantle heroes dismayed my father. Without them, his world was a poorer place, provisional, full of complexity and ambivalence, and his sense of certainty, bulldog-strong through much of his life, finally faltered.

That threw him back on the consolations of what was solid and material: every week through the summer, he cut the grass and stamped down the molehills on the lawn in front of the Chapel. He weeded and swept. These regular visits became a ritual of remembrance which soothed the anxieties, and restored them to their proper proportions in the long trajectory of history. The grasses grew, blushed with pink, on the bank beside the Hut, and the old lilac bloomed briefly every year at the entrance to the Plot. As the decades passed the Chapel aged well, and it represented one idea that held steady, of restitution for a life he had not expected to live.

9

Tues 17

A weapon of mass destruction

As Dad climbed up on to the scaffolding to build the Chapel, as he hauled the roof timbers up, he would have been able to survey the labour of a small army, as intent as he in placing its mark on the land. While my father poured his energies into one acre, what was going on around him over thousands of acres was the biggest transformation of the North York moors for several millennia. As he mixed the mortar and lifted the stones into place, other men were building tracks deep into valleys and up steep hillsides for the machines that were to clear the old woodland and heather moor and plough the soil. By the time my father had completed his work, the Chapel was no longer surrounded by open moor but by rows of sapling trees. The Chapel was a statement about war, and so also were these coniferous plantations stationed across the North York moors, all 60,824 acres of them.

Even on the map they look odd: the blocks of green, their edges and corners often drawn with a ruler, march over the moors, across streams, gullies, old quarries and tumuli and down hillsides. These were forests planned on an office drawing board. They're in sharp contrast to the older woods on the steep-sided dales, which follow the contour lines; their patches of green on the Ordnance Survey accentuate the sinuous path of rivers and streams cutting their way deep into the moor.

In the latter half of the fifties, hundreds of thousands of trees were offloaded from trucks and dug into the plantations. Moors that had not seen forests for over 4,000 or 5,000 years disappeared in a matter of a few months as the area was surveyed, mapped, drained, criss-crossed with tracks for heavy machinery, then fertilized and planted. On the Hambleton Hills, huge forests swallowed up Over Silton and Nether Silton Moors above Osmotherley and then sprawled across West Moor, Silver Nab and Windy Gill to create Boltby Forest. They spread through Southwoods, over the complicated contours of Hood Hill, and circled round the sides of Cockerdale before heading east through Byland and Wass Moor to Pry Rigg and Grange Moor Plantations. Some tracts of semi-ancient woodland which had fed and fuelled the villages along the foot of the escarpment had been clear-felled during the Second World War and were absorbed into new plantations. Old relationships to woods were supplanted, and only the names on the Ordnance Survey, such as Town's Pasture Wood or Elm Hag (a *hag* was a medieval coppiced wood), point to the past when the steep wooded hillsides of the Hambletons were an important local resource. The woodland had offered both pasture and a harvest of countless materials, from timber, coppice poles and charcoal to oak bark and kindling. There is still a scattering of clues to this old woodland management: there are remnants of old coppice stools, and on the track just below the Plot a grassed hummock abruptly rising twenty feet in the meadow is the remains of a lime-kiln built near its fuel source up in the hills. A Roman pottery was sited in the woods in the remote valley of Cockerdale neighbouring the Plot because of the ease of access to a plentiful supply of fuel. In old village papers from Kilburn there are references to the nineteenth-century schoolchildren who took time off to gather the bark from oak trees for leather-tanning to make a few extra pence to supplement the family income.

These coniferous plantations were a dramatic recasting of land and its use; their wood was never destined to be maintained or harvested by the local villages. It was never going to be part of the local, almost self-sufficient economy. They were imposed on these moors and hillsides with varying degrees of resistance, and their story is not related to local but to national and international circumstances. These blocks of conifers were a statement about twentieth-century warfare. The idea of their planting was the result of the First World War; their method of planting was the result of the Second World War; and their purpose was fully imagined to be in the pursuit of another, imminent, war. Now that it is barely economic to harvest many of them, they have also become in their own curious way a monument to twentieth-century war.

I see parallels between my father and his Chapel, and the foresters and their plantations: they were both working over the same few years in the fifties. Each arrived to stake out their claim to the land, each brimming with purpose and self-belief, each leaving behind them installations – albeit of greatly differing scale – that shape the land more than half a century later.

Having spent a lifetime walking through the plantations, smelling the distinctive pine resin, treading on their springy beds of needles or pulling boots through their thick claggy soils, it feels very odd to be sitting in the office from which those woods are managed, and to find it much like offices everywhere, with the nondescript sterility of beige carpets, water cooler and chipboard desks. It could be the office of an insurance company, but it's from here in Pickering, twenty-one miles from the Hambleton Hills, that the Forestry Commission runs the plantations that make it the biggest landholder in the North York Moors National Park.

So what did I expect? Muddy boots at the door at the very least, and some pinewood around, perhaps sanded and polished to show its brilliant sheen, creamy white, pale pinks and rich yellows, loosely veined with a darker grain. I expected a distinct smell of spruce, larch and pine – heaven knows the smell has been so widely imitated and commercialized, surely here I could find the real thing. Instead what I found was maps, plenty of them, compiled over the years, which told their own story of the plantations' past and how their future was being planned. I also found computers tracking the price of wood per ton, sawn wood or chippings; the cost calculations for haulage, which often amounted to more than the wood itself; and the country-wide network of customers from kitchen chipboard manufacturers in Wales to the ravenous new biofuel power station on Teesside, run by a company in Singapore, gobbling up 27,000 tons of wood a year from the North York moors alone.

The Forestry Commission is one of the last nationalized industries left, one of the few that the Thatcherite enthusiasm for privatization didn't reach (although it was mooted in the early nineties). It is rooted in the post-war era, the high-water mark of the power and confidence of the British state to plan, to organize – even to reshape its people and bring about a new model society. It was an era of unbridled optimism to some, whilst to others it was a time of comparably profound pessimism at the destruction of the particular, the distinctive and the eccentric. The Forestry Commission was the unloved, overlooked child in a brood that included the NHS, the coalmines and the steel industry, the Arts Council and a national education system. The Commission planted according to a model that owed much to the bureaucratic, imperialistic state that conceived it. Having run an empire for nearly two centuries, the British state was well used to the task of dividing up the earth's surface with a schoolboy's geometry set. It is to that overweening British state of the fifties, victorious in war and still ruling a large swathe of the globe's surface, that we owe the long rows of Sitka spruce that march up steep hillsides and across moors in North Yorkshire.

'The Forestry Commission was set up along the lines of empire, with district officers and conservators,' explains Brian Walker, who manages the forestry around Scotch Corner and has worked for the Commission in Pickering for over thirty years. 'Planting forests on this scale was a new venture and they copied the great forests of eastern Europe. The Commission ploughed up moorland and divided it into rectilinear blocks. It was a very militaristic organization in the forties and fifties: they used old military equipment, they employed a lot of veterans and they wore old army clothes. They drove Bren gun carriers to take plants on to the moors, and a lot of the engineers for building the roads were ex-army.'

The plantations were resented by many residents as a form of occupation; even now, some still feel that bitterness as keenly as when the saplings first arrived – a favourite view lost, a vista of moorland interrupted, the curves and twists of dale and hill contradicted by this sharp-edged state-sponsored intervention on the landscape. When the government brought in grants to encourage private landowners to plough up their moors for plantations, it set neighbour against neighbour. The Sitka spruce and lodgepole pine in particular became the villains of the piece. Both were imports from North America; the spruce, named after the small seaport of its homeland Alaska, was the most widely planted tree in British plantations. Its smooth, evenly textured pale wood is perfectly suited for high-grade chipboard. The lodgepole pine earned its name from use by Indians to support their wigwams or lodges, and because of its resistance to rot it is excellent for railway sleepers and telegraph poles. But what warranted the intense dislike was how, densely planted and never thinned, these species grew up as impenetrable thickets. Nothing grew beneath them, making the plantation floor a barren brown carpet of needles, and very few creatures could squeeze into the inhospitable density; a slim fox could possibly slip through, but rarely a deer. They offered little to British wildlife, displacing birds, animals and plants. As the trees grew, their branches stretched out over the tracks through the plantations, their tips close to touching, cutting the sky to a sliver and the track to a narrow corridor between green walls.

The plantations in the fifties were the first ruthless experiment in monoculture; ecosystems were ripped out by stripping the land, ploughing and fertilizing, thus altering permanently the composition of the soil; Walker estimates that, if left alone, it would take thousands of years for some parts to revert to moor because the ploughing brought up the lower layer of lime and broke up the top layer of acid soil on which the heather grows. The delicate wild grasses, the rose-bay willow herb, the patches of bilberry and heather were marshalled into thin strips along the ditches that edged the bulldozed forest tracks.

But in the fifties outright rebellion or more active resistance to this coniferous invasion was muted. These woods were planted to fight the Cold War; no one ever imagined they would end up supplying the raw materials for restless fashions in kitchen units, though that has proved their undignified destiny. However unwelcome these plantations were, objections were cowed by the sense of imminent threat from the Soviet Union, just as across the moors construction was beginning on the gigantic golfballs at Fylingdale which would dominate the *RBF* skyline for miles around and provide an early-warning system for Soviet nuclear attack. No place was sacred when faced with the exigencies of war. The plantations were needed to produce pit props for British mines; if timber supplies from Scandinavia or North America were interrupted, it was these saplings that would ensure that the miners could keep digging at the coalface so that the power stations would keep generating electricity and the lights on. Most haunting of all, it would be several decades before these saplings would reach maturity: the trees were planted in the expectation that Britain needed to be ready for war decades into the future. It was the permafrost of the Cold War, with its prospect of indefinite hostility.

These anxieties about wood and war were not a sudden, fevered creation of fifties paranoia. Their roots go down through centuries of British history, back to the publication of the classic *Sylva, or Discourses of Forest Trees and the Propagation of Timber in His Majesty's Dominions* by John Evelyn in 1664, in which he urged the planting of trees to meet the navy's need of suitable timber. It was a time when European nations such as France knew that proper management of timber supplies was critical to their capacity to build ships and thus extend their trading empires. Wood was the seventeenth-century equivalent of steel in the arms race of later centuries. Over the next 100 years this planting played a crucial role in establishing British naval supremacy in the early nineteenth century; Admiral Nelson's strategic skills would have counted for nothing without the huge timbers required to build his fleet and his own exquisite ship, now sitting like a carved wooden jewel in its concrete berth in Portsmouth.

But Evelyn's lesson was forgotten, and the primacy of iron and steel in shipbuilding obscured the continuing need for wood in the years leading up to the First World War. The focus of comparison between countries was on their warships and capacity for steel production, not on the vast forest reserves that Germany and the Austro-Hungarian Empire had at their disposal. Certainly, no one had envisaged that the Great War would use more timber than all the wars of the previous four centuries. In 1916, there were 2,000 miles of trenches on the Western and Eastern Fronts, and the only weapon against the sea of mud was sawn timber. Tons of shuttering and duck-boards were needed to floor, wall and roof the trenches, dugouts and tunnels. In addition, the most common fuel for cooking and heat on the front lines was charcoal; it was light to carry, quick to ignite and burned without the smoke that might give away the trench's position. Behind the lines, more timber was needed: huts were required to shelter troops, and sleepers were needed for the network of light railways. Ash was felled in the Lake District to make the handles for the thousands of shovels and pickaxes that dug out the tons of earth. It was wood that supplied telegraph poles for communications. The demand was vast as bombardment required a constant programme of repairs and replacements. In just one eighteen-month period (May 1917 to November 1918) the British Army needed 5.7 million tons of planking to build roads, 7 million tons of railway sleepers, and 365,000 tons of firewood.

The early years of the war were characterized by panic at this unforeseen demand. Up until 1914, Britain had been the biggest importer of timber in the world, sucking in huge quantities from Scandinavia, Germany and Russia through ports

such as Hartlepool (then one of the richest towns in the UK as
a port for the coalmines and timber trade). With the declaration
of war, the trade began a precipitous collapse; German supplies
stopped immediately, Russian supplies plummeted, and supplies from Scandinavia were first constrained by a shortage of
freight shipping – diverted to transporting men and materials
across the Channel – and then interrupted by German sub-
marines. As prices for timber soared, half a million acres of
Britain's woods were felled to make up the shortfall, and by
1916 the crisis had become known as the 'timber famine'. In a
book published that year on British Forestry, E. P. Stebbing
attempted a reprise of John Evelyn's *Sylva* with a paean of
praise to the man whose foresight ensured his descendants had
the timber they needed to build their ships. 'It is thus an illus-
tration of the duty which is laid on each generation to see that
sufficient planting is done in its time to ensure that the country possesses a sufficiency of timber in its hour of need,'
Stebbing concluded bitterly as he surveyed his own country's
hour of need and the dereliction of this inter-generational duty
to plant a legacy of timber. Britain had to resort to pleading
with the French for access to their forests, and by 1917 the
British Forestry Mission was paying a small fortune to France
for permission to fell timber in its forests behind the lines.

The Forestry Commission was set up in 1919 to ensure
that the nation's timber requirements were henceforth met.
It brought to an end decades of dithering in the nineteenth
century, when parliamentary committee after committee produced
worthy reports urging more afforestation but never committing
the state to any action other than cajoling landowners to do
something. It was the First World War timber famine that
convinced the sceptics that timber was far too vital a resource, the
investment too long-term and profit margins too small, for it to be

left to private proprietors – something that the French had long understood. Throughout the twenties and thirties, the Forestry Commission bought up land going cheap. In the massive sales of the early twenties a quarter of all English land changed hands as estates were broken up, crippled by the death of their heirs in the First World War, inheritance duties and the agricultural depression. Unemployed miners were drafted from County Durham to plant trees across swathes of the English uplands, but their efforts did not bear fruit in time to be of much help in the Second World War. Once again, shipping was disrupted and imports of timber from Scandinavia and Canada dramatically dropped, and prices rose as steeply as they had done in the First War. The woods that had escaped the axe twenty years earlier were now clear-felled, every tree chopped down. This was when the hillsides around the Plot, above Oldstead and along much of the Hambleton Hills lost woods which were centuries old. The pressing need now was for timber to supply the crucial pit props to keep the coalmines open; mobile tank warfare had no need of trenches.

Twice within twenty-five years Britain had been forced back on to its own timber resources, only to find them desperately inadequate. Twice a nation that prided itself on its technological mastery and its industrial might had found itself humiliatingly short of a humble commodity like wood. It was these crises that provided the Commission with its sense of urgency and, even more importantly, the legitimacy to clear and reorder the land – grubbing out ancient trees, swamping burial mounds in inaccessible forest and ploughing across moorland.

My father did not care much for the plantations, and in a small act of rebellion he planted several oak trees along the track to his Plot, which he checked every time he visited. But he accepted them stoically, persuaded of their need. His small oaks disappeared under the treads of a massive machine, at some point when they were clearing the track or felling the plantation. Only now, having learned some of the history of their planting, do I understand why I always hated the forests which surrounded the Plot, even before I was old enough to be interested in a view or aware of how we had lost it. I disliked their uniformity and the regularity of the long straight rows. Their dark interiors were intimidating; these were not woods to entice you in. You could not play in them. Squeeze through the spiky branches and your face and arms got scratched. Within a few feet, you felt trapped as if in a giant spider's web. You couldn't even climb them, that intoxicating experience for the small child who spends all their time looking up at people and trees. When we children wandered down the wide avenues of grass created as firebreaks for the plantations, it was easy to get lost. They may have looked like avenues but they came from nowhere and led nowhere, and every corner looked much the same as the last; the plantation was like some giant maze. It was a place defined by absences, a disturbing sense of empti-ness, the wind stilled by the solid green walls that boxed us in.

I was absolutely certain that this was not what a wood should be like. I measured the unnaturalness of these plantations against other woods I knew. I played with trees like some small girls play with dolls; I talked to them, I named their parts, I sat with them for what seemed like hours, up in their branches, spying the comings and goings of the family and the village between their leaves. My favourite was a horse-chestnut tree at the end of our garden whose smooth, powdery green limbs became a hideaway from a noisy family and household chores. Trees were places to dream in as well as places to domesticate:

branches became kitchens and there were bedrooms in the airy green turrets. Behind our cottage, sycamore woods stretched up the steep hillside, and they were our playground; this was where I agreed, in a bid to impress my siblings, to be hung by one foot, upside-down, from a rope and swung out like a flying starfish over the roof of our cottage. This was where I mapped base stations and outposts for an elaborate game of spies which no one wanted to play with me. This was where I daydreamed, lying amongst the bluebells and the wild garlic with my books, gazing up at the pattern of green sycamore leaves against the sky.

There were more woods at my school, Duncombe Park. We played under the oaks, yews and beeches, escaping far enough in its woods to lose all our fellow classmates. We were explorers there, every day finding new territories well beyond the reach of adults. Only now do I realize quite how extraordinary this playground was. Duncombe Park has some of the most magnificent trees in the country and many of them are 250 years old or more. Rich in wood-feeding insects, rare fungi and a wide range of birds including the elusive hawfinch, the woods are among the most important in the north of England.

In comparison, the plantations felt like forbidding imposters who had colonized the land. In my mind, I conflated my father, the coniferous trees and the Chapel: they all intimidated me. It felt like a male, military landscape and as though I was there on sufferance, an irrelevance to the important themes of war and masculine honour. Now I return as an adult, nearly twenty years after the end of the Cold War, and the planners' self-importance seems like hubris. In the fifties' rush to plant, the presumption was that labour would continue to be as plentiful and cheap as it had been in the thirties; no one paused to consider the cost required to maintain these forests. The dense thicket I so disliked as a child was the outcome of rising labour costs: a twenty-five-year-old plantation needs thinning, but by 1970 it no longer paid to put a man, even if he had a chainsaw, into such a wood. Ideally, by then one row in nine would have been felled and the timber extracted, along with smaller branches, amounting to one fifth of the timber. Access routes would have also been cut to allow subsequent thinnings. This is fiddly and yet also bulky work and much of it has to be done by a person on foot: you can't drive large machinery into rows of trees only a few feet apart. In many places the thinning was never done, and without it the trees never flourished. They grew up corralled in their blocks, too spindly to make good sawmill timber, their root systems undeveloped and their growth slow; they prop each other up and any felling can now bring a whole stand down like a pack of cards. They're giant weeds. The costs of felling, particularly on steep hillsides which are inaccessible to the machines developed for the plains of northern Europe and the US, often make it un-economic. The timber is only good for wood pulp or fencing. It is worth so little that, even if it is felled, it can end up rotting in heaps on the roadside, the cost of haulage exceed-ing the sale price.

In 1995, the plantation along the track down to the Plot was clear-felled. Because the land is relatively flat, they could bring in the machines and it was thus sufficiently profitable to war-rant felling. For a while, before it was replanted, the site looked like a First World War battlefield, with nothing but rotting stumps and the debris of branches turning silver as they died. But within a year, fresh growth sprang up between the newly planted saplings. For the first time in my memory, it began to look pretty. Seeds that had lain dormant in the soil for nearly half a century under that thick coating of needles flourished.

Trees such as silver birch and flowers such as rose-bay willow herb mantled the dead wood with green. The replanting has been done with care: broad-leaved saplings have been planted along the edges of the forest and the conifers are concentrated in the centre. There is no new Sitka spruce.

Trees pass down the generations, like a message in a bottle. In full growth, they reflect the preoccupations of two generations earlier. The coniferous plantations were an expression of the anxieties and fears of the forties and fifties, and it will be several more decades before we have eradicated their legacy. Brian Walker and his colleagues are now planning fifty to a hundred years into the future, creating habitats that perhaps their grandchildren will experience, but they certainly will not; few other jobs require a time-frame so far in the future. In a world where predictions of apocalyptic catastrophe have become commonplace, it is hard to imagine devoting one's labour to planning forests for the end of the twenty-first century. Walker makes few predictions about the future other than to conclude that he believes people will still need wood, and they will also need places to play.

What was created to fight a war is now about pleasure. The Forestry Commission talks of making places for recreation, with bicycle routes and picnic spots. Its new priority is pleasuring the eye. The Commission is trying to coax back the bilberry and the heather on Wass Moor along the A170 near the Plot, one of the main access roads into the National Park. The visitors arriving from West Yorkshire don't want to look out of their cars on to a wall of coniferous trees, they want the distinctive vegetation of the moors, above all the heather. Maps in the Pickering offices now measure what people can see and how many see it; the coniferous trees are tucked into unseen crevices, hidden from view. Those blocks of Sitka that remain are being slowly eased out; there are even some grants to assist their felling and, even more promisingly, the new biofuel station at Teesside might finally make it economic to clear even the hillside plantations which are the most expensive to fell. The plan is to replace them with broad-leaf trees such as oak, hazel and ash, the trees that have thrived on these hillsides from the end of the Ice Age. There are even plans to fell the trees in front of the Chapel; perhaps the Plot will get its view back. The wheel is slowly turning full circle.

DATES	11th	12th	13th	IN THREE DAYS
	396	163	328	= 887
	2	2	2	= 6
	8	28	11	= 47
	7	164	105	= 276
	1			= 1
VARIOUS.	1. Woodcock 4	9	1. W. Cock 4	= 19
TOTALS	419	366	451	= 1236

GUNS

Lord Mountgarret
Lord Darnley
Mr T. Wood
Mr F. Fane
Hon S. C. Lister
Sir R. Payne Gallwey
W. Payne Gallwey

R. P. G. inv. 1891.

10

Thur 19

A killing game

On chilly November days, when the hillsides are reverberating to the crack of gunfire, the history of war seems very present on the Plot. Close the eyes and a civil war seems frighteningly imaginable. Of course it is no such thing, just pheasant-shooting, a routine occurrence in these woods. To visit the Plot's nearest neighbours often requires a call to check on the shooting; it always seemed plausible that a timetable might slip, a shoot overrun, and a shot might come whistling through the windscreen or narrowly miss my shoulder. Everywhere in the forest and around the Plot there is the paraphernalia that accompanies the breeding and nurturing of the birds to be shot: old metal canisters are recycled as maize feeders and trailing hosepipes bring water. It looks much like rubbish dumped by careless visitors. But no one is complaining; the Forestry Commission rents out the shooting to a syndicate of local farmers and their associates. It brings employment to the beaters and sport to the shooters; this is North Yorkshire asnd no one argues with killing game.

One of the longest-lived, most continuous human activities on the moors has been hunting. There were royal hunting grounds on the North York moors around Pickering from Norman times. Thirty deer parks enclosed by stone walls were dotted along the edges of the moors and originate from the Middle Ages. Land ownership here has been determined by hunting more than the productive capacities of the soil. Until very recently the moors were busy with different forms of chasing, killing and their attendant rituals. The hunt came to visit our village of Oswaldkirk every year, and the hounds swarmed across our gate and all over the garden in front of my tolerant parents while the hunters in their pink coats sipped sherry in front of the manor opposite. My brother became master of hounds of his school beagle pack, and introduced a proud father to the sport. Long after my brother had left Yorkshire, Dad continued to follow the beagles every Saturday up until the last few years of his life. In his olive-green anorak, he would crane his head over the top of hedgerows as he went up on his tiptoes (he was very short) to spot the small figures racing across the moors after the beagles which were racing after the hare. Then, jumping into his rusting car, he did his own racing along single-track roads, in a convoy of farmers' muddy Land-Rovers, to arrive at another hedgerow. I could see that it was companionable in a terse kind of way – a tip of the cap, a nod, a 'John' – and it was of course hunting on the cheap, requiring no fee for joining a syndicate, but its appeal seemed pretty elusive to me. He insisted I accompany him on rare weekend visits and I got cold and very bored.

Hunting with dogs for live quarry was banned in 2004, but the complexity and local unpopularity of the legislation has left plenty of scope for both beagling and fox-hunting to continue on the moors. Pheasant-shooting is even more prevalent in North Yorkshire: across the UK every year 20 million are released from their pens and waddle from feeder to feeder to gorge on maize like the fat Chinese chickens that they are, and 15 million of them are shot. But the really serious sport on the North York moors is grouse-shooting.

On a blustery May day, I'm walking down off Black Hambleton. It's like falling out of the sky, with the view laid out around me and the chimneys of the Teesside industrial plants just visible over the Cleveland Hills. It is too early in the year for new bracken and the moor is still made up of winter-bleached swathes of pale browns. Only the bilberry bushes sprawl a brilliant green, as if some giant had splashed paint. As I crash down the slope of thick heather, a bird shoots into the air just a few yards ahead of me with a shrill cry of alarm. Its wings work furiously to propel its frail body up into the sky as quickly as possible. Very soon it is a grey speck against the scudding clouds. That's as much company as the grouse ever has to offer the walker, a punctuation point – unpredictable, noisy, frightened and brief. It makes even the most experienced walker start, a small moment of shock to remind one that the moors have for a very long time been a place for the hunted and the hunter.

Red grouse are relatively rare; their only habitat in Britain is moorland and in many places their populations are now considerably reduced. Yorkshire, Northumberland and the Peak District are the only upland areas where there is a reliable 'croppable surplus' – as the hunting fraternity briskly describe the population distribution required for shooting. It is sheep – in the right quantities – that ensure the ecological niche for the notoriously particular grouse, which requires considerable additional encouragement from gamekeepers charged with a schedule of heather-burning. The latter provides the grouse with the mosaic of differently aged heather that caters for every stage of its life cycle, from the green shoots of new growth (for feeding) to the older woodier stems (for nesting). Even with such zealous assistance from both man and sheep, grouse populations soar and crash in a roughly seven- to twelve-year cycle driven by the bird's own parasitic burden – the organisms that feed and multiply on grouse and eventually inflict the epidemics that kill them. This is a bird that has remained stubbornly wild, beyond human ingenuity to propagate, or rid of disease with drug-laced feed, unlike the pheasant.

It is the wildness of this beady-eyed bird that gives it kudos as prey. What delights the hunter is the speed and erratic nature of its flight which can reach up to 80 mph. It was only when a reliable, fast-loading gun had been invented in the nineteenth century that grouse-shooting became such a fashionable sport for city gentlemen. As the technology of the guns improved, the desire for record quantities of birds became paramount; estate workers were put to the task of driving the grouse, and shooters hid themselves in butts – stone-walled shelters concealed in the heather. Hunting no longer involved much physical prowess, stamina or skill; it did not require stalking or arduous hours in the saddle. It had become a matter of technology and marksmanship. At the same time another form of technology, the railway, was for the first time offering easy access to the moors where grouse could be shot. Yorkshire was accessible from London for holidays, and the pattern of social life shifted to accommodate the shooting season. Queen Victoria's eldest son, Edward VII, gave the pastime the royal imprimatur.

By the 1880s British moors had become killing fields, and the annual bags on estates across Britain soared in the decades leading up to the First World War. In 1888 the 6th Lord Walsingham wanted to set the record for grouse shot in one day with one pair of guns 'by having every bird on his

Yorkshire estate driven over him, with a plan of campaign more appropriate to a battle between nation-states and every tactical consideration given due weight'. His bag was 1,070 grouse in the course of fourteen hours and eighteen minutes. It was said that the grouse were so repeatedly driven over his guns that some dropped out of the sky from sheer exhaustion.

One of the most prominent figures in the Edwardian shooting world was another Yorkshireman, Sir Ralph Payne Gallwey, author of such books as *High Pheasants in Theory and Practice* and *Letters to Young Shooters* and inventor of Payne Gallwey gaiters, shooting-sticks and gun-cleaning kits. He took up residence in Thirkleby Hall, just at the foot of the Hambleton Hills, four miles from the Plot and within easy access of the grouse moors. Here he installed an indoor rifle range and, fascinated by ballistics, built models of ancient siege engines. He died in 1916 while European armies were demonstrating more ballistics in Flanders than even he could have imagined. Again and again in the history of Edwardian England's love affair with shooting there are premonitions of the slaughter of human beings that lay only a few years ahead. England's enthusiasm for the sport was shared by its future enemies, Germany and Austria-Hungary; the German emperor was a regular shot in England, and the game larder at Sandringham was copied from one in Hungary, built to hang thousands of birds from a day's sport.

At the turn of the century, this appetite for killing became near-indiscriminate. The tally recorded in household game books now makes chilling reading, charting as it does the British Empire's pattern of slaughter across the globe. The game book of the Marquess of Ripon included rhino, tiger, pig, deer, pheasant, grouse, wild duck and rabbit; he was once regarded as the best shot of his age, and was reputed to have shot twenty-eight pheasants in a minute. Every year the pheasants' death toll ran into thousands, reaching a total of a quarter of a million on his estate in just over half a century. Hares peaked at 19,000 in 1894 and never dipped below 11,000 a year over the entire period 1867–1923, not even during the war. Long before English gentlemen arrived at the Western Front in the First World War, they had perfected their shooting skills on the wildlife of the British countryside.

The black and white photos of the kill after such shoots are jarring. The prey were laid out in rows on the verge and hung on the fence, ranked by species – rabbits next to hares, and then birds. With a look of proud self-satisfaction, the men survey their dead quarry, guns under arm, while the women look on, wrapped in furs. The dead of this killing field were a cause for pride, a celebration of the supremacy of human ingenuity over nature; the photos were to be displayed, framed and hung on the wall.

There were qualms in some quarters – the Duke of Portland admitted that, looking back at his game book, he was 'ashamed of the enormous number of pheasants we sometimes killed. This is a form of shooting I have no desire to repeat.' But the appetite for grouse-shooting has remained steady. Their wildness was once their best protection and made them elusive quarry; now it prompts even more determined pursuit. One farmer up on Snilesworth Moor talked to me of £30,000 for the privilege of shooting grouse for a day, others put the cost at less than a third of that, others preferred to keep the whole thing discreet; the point was that the dizzying sums involved for a party were several multiples of local salaries, tilting scales of value and generating rumour and exaggeration. This is a globalized business. Agents sell shooting to customers from the US, Germany and Russia; one five-day shooting mini-break, before the credit crunch, for a party of Americans and their wives, was priced at a quarter of a million pounds.

Grouse-shooting has become inextricably tied up with the privileges of ownership. It was used as a justification to refuse ramblers access to the moors of northern England in the 1930s, penning urban populations into their cities. It has expanded with new money throughout the twentieth century from bankers to car dealers and hotel dynasts. The combination of olive green, guns, Land-Rovers and dogs is accompanied by an easy assumption of authority and the steely statement of priority claim. Without grouse, the area would never have attracted the money that has transformed humble market towns such as Helmsley into collections of expensive little hotels and designer clothes shops. When the shooting lobby's Moorland Association produced an analysis of the economic benefits of shooting, it quaintly included 'wives shopping' (a question mark was the only estimate of how much that might amount to), although the future of this micro-economy is uncertain as a deepening recession is likely to hit this kind of luxury industry hard. Grouse wealth is discreet, unlike fox-hunting with its public ritual of the meet and the popularity of following the hunt. The only indication of a major shoot is a fleet of dark-green Land-Rovers in convoy on the narrow lanes over the moors. The shy, gawky grouse has found itself at the centre of a small social eco-system designed to encourage its reproduction and enjoy its mortality.

No part of this account fits the public-relations exercise now required of the shooting fraternity if it is to ensure its sport's long term survival. They feel beleaguered, having seen other field sports fall by the wayside in recent years, so when I ended up in the cold dining room of an eighteenth-century shooting lodge on the moors, the Moorland Association's spokesman was emphatic: it is to grouse that we owe the beauty of the open moor, I was told in no uncertain terms. Grouse-shooting was the only form of land use that maintained the moor without subsidies from the taxpayer, unlike sheep or wind-generated electricity. The gamekeepers' schedule of heather-burning helped prevent the build-up of dead wood and thus reduced the fire risk, while bracken was controlled by spray from helicopters and further treatments on the ground every year. All of this was expensive, hence the high cost of shooting, but it made for the best conservation strategy for the Yorkshire moors. He had a point, I conceded, but perhaps an even better conservation strategy for the moors would be reverting to scrub, and eventually forest? He was scathing in response: we have plenty of woodland, why would we want more? He spoke with the brisk irritation of someone who believes they are providing a public service for which no one seems to be grateful.

These encounters and histories remind me why the Plot was never a place where I felt I belonged, why I always felt our family were outsiders, only ever politely tolerated by those whose families had lived and worked there for generations. We were from London, and, even more odd, we were Catholic. In the eyes of the North Yorkshire landed middle classes, we lacked the money to overcome either of those considerable disadvantages. The place could still madden me by the casual condescension of its minutely observed social hierarchy, but none of that had ever bothered my father. On the contrary, he loved the apparatus of the English upper classes. He read histories of obscure aristocrats and could recount whom they had married and how their connections spanned the county and the country with a level of knowledge that always left me baffled as to why he wanted to know this stuff. There was still so much to understand about this man.

The key fob had taken me on a trail that had led to a better understanding of my father and his Plot. It had given me insight into what lay behind the bluff machismo of a man who missed his war. I've been trespassing, because this was not territory he ever expected a daughter to investigate; my father never made much effort to conceal his misogyny. It's a relief to turn to other explanations of the Plot. When I visited one of my father's pupils, the sculptor Antony Gormley, in his studio in London he told me, 'This book will be a liberation.' I was heartened by this, and decided it should be a prophecy.

I wanted to go gliding. More than ever I was looking forward to that distant perspective on the land from high up in the sky. I heard on the radio of an extraordinary experiment in pain relief: researchers at Cambridge University set a group of people with chronic pain to spend some time every day looking through binoculars at the part of their body where the pain was occurring. But the binoculars had to be the wrong way round – the ankle, knee or hand had to appear as if very distant. They found that, in comparison with the control group, the binocular watching had considerably reduced the experience of pain. Could gliding have the same effect?

August 2007: it feels like it has been raining ever since we were last in Yorkshire. As we drive up the M1 through a waterlogged England, I glimpse something of what Noah might have felt when he released his dove. I'm juggling mobile phones, contacts book and maps; we're heading to the Dales but I've extracted agreement that I can try again to go gliding and we are taking a detour via the Yorkshire Gliding Club. It's that cheerful voice again. 'Possibly,' she says, unflustered by my protestations of how rarely I'm in Yorkshire and how far I have to travel, 'we're just getting briefed on the weather.' I call back, ever hopeful. 'No,' she says finally, 'try next weekend.' But next weekend is impossible: we'll be deep into term-time with the winter looming.

Is it me or do I detect a note of impatience behind the firmness: a hint of I-don't-organize-the-weather, you know. Or an unasked question: when are you southerners going to learn the Yorkshire bleeding obvious, namely that weather is never predictable and always liable to upset the best laid plans? You can't schedule the Atlantic, Pennines and North Sea according to your diary needs.

THE COUNTY MAP OF YORK 1775 MAP 4

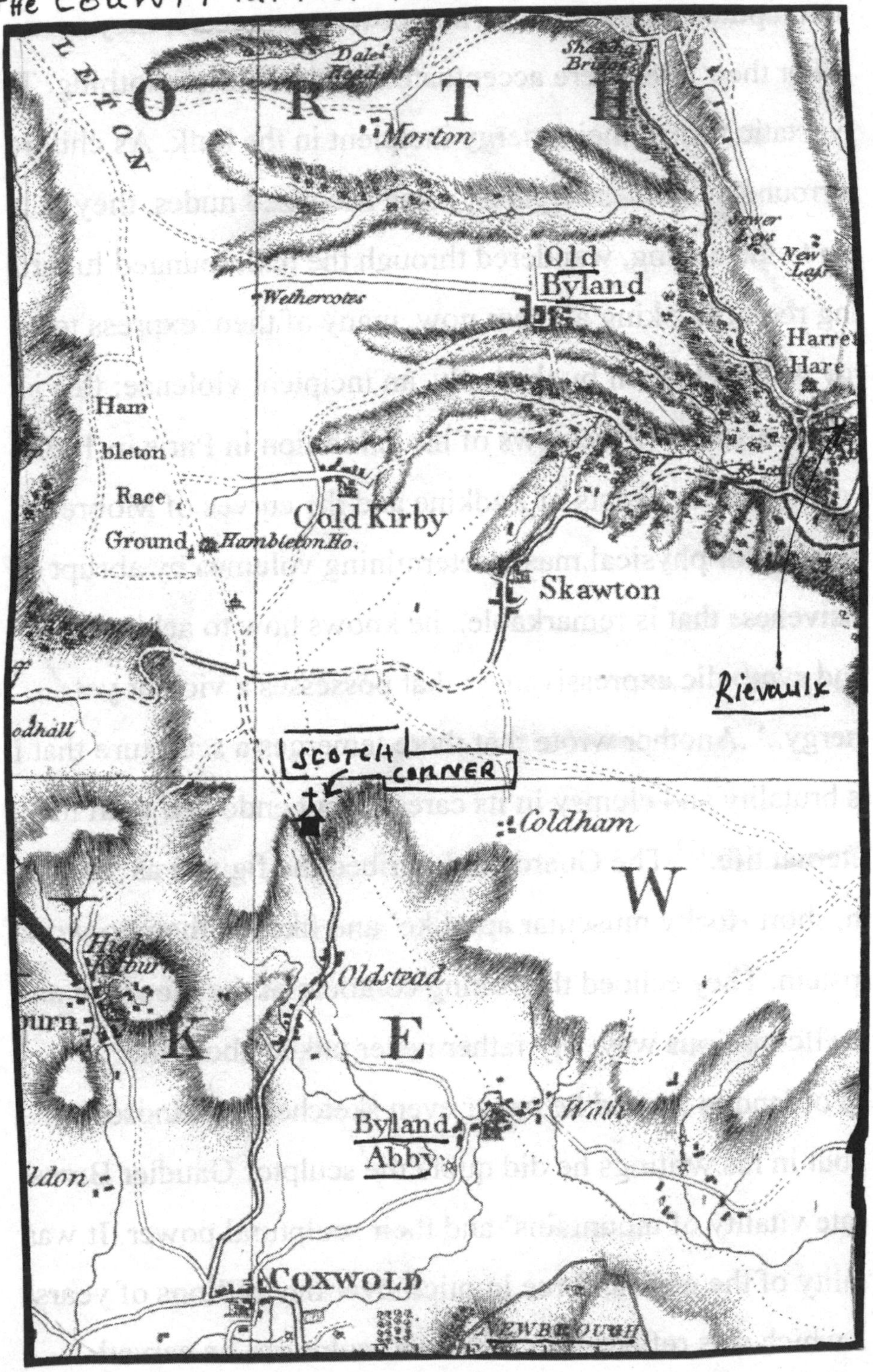

Part III: The Promised Land

11

Sanctuary

It was a brilliantly clear day in midsummer, and we were escaping. My sister, a friend and I had left a total of eight children and three husbands, and slipped out of our domestic routines, catching the train with nothing but small overnight knapsacks. Standing in my brand-new walking boots on the London platform, wedged between commuters, I felt the thrill of the runaway. We had three days to revel in the irresponsibility of leaving our chores behind, the email inbox filling up, the phone messages going unanswered. We were answerable to no one, unconfined even by a car with its family detritus of parking tickets and sticky sweet wrappers. We would get up when we wanted, start walking when we wanted, stop when we wanted; there were no complaining children to conciliate or tired ones to coax. The only limit was that of our own physical capacities, the strength of our bodies, our legs, feet and the shoulders on which we carried our knapsacks. All of which we were to feel in new ways by the end of the three days, but in those first hours, escape brought its own edge of sweet exhilaration.

We spent a day walking the Drovers' Road along the

Hambleton Hills, picking it up above Osmotherley at Square
Corner and following it over Black Hambleton and across
Arden Great Moor under a blazing sun. We ran out of water and
in that great sweep of land there was neither a farmhouse nor a
stream to refill our bottle, so we were thirsty until we reached
High Paradise Farm, several miles further on, where we set the
dogs barking and a kindly lady lent us her tap. Seven miles and
several hours later, the shadows were lengthening when we
finally reached the Plot, footsore and still with several miles to
go before we reached the pub at Kilburn where we were to stay
the night. We sat down on the low wall for a brief rest, watching tiny flies dancing in the shafts of evening sun. Then we
rallied our aching legs and pressed on, eager for supper. By
the time we arrived in Kilburn, the sense of achievement was
immense.

This was a land now overlaid with the memories of our conversations; the chatting about family and work was linked in
the mind to the stone walls, the patch of sheep-cropped grass
where we stopped for lunch and the wizened hawthorns bowed
by winter winds. Our laughter and the anecdotes of dramatic
births told by my sister, a midwife, had become part of the
landscape. When I return now, I remember those snatches of
conversation alongside my father's marching, his irritation and
rambling monologues.

Later that evening, the name of High Paradise Farm came
back to me and looking at the map I found its counterpart,
Low Paradise Farm. There are similar names thinly scattered
across the moors, usually in the emptiest places. They mark a
rare expression of extravagant idealism in the most unlikely of
contexts, the hard, lonely life of farming families. But it struck
me that the North York moors have long been a place of
refuge, of sanctuary, of escape and of new beginnings for the

spiritually or materially dispossessed. It's a use of the land that connects the hermit to the socially ambitious, the dissenter farmer to the outlaw over the span of one and half millennia. The North Yorkshire moors are something of a dead-end; only the Drovers' Road along their western edge was a thoroughfare. The moors were a place to avoid; they were not on the way to anywhere important such as a great city, port or industrial conurbation. They have never been a corridor, only an unlikely destination, and that is part of how they kept their distinctive character in this small island well into the nineteenth century. This intensity of local identity is captured in Canon John Atkinson's diaries, *Forty Years in a Moorland Parish*, published in 1891, which begin with an account of his difficulties in finding his new parish of Danby as he rode across the moors from Scarborough. There were no signs, the tracks were not clear and there was no one to ask for directions; this was not a place that expected to be visited. This was a land to get lost in, and a place to hide. To some this has been a deterrent, but to many others it has been its attraction: there are always those who wish to be lost. Again and again in Yorkshire history one stumbles across those who ran away to the moors to escape their reputation, or the law, or the world and its corruptions. It's a gallery of rogues and mystics, preachers and dreamers.

The topography of the land immediately around the Plot lends itself particularly well to escapes; the valleys of Cockerdale and Hell Hole are folded into the wooded hillsides, only reached by discreet tracks. Both have been used as retreats. The names Hood Hill and the Thief's Highway are a reminder of how the reach of the law was intermittent at best into this crumpled land of crooked valleys and hidden ravines, where bandits and highwaymen lasted well into the eighteenth century. Far more prestigious but also intent on relaunching his life, Sir Charles Duncombe, the London banker, arrived in 1689 to buy himself the medieval castle of Helmsley – the estates of a former royal favourite – and the social status of a landowner. (The poet Alexander Pope commented scornfully, 'And Helmsley once proud Buckingham's delight/Slides to a Scrivener or a City Knight.') Many of the socially ambitious have followed his example, buying moorland to prop up their claims to privilege and demonstrate their taste and wealth, or simply escape to build their private utopias.

Researching this book, I came across a parallel story to my father's: in the 1950s a family lived out their own dream of escape and self-sufficiency at Silver Fox Farm, less than a mile from the Plot along the Hambleton escarpment. Within a year they had had enough and sold off the farm, and the wife wrote a book about their adventure. The search for a promised land has proved persistent. Two years after this family, my father, filled with comparable enthusiasm, was also hauling building materials and furniture up the steep hill to make a small corner of these hills homely. It is what draws the millions who holiday on the moors, those who come here to retire and those who commute hundreds of miles a week so that they can live here. Of all the characteristics of the land, this was the most important to my parents, both of whom had decided that adulthood required an escape. North Yorkshire offered the opportunity to create their Promised Land.

The next day, we plotted a path that unwittingly linked different stories of the promised land. In the crisp sunshine and vibrant green of midsummer, we walked from the Plot across the valley of Cockerdale. In the bottom of this privately owned valley, out of sight of any other human dwelling, sits Cockerdale Farm and its immaculately tended garden. Colin

Furness, the owner, later told me how, foreseeing the lean times ahead for agriculture, he had sold up his farm in Northumberland and retreated to this hidden valley. He had to clear out tons of rotting slurry which had nearly turned the valley floor to a quagmire; he planted hundreds of trees and bred horses. We climbed up steep tracks through the forestry plantations to come out at Cam Farm, where radios were blaring out music above the bleating sheep gathered for shearing or dipping. After several fields we were back in woodland, following a path which directed us through sun-spangled birch and oak woods where moss lay spongy and deep green beneath our feet. At the edge of the escarpment, we reached Mount Snever Observatory, John Wormald's private retreat.

From Mount Snever we scrambled east along the escarpment, ducking from one path to the next on a thickly wooded hillside criss-crossed with tracks. We stumbled onto a broad path where the ground felt surprisingly even; perhaps it was an old track for the monks from their farm at Camm Grange and the pastures on the moor down to Byland Abbey. The path dipped gently down through woodland so dense one could not see to the valley beyond. Above the village of Wass, the path stopped abruptly and we headed in what we thought was the abbey's direction, floundering through gloriously rich green bracken that came well over our heads. There were glimpses of clear blue sky ahead so we plunged on down the steep slope, pushing blindly through the bracken stalks and fronds, last year's growth crunching under our feet. All of a sudden, we burst into bright sunlight at a fence with green sheep pastures beyond. There below us rose the glorious stone ruins of Byland Abbey, one of three great medieval Cistercian monasteries of northern England. We had been anticipating it for several hours, but even so, the moment of revelation brought with it a

proper thrill of surprise, and a deeper sense of awe. Byland
Abbey has always been astonishing in this rural landscape, no
less so now than it was on its completion in 1195. Coming
down off the hillside as we did on our walk that summer day,
in the company of a pair of curlews who cried and whirled
above us, we watched the ruins sail into view like a great
galleon over the meadows, the ruined walls like ragged sails
against the sky.

The Byland monks arrived in the area in 1137, a ragged band of
a few men with their possessions loaded onto an oxcart. They
had been forced to flee from Calder in Cumbria, where their
small monastery had been raided by the King of Scotland.
They were members of an obscure order known as the
Savigniacs which thirteen years later was absorbed by their
more successful rivals, the Cistercians. What drew these men
to this part of England was its wildness: North Yorkshire had
still not recovered from William the Conqueror's depredations
sixty years before. The names of some of the grange farms
Byland founded are a reminder: Wildon Grange near Oldstead
is derived from the Saxon for 'wilderness'; Stocking, the original name for Oldstead, was a term used for partially cleared
woodland where the stumps were still standing.

The appearance of the white-robed monks in the early
twelfth century was to presage the most significant and enduring human intervention in this landscape's history. The
Cistercians' tenure of the Plot and the surrounding area was to
last 400 years, and their legacy has lasted nearly another five
centuries. The Plot's acre was one of the many given to the
Byland monks by the Norman landowner Roger de Mowbray.
It was part of a large belt of woodland from which the
Cistercians drew plentiful timber for their construction work.

They required wood for fuel to burn the lime with which they made their mortar; they needed charcoal for cooking; they needed oak bark for tanning. The Cistercians' choice of sites for their monasteries was always determined by plentiful woodland and water, and this was to be one of the Plot's main uses for centuries. Many of the woods around the Plot were coppiced for sticks used in fencing.

Almost every aspect of the Plot and the area bears the hallmarks of the Cistercians' long tenure and their shrewd ambition. They were the first to develop the North Yorkshire moors for sheep-rearing; they built up the trade with Europe, collecting huge quantities of wool to export from Hull to merchants in Flanders and Italy. So brilliantly successful were they at developing this trade that it endured for another half-millennium after their demise. At the Reformation the monks were pensioned off and the monastery crumbled, but the ambition that had shaped the land endured: the new landowners inherited their skills at sheep-farming and their trading networks.

The view over which the Plot once looked is a landscape still marked by its one-time Cistercian owners. Many of the farms date from Byland's tenure, as their names reveal; 'grange' was the term applied to the distinctive Cistercian system of outlying farms run by lay brothers, and many of the farms indicate their monastic origins: Oldstead Grange, Camm Farm Grange, Wildon Grange, Osgoodby Grange, Thirlby Grange, Balk Grange, Low Kilburn Grange, Scencliff Grange. There are still ponds which the monks designed and built; the fields around Byland are pocked with the ditches and dykes that once made up medieval England's biggest water-engineering scheme. Some fields around Oldstead even carry the names of the individual monks who cleared them. Subsequent generations have benefited in myriad ways from the monks: they still use the fields the Cistercians shaped to make best use of the contours for good drainage, and many cottages around Byland have incorporated the quarried stones taken from the post-Reformation ruins to build new homes. The monks were the first to see that this 'wasteland' could be a promised land, and everyone who has come since has inherited their legacy.

It is hard now to imagine quite how dramatic the arrival of the Cistercians was in this half-empty land. They wanted to be 'far from the concourse of men' and they cited the aim of the fourth-century desert mystic John Cassian: 'the world forgetting by the world forgot'. They chose a forgotten corner of England to emulate the example of Citeaux, their founding monastery in France, whose location was described as a 'place of horrors, a vast wilderness'. Just as the early Christian mystics had gone into the desert to find God, so the Cistercians sought out the forest – medieval Europe's equivalent of the desert – which was the refuge of outlaws, the dispossessed and wild animals. North Yorkshire was soon dotted with their monasteries, and the Plot found itself surrounded: Rievaulx lay just six miles to the north-east, whilst the monasteries of other orders sprang up across the valley at Newburgh, and a convent along the Drovers' Road at Arden. Here in this wilderness, these men and women dedicated themselves to finding *quies*, the peace of a quiet conscience.

The Cistercians believed the world so corrupt and corrupting that salvation was only possible for those who succeeded in removing themselves entirely from its temptations. The dangers of wild animals or famine for pioneer occupiers of the land were small in comparison to the threat of the world's corruption for their souls. St Bernard of Clairvaux encouraged his brother monks by telling them that he found 'no terror in the hard mountain steeps, nor in the rough rocks nor in the hollow places of the valleys, for in these days the mountains distil sweetness and the hills flow with milk and honey, the valleys are covered over with corn, honey is sucked out of the rock and oil out of the flinty stone, and among the cliffs and mountains are the flocks of the sheep of Christ'. It was only in the wilderness that the Cistercians believed it was possible to search for God. Their promised land was a utopian dream of total detachment from the world. For a century, this promise proved compelling to thousands of young men all over Europe, who flocked to join the austere Cistercians, and the order expanded from a tiny handful of monks to 700 monasteries. Men from even the wealthiest and most powerful families rejected the world and found themselves donning the coarse undyed wool of the Cistercian habit to work on rough, uncleared land like the Plot. It was here they hoped to find God.

It was an extreme response to an age of rapid social and economic change and violent conflict. The twelfth century experienced dramatic population growth, and a new urbanization saw towns and cities expanding rapidly. It was an age of anxiety. A cash economy was re-emerging in Europe for the first time since the Romans, and trade was accelerating. There were repeated laments about the commercialization of human relationships. Older traditions of gift, patronage and honour were being supplemented by new professions such as lawyers' and bankers' in the growing towns; 'everyone has their price' was a common and bitter refrain. An unprecedented number of people were on the move, as migrants, pilgrims or vagrants. With these changes came a new impersonality, as strangers became customers and neighbours in the cities. It all caused great insecurity; money was frequently excoriated as a form of pollution. Greed was the great sin of the age, placed alongside pride at the top of the catalogue of human evils, and moralists urged the faithful again and again to be wary of entrapment. The great Cistercian St Bernard declared that 'the avaricious man is like hell'. Avarice was charged with 'destroying friendships, breaking up families, causing wars, nourishing controversy'. There was an acute fear that the social order was collapsing and that the end of the world was imminent. It was a time of deep pessimism, haunted by vivid visions of tortured damnation in the afterlife.

It was also a time of war. The great expansion of the Cistercians in Yorkshire in 1135–55 coincided with a twenty-year civil war as the nobles sought to secure their power and King Stephen fought to keep the English throne. Many nobles and their protégés were sucked into betrayals of family, neighbours and allies. Byland's great benefactor, Roger de Mowbray, lost a fortune during the civil war, later improving his situation through his prowess as a keen Crusader, only to suffer further setbacks by backing a rebellion against Henry II. The Cistercian monasteries absorbed a steady supply of former knights anxious to secure redemption from the atrocities they had committed or witnessed. The monasteries also benefited from wealthy patrons equally anxious to secure redemption via large donations, which were part of a strategy on the patron's part to neutralize tracts of land, create alliances and build up an economic base from which to profit. For both the knight in battle and the feudal lord running an estate in such 'unsettled times . . . it was hard for any to lead the good life unless they were monks', commented Brother Walter Daniel, the biographer of the great abbot of Rievaulx.

The Cistercians' response was a utopian dream of total detachment from the world; their aim was to withdraw entirely from the economic system. One of their guiding ideals was *paupertas*. This was not just a matter of rejecting material wealth but also worldly power. The two were intimately linked in the feudal concept of ownership, which included powers to exact taxation and dispense justice. The feudal landowner was entitled to impose dues on beer-brewing, milling, pasture, passage over his land and the use of bridges, as well as issuing demands for labour and military service. Such dues could amount to as much as half a peasant's income; if he did not pay, the feudal lord could summon him to his manorial court and impose fines. The Cistercians believed feudalism licensed the arbitrary power of the wealthy and exploited the poor, and they wanted no part of such a corrupt system; unlike other monastic orders of the time, they initially insisted that their monasteries had no serfs and no income from feudal dues such as tithes. They accepted vocations from every level of society and instituted their own system of labour, the *conversi* or lay brothers, to work the land. Indeed, such was their loathing of feudalism that they were known to relocate a village if it was in the way of the development of their monasteries, to avoid any contamination. In the early days, they refused even to build mills, for fear this would entangle them in charging dues to those in the neighbourhood. They set out to produce everything they needed for themselves, from the metal to the tiles, timber and stone for their churches, from the wool for their habits to the bread and fish for their table. Many of these rules were relaxed as the centuries wore on, and these monastic institutions acquired unimagined wealth and influence.

But in the early years, hard labour was required; rejecting the example of other orders, the Cistercians did not spend large portions of their day on elaborate rituals, copying manuscripts and prayer, but on manual work. 'Believe me, I have experience you will feel fuller satisfaction labouring in the woods than you ever will in books. The trees and the rocks will teach you what you can never hear from any master,' wrote St Bernard. The men finding this satisfaction in the woods around the Plot lived harsh lives. Their diet of one vegetarian meal a day was inadequate and many monks suffered malnutrition; it's been estimated that the average life expectancy for a Cistercian monk in these early years dropped by seven years to just twenty-eight. Only one room of the monastery was heated in winter, the *calefactorium*, and the monks had to stuff their stockings to prevent their feet from freezing. As St Bernard warned new arrivals, 'leave your body behind when you enter these gates, only your soul is needed'. Contemporaries were impressed: the Cistercian monasteries were the 'surest way to heaven', wrote William, the Benedictine librarian of Malmesbury in 1124, while another non-Cistercian commented that 'by the great good they do they shine out in the world like lanterns burning in a dark place'.

Cistercianism was an austere discipline, but for the early Byland monks it was unusually so. Their first forty years in the area were troubled as they moved three times in search of the right site. Several times they travelled up and down along the Drovers' Road across the Plot; the first donation of land they received, in 1137, was at Hood, just a mile south-west of the Plot, but it was not large enough so they moved north a few miles further along the Hambleton Hills to Old Byland. But the monks at the neighbouring new monastery of Rievaulx complained that they could hear Byland's bells chiming, and besides, the land up on the top of the escarpment was exposed, and harvests would have been late and vulnerable to bad weather. So in 1147 the Byland monks travelled back down the Drovers' Road, over the Plot to the bottom of the hill and the village of Stocking, now called Oldstead. They stayed there thirty years as they prepared their final move to Byland, clearing the land of trees, diverting five streams to provide an adequate water supply and building their church. For nearly half a century, this monastic community had been involuntarily itinerant, arriving each time to begin the back-breaking work of assarting the land – felling trees, uprooting the stumps, clearing brush and brambles. They worked with inadequate tools, breaking up the soil by spade or even hand because their ploughs were often too inefficient to do more than scratch the soil.

After three false starts, the monks were intent on constructing a building at Byland that would announce they had overcome this inauspicious beginning, determined it would be England's biggest, most ambitious Cistercian church. At the time it was built, Byland Abbey was the largest abbey church in the country, the equal of any European cathedral of its time. It was a triumph of determination, and the exuberance and radicalism of its architectural ambition reflects that determination. Byland was built in a Gothic architecture that was still novel, and a stark contrast to the extravagance and gaudily painted interiors of the Romanesque; frescos were banished and the walls were white; the huge windows were filled with plain silvery glass called grisaille. Shockingly severe to contemporaries, gothic expressed discipline and simplicity; carved capitals, elaborate altars, tombs and stained glass were frowned on by these early Cistercians. The emphasis in Byland Abbey was on light: the walls of the nave were punctured with expanses of glass to allow light to flood in. The building was designed to illustrate the dualism of the medieval world-view – day and night, light and dark, good and evil. Now, these great windows have left the nave's walls ragged, revealing great slabs of sky or hillside beyond.

Byland's ruins are dominated by the most ambitious of its architectural features. Above the main entrance door in the western façade the monks built a great rose window with twenty-four spokes. It was later copied across northern England and is believed to have been the model for York Minster. The west front of the main abbey is the most complete section of the ruins, and the façade is topped by the last fragment of this rose window, a semicircle of stone frame, one side capped with a pointed pediment as if indicating heaven. The rose window was a symbol of the wheel of fortune, of how the rich and powerful one day are cast down the next, a much-repeated theme of medieval life. Byland's rose window was not just an architectural vanity, it was a powerful statement about the cruelly insecure age of which these monks had had bitter personal experience.

After the Reformation the abbey was left to disintegrate, its roof stripped of valuable lead, and over the following centuries the ruins were pilfered as a source of cheap stone. But the frame of the rose window and its warning of the precariousness of fortune persisted, ominously silhouetted against the sky, as eloquent to new generations as it was to its builders, both prediction and epitaph.

There was plenty in this search for sanctuary in a period of political turbulence, in this astonishing creative achievement in the wilderness of the moors, in this distrust in the fortunes of the world, that must have proved utterly compelling to the teenager who arrived in the middle of the Second World War in North Yorkshire to attend boarding school. This was the history in whose shadow my father wanted to take shelter as a new dark age, he believed, took grip on a world in chaos.

He arrived in 1941 by train on a long journey disrupted by

wartime exigencies, leaving his family in a London under nightly bombardment. My grandmother had resolved that her son, brimful of enthusiasm, ambition and energy, was to be educated to become a Catholic gentleman; my grandfather was less convinced that expensive fees at a school like Ampleforth were something the family could afford, but he was prepared to indulge his wife. He himself had left school at fourteen – his own father at twelve – and what he really wanted was my father to help him in the family business as soon as possible. However dearly my grandmother cherished the idea of a good education, the family barely had the means to pay for it; the decision to send my father all those hundreds of miles away I see now as a gamble to secure a precarious middle-class status.

My father's family history contained such sudden turns of fortune that it provided plenty of grist to his claims that a civilization was in chaotic decline. As we were growing up we learned very little of this turbulent story, but in his later years my father was keen to leave an accurate record, and he wrote a remarkably frank pamphlet. Some of the alcoholism and suicides of which the family seemed to have had more than its fair share made an appearance, along with a story of huge ambition. The man who dominated the story was his own grandfather and namesake, John Joseph Bunting. My great-grandfather glowers from the photos with a heavy, set face and stocky build much like his grandson. One of seven children brought up by a seamstress who had rejected her alcoholic husband, he worked his way up from office boy selling newspapers to manager in one of the biggest tea-trading companies in the City. In 1915 he left to set up his own business supplying the English and Scottish Wholesale Co-operative with tea, cocoa and cocoa by-products. He was a brilliant businessman and within five years his staff had grown from three to seventy.

He bought a rambling mansion in Highgate to house a growing brood of children from a succession of wives (they had a habit of dying or disappearing). The success continued and by 1927 he had bought a 1,600-acre country estate in Sussex called Coghurst. It was a large Victorian baronial hall set in parkland and approached by a grand drive which swept between rhododendrons around three landscaped lakes. John Joseph bought the house fully furnished, right down to the curtains and crockery. The photo of the main drawing room shows a massive chandelier, gilt furniture and huge mirrors 'in the semblance of a stateroom in some Ruritanian palace', my father commented wrily in his history.

It was an instant stately home at a time when such things were going relatively cheap as old families, impoverished by agricultural depression and the loss of their heirs, were forced to sell off. The oak-panelled hall came already equipped with the stuffed trophies of big-game hunting. Here the former newspaper boy could style himself as a gentleman, indulge his taste for cigars, wear tweed plus-fours and place himself at the centre of the photos of his large tribe. The house was large enough to accommodate the arrival in the holidays of fifteen grandchildren with their parents and nannies. My father learned to row and swim on the lake amongst the lily pads; he helped do the milking on the estate farm and sneaked into the walled vegetable garden to pick ripe fruit. He talked of this 'earthly paradise' all his life, repeatedly referring to its grandeur and opulence. It was one of the few things he wanted us all to know: that the family had seen better days, that we had been dispossessed and that by rights we should be enjoying the rhododendrons and the lily pads.

The history my father inherited from his mother was almost as flamboyant. My grandmother was two generations from a penniless Irish immigrant who fled the potato famine and came to London to sell coal from a handcart. He built up a coal-haulage business which transported his two sons and six daughters into middle-class respectability in a large house in Highgate and a modest property empire. But his daughter Margaret made a disastrous marriage to an Irish American who abandoned her and their two small girls, the elder of whom was my father's mother, Bridget. (Such was the stigma of marriage breakdown that everyone was told he was dead.) She grew up in a household struggling to maintain respectability, dependent on hand-outs from the family business. The marriage to John Bunting's son, Bernard, provided stability at last. The photos of my father's childhood with his three sisters in Friern Barnet, north London, depict a quintessential middle-class domesticity: my grandmother in her signature pearls, my grandfather portly and pleased, cigar in hand. The clutch of children posed clean and obedient in the large garden. There were photos of sailing holidays and golf tournaments. This was the springboard my grandmother hoped her children would use to ensure that they left behind the insecurity and poverty that had dogged their forebears.

By the thirties, John Joseph Bunting, the Tea King, was the most powerful man in the London tea trade. The climax to his career came in 1935 when the Lord Mayor of London, accompanied by the Sheriffs and Aldermen, laid the foundation stone for John Joseph's biggest investment to date, a dedicated office block on Fenchurch Street to house the tea auction room and the rubber exchange. Plantation House was one of the most lavish City office complexes of its time. Its completion, a year later, was marked with a staff dinner in Claridges, and John Joseph celebrated his new status and affluence by buying a large, newly built first-floor flat overlooking Marble Arch.

Within four years, everything was lost. The tea company had gone into voluntary liquidation after a disastrous lawsuit: John Joseph's main customer had accused him of buying up stock to fix the price and refused to honour its contract. The whole edifice of opulence and respectability came crashing down as rapidly as it had been erected. Coghurst and Plantation House were both sold in 1940, and John Joseph retreated, bitter and defeated, to a small house in Highgate and an irascible old age. Bernard struggled on under the liquidator and wartime rationing to pay off the £750,000 still owed to creditors (a task finally accomplished in 1953). In his later years he was forced to pack the tea himself in a former broom cupboard of the magnificent office block his father had once built. Money was so tight that it began to show in the shabbiness of his worn suits.

Coghurst and Plantation House lived on in my father's imagination, icons of a family wealth that in his childhood he was briefly led to believe would be his entitlement. In the early sixties, he took his own small son back to visit Coghurst, on the outskirts of Hastings. He found to his horror that the house had been largely demolished, and an estate of bungalows had colonized much of the parkland. Around the lakes were ranks of brightly coloured caravans. The lodge gates, destroyed by a bomb, had been replaced by a bus depot.

If what happened to Coghurst was painful for my father, what happened to Plantation House was bewildering. In the late eighties, it was bought by property developers who invested millions in refurbishing it, paying particular attention to its history as a central institution of the imperial tea trade. They unearthed the original dedication plaque; contact was made with my father and he cast a relief of his grandfather's head in bronze for the new development. There was a grand ceremony in 1991 when the refurbishment was completed, which my delighted father attended, and he sent us all the commemoration mugs that were produced. History, it seemed, was finally being honoured. But it was not to last; a few years later I asked my father if he had kept up the connection with the City, and his answer was brief. The building was being demolished – within a decade of the expensive refurbishment – to make way for a new development, which was finally completed in 2004 as Plantation Place.

It was a very British experience of the turbulence of the twentieth century; it involved only a fraction of the bloodshed and suffering experienced across the continent by comparable generations, but its chaotic discontinuities, the fortunes made and lost with brutal abruptness, are striking for how they have been tidied away in a mainstream narrative of increasing postwar prosperity. One suspects it is not that unusual a tale of the precarious world of the lower-middle class in the first half of the twentieth century; a few turns of the wheel of fortune could propel them into unprecedented wealth – and equally, a few more turns could plunge them into a desperate struggle to keep up appearances, the latter all the more poignant since etiquette insisted it should be a strictly private battle.

My father's conclusion was that capitalism was too fickle a mistress to tempt his hand. He had no wish to be so roughly treated by trade in a city that had made and broken fortunes with such reckless chance. Byland Abbey's ruined façade with its stone frame for the rose window, a symbol of the wheel of fate, was no medieval superstition for him, but an accurate comment on the instability of his own century.

Our family life was framed as much around my father's understanding of the Middle Ages as around the century we

were living in. The ideals of medieval monasticism dominated his imagination – as an inspiration to his faith, his art
and his fascination with history. In his later years, he would
often join the Benedictine monks at Ampleforth for a lunch
conducted in silence except for the reading of a devotional
text. He lived almost all his life in close proximity to the
ideals and way of life prescribed by the fifth-century Italian
monk St Benedict in his *Rule* – its present practice as well as
its glorious past, when the Cistercians launched their dramatic
twelfth-century reform of the *Rule* and built monasteries from
the Baltic to Portugal. To his mind, the Cistercian ideals had
been unjustly and brutally destroyed by the great calamity of
the English Reformation. Like all English Catholics, he
prayed fervently for his country to return to the 'faith of our
fathers', in the words of his favourite hymn. These beliefs of
his were not a matter for discussion, let alone for a difference
of something as indulgent as opinion; they formed a bedrock
of unquestioned, unquestionable, very private faith. He never
missed Mass on Sunday nor holy days of obligation, and I
suspect he never missed his nightly prayers. But he didn't
talk about his faith, and he never even commented on the
lapses of his children. After he died we found a handwritten
prayer in his wallet; the Catechism truths he had been taught
as a child lasted his lifetime. The ruins of Byland – and
Rievaulx four miles to the north as the crow flies – were symbols for him of a time when his faith had had its rightful place
in England.

High up on the façade of the Chapel is a niche containing a
Madonna and Child. She has aged well over the last half century, the York stone touched with the grey-green mildew to
which it is prone. But she looks over her baby's head into the
forest with as much stout defiance as when she was first

levered into place. Then, she would have looked out to the young saplings, and over the fields and hills towards the ruins of Byland, two miles away. Her prominence was an emphatic assertion of Roman Catholicism, a reclamation of the land for the true faith. My father may not have been able to bring England back to the 'faith of its fathers', but he could ensure that one English acre was Catholic again.

12

A manifesto in stone

Just across the road from Byland's ruins stands a pub. Sitting in a corner on a cold winter's day with the fire roaring, it's a good spot to watch the rain beating against the old stones of the grand west façade and the fragment of the famous rose window. As the eye returns to one's pint, it might just catch sight of a curious carved stone head, inserted into the fashionably exposed stonework of the bar wall. It's much the same size as the stones amongst which it has been inserted, and it's the same colour and texture. It's easy to miss. By now, curiosity might quicken because there's another carving. And another. In fact, dotted in the walls of several of the connecting rooms are carvings: heads, and small figures, often oddly shaped. Some are darkened by the touch of many hands, others seem to have gone unnoticed.

When I ask the bar staff about them, they don't know who did them or where they came from; nor do they seem much interested. This is a busy gastro-pub with rooms at £200 a night which are billed as the 'perfect getaway' and offering 'exclusive tranquillity'; venison T-bone with fat-cut chips and chocolate fondant are on the menu. The Cistercians would be horrified at how their promised land has become a luxury weekend break.

But of course I didn't need to ask the bar staff who did the carvings; I was just curious to know if they knew, and a little shocked to see how short memory can now be, even in North Yorkshire, even in Byland Inn, a place that makes so much of its living from memory. But the bar staff are as likely to come from Vilnius or Krakow as North Yorkshire, and the pub has changed hands relatively recently: what did I expect?

Dad carved them in the early nineties, and he was paid in lunches. I do not know how many meals he got for each but I had the impression that the arrangement with the couple who originally renovated the old-fashioned pub lasted quite a while, to mutual satisfaction. Dad had some excellent meals, and the couple were very appreciative of his services.

To my mind, the pub's quaint carvings are a wonderfully suitable statement on the man, more so even than some of the much grander sculptures over which he laboured for years, which stand around the wider Ryedale area and in schools and hospitals across northern England. They reflect his irrepressible love of carving, his delight in the material so that any piece of stone, however awkward, could yield a form.

The carvings sit beside the pub's tables and chairs, which were made by Robert Thompson, the village carpenter who first taught Dad, as a fourteen-year-old, to carve. Here were the inspirations – the monastic ruins, the carpentry – that made so deep an impression on this boy that they shaped his greatest ambition – the building of his Chapel on the Plot – and how he wanted to live his life.

Thompson's furniture had been one of the first things my father noticed when he arrived at Ampleforth. While other boys were probably comparing cricket scores and squabbling over rugby boots, my father wrote how he 'recognised the adze mark and the mark of the carver's chisel' on the school's tables and chairs. From a precociously early age he had been interested in the Arts and Crafts tradition of William Morris, but it was Thompson, the carpenter from the small village of Kilburn, who brought that interest to life and introduced him to a passion he never lost. Kilburn is just over a mile from the Plot, one of the pretty villages that make up the view from the Hambleton Hills; once, it would have been possible to glimpse a few of its rooftops from the Plot. In the 1940s, Thompson was beginning to acquire a name for himself as a talented craftsman in the tradition of the Arts and Crafts movement, making thick-set oak tables and chairs which were commissioned by churches and institutions across the country. His signature was a small mouse discreetly carved on a leg or underside, but it was not the mice that caught this schoolboy's attention, rather the undulating surfaces left by an old-fashioned tool, the adze, and the flaked ripples of the chisel on the English oak; it was the visibility of hand and tool in the form that intrigued him. Looking back on his early days at Ampleforth over fifty years later, my father wrote:

> I lost no time in walking on a free afternoon to
> Kilburn, ten [*sic*, in fact four] miles distant. [A journey
> that would have taken him past Byland.] Here, Robert
> Thompson had a workshop where he employed carvers
> and joiners making furniture for domestic and
> ecclesiastical purposes. I met Robert Thompson and I

was enthralled by the smells of oak and leather and
bees wax; by the sight of men working, carving and
assembling pieces of furniture. The journey back in
rain and in the dark could not dampen the ardour such
a scene had aroused in me. I made a number of visits,
and for the holidays I took home a piece of oak and
some chisels Robert Thompson had given me and I
carved a face in relief of an Indian. I made a workshop
for myself at the top of the house in a spare room
where I carved book ends. Tim [a friend] and I went to
shops in London and came back with orders and I soon
found myself lucratively employed in my holidays.

He had found his passion, and throughout his school life he
fitted visits to the workshops at Kilburn between his rugby
matches. In due course, his father insisted that his son had
had enough expensive education and that it was time to leave
Ampleforth, but Dad managed to persuade his parents to let
him return to work for Thompson for a few weeks. He took
lodgings in Coxwold, and walked to and from Kilburn twice a
day (twelve miles in total), returning after supper to the
workshop to do his own carvings. In 1948, after his National
Service, he came back for another stint of several months.

It was not just Thompson that drew my father back to
Yorkshire, but his village. My father was a stubborn romantic:
he needed idealizations of places as he did of people, and he
focused them on this small village:

Kilburn village when I knew it in 1941, in 1945 and in
1948 had hardly changed its way of life since the
beginning of the century. Horses were still used and
there was a blacksmith. Most villagers kept a pig for

ham and bacon. Milk was delivered from a churn and measured by the imperial pint. There was a butcher and an inn. The innkeeper and his two sisters were in their eighties. Beer was drawn by a white jug from wooden barrels . . . The people in the village grew most of the food they required. They made their own butter and baked their own bread . . . Life was slow and steady and generally long-lived. It was as near as England could ever get to the idea of a peasantry based on land. I was able to glimpse all this and to share in the life of the village before it all vanished in the 1950s . . . when I knew Kilburn and Coxwold there was little changed from the time when Laurence Sterne lived and wrote *Tristram Shandy* in his house at Coxwold.

The four-mile walk from Ampleforth took him past Byland's ruins and the villages of Wass and Oldstead to arrive at the pretty village of Kilburn. A stream runs down its length, bordered by cropped cushions of green lawn which run up to the charming stone cottages. An old church stands at the top of a small square, now used as a car park, overlooked by the quaint pub. High Kilburn, a half-mile away, is organized around a large green where the handsome, slightly grander houses sprawl out with plenty of space for gardens, vegetable plots and privacy. This was where my father believed he had found the Promised Land. He saw it as a gentle world where life had a calmer, more predictable pattern and families could pass on their plots from generation to generation. Security was rooted in simple needs and self-sufficiency. He projected an untroubled timelessness onto Kilburn's landscape of old churches, wooded hills and twisting valleys, which he believed had been bypassed by much of the previous hundred years. More importantly, it held out the promise in the forties that it would be bypassed by much of the next century as well. He believed these quiet stone villages offered some degree of sanctuary from the twentieth century. Just as the Cistercians had sought the wilderness to escape from their age, so did my father. In 1957, as he cleared the Plot and built his Chapel to overlook the villages he so loved, he would have seen the parallels with the labour of the monks so many centuries before. His Chapel was a small, quiet comment on their immense efforts. He had inserted himself into a medieval artistic tradition, 800 years old, and into the geography of this corner of North Yorkshire, and he drew inspiration from both all his life. Even into his old age, the sense of relief at having found this sanctuary was still palpable. There was more to his escape than the family history. It wasn't just the precarious insecurity of the twentieth century that drove him into this rural retreat, but an entire civilization which he believed to be irredeemably corrupted. And, for him, nowhere was this more evident than the suburbs where he grew up.

Dad only ever referred to the suburb of Whetstone in terms of contempt. His sisters remembered the place with great affection, and I was curious as to what had made him dislike it so intensely. I had never been to his childhood home so, on a cool grey June morning in 2008, I went to have a look.

The suburbs of London are where the city comes to play golf and be buried. The handsome Edwardian house in Friern Barnet Lane, Whetstone, where my father's family lived is still there, and I knocked on the door. The current occupants have lived there for three decades, and they kindly let my aunt and me take a walk back in time. To my aunt's great delight, small details such as the solid oak banisters and newel post running from top to bottom were still there, as were the panelled doors and pretty stained-glass windows. We sat in what had been my father's bedroom in the attic looking out over the hills of this northern fringe of London across to Enfield. Nowadays the view is lush with mature trees so that the surrounding streets are barely visible. Next door was the bedroom my father took over as a workshop for his wood-carving; here, he would have looked out over the North Middlesex Golf Club, now screened by a huge wall of mature trees. Despite its suburban surroundings, the attic is like an eyrie in the trees above London.

The garden is a lavish 250 feet in length, running down to an area of wilderness in which a magnificent ash tree grows – comfortably old enough to have offered my father his first adventures in tree-climbing. Next to it is a lime tree into whose trunk, my aunt told me, my father had cut notches for his younger sister to climb up; I scrutinized its rough grey bark, imagining that perhaps I could see in the shifts of colouring and texture the marks Dad made seventy years ago. The fruit trees planted by my grandparents are now wizened and knobbled with age but are still bearing fruit. What was there to have taken such a deep dislike to?

The confusion deepened when I visited the local park. Only five minutes' walk from the house, this was where my father was taken by his nanny for walks. The formality of the evergreens and rosebeds, the immaculate bowling green and grandiose Edwardian statue might have looked much the same in the thirties. Down one side of Friary Park, a little stream ran between banks of cow parsley and under an old humpback bridge. It was a remnant of Whetstone's past as a small village beyond the reach of the city and its commuter rail

lines. There were still a blacksmith's and a farm in Whetstone in
the thirties, remembers my aunt.

But it was a rural village slowly transforming in front of my
father's young eyes into a suburb as a greedy city gobbled up
the countryside around them. The streets behind Friern
Barnet Lane were being built as my father grew up; he could
have watched the houses on Church Close, Church Crescent
and Church Way going up from his bedroom window. The
trees which have now matured so handsomely would have
been skinny little things in the thirties and could have done
little to soften the newness of the bricks and tiles or the bald-
ness of the regimented rows. My father in his attic bedroom –
he had his sister put his breakfast into a basket for him to
haul up on a pulley for his convenience – had a bird's-eye
view of one of the most dramatic periods of British urban
development.

The inter-war years saw a huge expansion of suburbs
around all of England's major cities, and thousands of acres of
farmland disappeared. Light industry sprawled along roads,
and suburbs were transformed from the preserve of a wealthy
minority to the home of an expanding and newly prosperous
population. It was the most intense house-building programme England has ever seen and is still to be equalled: a
third of all the houses in England and Wales today were built
in a twenty-one-year period between 1918 and 1939. In 1934,
1,500 houses were going up every week in Greater London;
the population of the capital's suburbs increased by 810,000
in the ten years after 1921. In the thirties, it increased again
by another 900,000 in eight years. By 1939, London had
reached its historic maximum population of 8,615,000, a
figure still to be surpassed. Counties like Middlesex, south
Hertfordshire, Buckinghamshire, Essex, northern Kent and

Surrey were transformed. In contrast, when my father arrived in North Yorkshire, he found a part of England untouched by this dramatic expansion. Far from any major industrial centre (unlike the west or south of the county) its pattern of small villages of stone cottages and modest market towns had not changed, and the spaces between them had not become building sites.

In Whetstone, my father was on the front line of this rapid suburban expansion as the pebbledash and fake-Tudor semis crept across the land. On Sundays, when he walked with his father or went cycling into neighbouring Hertfordshire, he saw at first hand the digging up of the fields, the felling of the old trees and the uprooting of hedgerows for the new housing estates. To his mind it was a triumph of all that was dull, meretricious and fake. Sixty years later, in his autobiographical pamphlet, the memory was still vivid; he never forgot what he had run away from:

> North London was untroubled but uninspired. The
> rows of shops along the Great North Road, already
> busy with increasing traffic, may have been practical,
> but for me it held little charm. There was plenty of
> middle-class respectability and golf clubs, but no
> splendour. There was not much visible poverty and all
> through the decade in which I was growing up more
> and more fields were being devoured by drab housing
> developers. From my bedroom window at the top of
> the house, I could see Alexandra Palace in the distance
> where television broadcasts would soon be hazily
> transmitted. Many fields stretching across to Cat Hill
> and Enfield would soon be built over and turned into
> the outer sprawl of London. The people whose lives

seemed to reflect the uniformity of the architecture
shared in the uniform monotony of suburbia.
Doubtless they were worthy people and had
respectable jobs in the City, but there was nothing
about their lives or their ambitions which could
impress me or do anything to inspire me. Many of our
neighbours had become prosperous by their industry –
insurance brokers, stock brokers, industrial architects,
petroleum, journalism – whatever were the rewards of
their labours, the lives they led did not seem to offer
any recompense of the fuller life I had glimpsed in the
country at Coghurst.

My father was a child of his times: his idealization of
Coghurst – the estate farm and the gardens – was not just
about privilege but about an intense rural nostalgia. He
absorbed one of the dominant cultural responses of the
decades in which he was born and grew up. In the twenties,
England was emerging from the trauma of a catastrophic
war that only intensified as another war loomed on the horizon. It was an era in which the nation needed to be defined;
not only did it have enemies against which it had to rally,
it also had new technologies of communication – the radio and
the popular press – with which to reach a more literate
mass audience. The industrial, urban centres on which British
imperial power was based and which underpinned the
massive war effort twice within a generation were places of
self-evident conflict, home to the victims and the perpetra-
tors of exactly the tumultuous change that so many feared.
Politicians, writers and artists turned to a neglected, shabby,
relatively poor countryside for their images of nationhood in
the inter-war years. The contours, colours and sounds of rural

England became romantic symbols of identity. What was idealized however was a southern landscape, often the rolling chalk downlands of the Home Counties, not the bleaker windswept uplands of northern England such as Yorkshire; this was a myth of consolation and nurture.

In 1924, three years before my father was born, Stanley Baldwin, the Prime Minister, famously articulated this vision of England:

> The sounds of England, the tinkle of the hammer on the anvil in the country smithy, the corncrake on a dewy morning, the sound of the scythe against the whetstone, and the sight of a plough team coming over the brow of a hill, the sight that has been seen in England since England was a land, and may be seen in England long after the Empire has perished and every works in England has ceased to function, for centuries the one eternal sight of England. The wild anemones in the woods in April, the last load at night of hay being drawn down a lane as the twilight comes on . . . and above all, the most subtle, most penetrating and most moving, the smell of wood smoke coming up in an Autumn evening . . .

It was a superb denial of reality. Baldwin disregarded the fact that the vast majority of the English population lived in industrial cities and had little experience of the country he was describing. He chose to overlook the fact that the countryside was in the grip of a harsh agricultural recession which left fields and farms derelict and which was to contribute to the Great Depression of the thirties. Baldwin was not describing a landscape he had ever worked himself; he had never used that scythe or brought in the plough team. He clearly knew nothing of the animal shit, the sweat and sheer hard labour that constituted farming life. What Baldwin was offering was a landscape to console and reassure a nation still traumatized by the Great War; the countryside was somewhere to retreat to, no longer seen a place to work but one in which to rest.

The picturesque 'rural retreat' became a middle-class cultural icon which endured through the twentieth century, coming into sharper focus at times of anxiety in subsequent decades such as the seventies and eighties. The countryside was no longer seen as an underdeveloped provincial backwater but as a place for contemplation. Once in your damp cottage without its modern comforts of running hot water and daily newspapers, your purpose was to experience a rural timelessness. It was as if there was an inverse relationship between the growing obsession with time in urban industrialized England – timetables, clocking in and out, time efficiency, time-wasting – and the fetishizing of the countryside. The countryside became the repository for a romanticized rhythm of sun and seasons. Baldwin's idealization went even further: as religious faith in a Christian God outside time faltered, he was – absurdly – offering the English countryside as 'eternal'. Baldwin was using ideas that were to gain a stubborn currency in the English imagination in the twentieth century. They gripped my father, but, he concluded, this real, unchanging English countryside, he concluded, was not to be found anywhere near Barnet. There was nothing eternal about the fields on Cat Hill and Enfield that were being ripped up in front of him. England was disappearing, consumed by a voracious urbanism, corrupted by mass consumption to meet new, cheap tastes.

It was a subject to which George Orwell devoted his novel *Coming Up for Air*, published in 1939. Orwell drew on a recurrent theme of popular fiction in the inter-war years, of the First World War soldier who returns home to discover that the country for which he has been fighting so bravely has been destroyed from within. Orwell's hero George Bowling, an insurance salesman, asks:

> Do you know the road I live in – Ellesmere Road, West Bletchley? Even if you don't, you know fifty others exactly like it. You know how these streets fester all over the inner-outer suburbs. Always the same. Long, long rows of little semi-detached houses – the numbers in Ellesmere Road run to 212 and ours is 191 – as much alike as council houses and generally uglier. The stucco front, the creosoted gate, the privet hedge, the green front door. The Laurels, the Myrtles, the Hawthorns, Mon Abri, Mon Repos, Belle Vue. At perhaps one house in fifty some anti-social type who'll probably end up in the workhouse has painted his front door blue instead of green.

Bowling looks back to his own upbringing before the First World War in a country village with deep nostalgia and his bid for 'air' translates into a return visit to this childhood idyll. But the village has become a town, the fields and gardens where Bowling fished and swam are now covered with bungalow housing estates. He's trapped into a life of meaningless and soulless routine, all the while forced to scrabble in a tedious job for a meagre measure of security.

Orwell – and even more so my father – disregarded the fact that the new suburbs were a promised land for many people.

They brought novel comforts such as gardens, indoor lavatories and accessible green space to urban populations. The development Orwell was satirizing was that of a new lower-middle class – white-collar workers in the expanding new bureaucracies of industry, commerce and state – with a little spare money and some leisure. It was the emergence of a mass consumer society and the leisure age – both of which were to define the latter half of the century. But for Orwell and many others, including my father, these changes prompted a deep anxiety about the loss of a distinctive sense of place, of authenticity and, even more importantly, of the freedom and autonomy of the individual.

Orwell's anxieties were shared by an influential movement, preservationism. The Council for the Preservation of Rural England was founded in 1926 and alongside it grew up a group of 'ruralist' writers who brought to their critique of modernity an intense romanticism; they lamented the decline of traditional English crafts and the vitiation of English village life, and descried the ribbon development and roadside advertising of the dawning age of the motor car. George Sturt wrote panegyrics to the agricultural crafts of his native Farnham in Surrey, most notably in *The Wheelwright's Shop*, published in 1923. The prominent preservationist H. J. Massingham poured out books throughout the thirties on different aspects of English country life, including tributes to landscapes in the process of being transformed such as the Chilterns, the Cotswolds and English downland. The young John Betjeman wrote gloomily of the 'brick built breeding boxes of new souls'.

In this panic about the new urbanization, there were strong streaks of misogyny, misanthropy and snobbery. The long lists of pet hates ran from pylons to petrol stations, from billboards to telegraph poles; in one CPRE pamphlet in 1930 the complaint was that there were too many tea rooms and that 'the owners are small men and anxious to attract attention, and have neither the means or education to build anything very decent'. In 1934 J. B. Priestley published his *English Journey*, in which he offered three categories: the Old England of cathedral towns, Industrial England, and the third England which 'belonged far more to the age itself than to this particular island'. This category was a cultural no man's land homogenized by new technologies of entertainment, mobility and consumerism. As Priestley explained:

> this is the England of arterial and bypass roads, of filling stations and factories that look like exhibition buildings, of giant cinemas and dance halls and cafes, bungalows with tiny garages, cocktail bars, Woolworths, motor coaches, wireless, hiking, factory girls looking like actresses, greyhound racing and dirt tracks, swimming pools and everything given away for cigarette coupons. If the fog had lifted I knew that I should have seen this England all around me at that northern entrance to London, where the smooth wide road passes between miles of semi-detached bungalows, all with their little garages, their wireless sets, their periodicals about film stars, their swimming costumes and tennis rackets and dancing shoes.

Priestley was describing my father's London. Long after the intellectual agenda had moved on and this preservationist impulse was discredited as romantic nostalgia, my father would lapse into a comparable irascibility. We heard only the snobbish contempt, but looking back I can see how it was rooted in a belief that modernity had homogenized, trivialized and functionalized: it was a version of bread and circuses that demeaned human dignity, labour and relationship. Industrialization had reduced the labourer to an adjunct to a machine, and it alienated people from their true nature and the product of their labour. It was dehumanizing – as two world wars and the brutal mechanization of killing had amply demonstrated. Human nature had sold itself short, my father bitterly concluded, falling for the cheap tat of consumerism and abdicating any larger ambitions towards meaning or transcendence.

In an edited collection, *Britain and the Beast*, H. J. Massingham described the 'internal decay' of rural England. Suburbanization 'expels the native population, pulls down its cottages or puts them in fancy-dress, builds houses of its own as characterless and innocent of design as are all its acts, debases the neighbouring countryside and suppresses its crafts and husbandry'. He picked out for particular scorn the mock-Tudor housing and hostelries with their planks of stained dark wood nailed on to resemble half-timbering. Skill was being disconnected from locality, making redundant the craft traditions that had been specific to the particular building materials of a place. Yet such skills were a crucial element of the authentic distinctiveness of place. Priestley wrote in an essay, 'Britain in Danger', published as the conclusion to the anthology *Our Nation's Heritage* on the eve of the Second World War, that 'It took centuries of honest workmanship and loving craftsmanship to create the England that was renowned for its charm and delicate beauty. In twenty years we have completely ruined at least half of that England.'

My father believed that the villages he found in North Yorkshire, especially Kilburn, belonged to that other half of England, still uncontaminated by arterial roads, pebbledash semis and suburban streets. Here the half-timbered houses were not made of nailed planks but of the original ancient, worm-infested timber, perhaps a half-millennium in age. There was no threat that suburban housing estates would come marching over the hills or lines of shopping arcades and dance halls would sprout alongside widened, straightened roads. Far from urban industrial conurbations and before the age of long-distance commuting, these villages were insulated from change. In North Yorkshire, amongst the crumpled fields, moors, sleepy villages and ruins, Dad, defiant of family and convention, chose the histories he wanted to live with.

My father resolved that the only way to be truly human in such a corrupted age was, like the Cistercians, to set oneself against one's age. He carved out a life of small rebellions, and that is what the eccentric art student, in his country-market three-piece worsted suit, set out to achieve in post-war London.

He tried to recruit possible allies: he turned up unannounced on the doorsteps of the artists he most admired – Henry Moore, Jacob Epstein, even Brancusi in Paris. Epstein's maid dismissed him on the spot; Moore kindly sat down with the art student and discussed carving Madonnas over a glass of wine.

His parents were horrified: they had expected him to help his father in the failing family business. But what attracted this young man was a way of life focused on the making of things. He admired the home-made and the hand-made. By the age of ten, he had developed a keen interest in the ideas of Eric Gill, a Catholic sculptor who founded a number of communities in the first half of the twentieth century based around ideas of self-sufficiency, art and craft. My father was fascinated by the craftsman's skill and how it developed through a self-evaluating intelligence. It was why the flint arrowheads from Scawton Moor sat on his windowledge. Craft and art were inextricably linked; in an essay he wrote on the subject, he quoted from a 1930 pamphlet by Eric Sharpe, a follower of William

Morris: 'And herein lies the argument for hand-made things. For the mind works through the hand, guiding the tool, more directly than through the machine, and the article made acquires a more human quality, and conversely the appeal is more direct back to the mind that uses and enjoys it.' The hand-made was not just aesthetically superior, but spiritually enriching for both those who produced the object and those who used it. Working with your hands and developing a skill meant autonomy and self-expression, crucial qualities of one's dignity as a human being that found no home in an industrial consumer society.

Gill looked for inspiration even further back in the past than the preservationist movement. To him and to William Morris it was not so much a matter of preserving traditional craft skills as of regenerating an entire artistic tradition, which they believed had last flourished in the Middle Ages. In their idealization, it had been an age in which craftsmanship and art were still connected and both were an expression of the everyday experience of the masses. Art, then, was not the pursuit of an élite for aesthetic pleasure, but a means of spiritual enlightenment for a whole culture. Art 'cannot exist in isolation, or only one man thick. It must be a thousand men thick,' summed up W. R. Lethaby. Art was not the creation of an individual genius, but rooted in a particular set of social and cultural relationships. This idealization of the Middle Ages went even further: it was a lost golden age in which belief was the subject and inspiration of art, part of a seamless whole of sacrament and sanctification which gave purpose and meaning to life and labour. The ideal of the hand-made and the home-made was extended into every part of domestic life by Morris and, in turn, by Gill.

These were the ideas I found, after my father died, in the

essays, articles and reviews he had written and stuffed into boxes which had piled up in the cupboards of his cottage. His writings read as he had often sounded, repetitive, grandiose and yet intriguing: a jumble of ideas, the absurd alongside the thought-provoking, the banal beside ambitious self-belief. Here, I found the fragments that helped me understand that the Chapel was his credo.

One man he mentioned frequently was a French desert hermit, Charles de Foucauld. A former soldier, he founded a hermitage in Algeria on the edge of the Sahara before he was killed in 1916 by Tuareg horsemen. My father travelled to Algeria in 1955 to see de Foucauld's chapel at Béni Abbès, and the pastel sketches he drew of his visit were hung on the walls of the Hut at the Plot. De Foucauld's emphasis on physical labour echoed that of the Cistercians. He talked of the ideals of the 'hidden life' of Christ, when he had been a carpenter before his public ministry; my father wrote, 'the toil of everyday life at work and in the home was made the fitting means of our sanctification'. De Foucauld developed the hidden life into the core of the new religious order he founded: 'the life of Nazareth in its simplicity . . . not less than eight hours of manual work a day . . . neither large properties, buildings or alms, but real poverty'. This ideal of the hidden life expressed itself in an architecture of humble simplicity, using local materials and skills; de Foucauld's church on the sand dunes of the western Sahara was made of mud bricks, the roof was of palm-leaf thatch and the floor of yellow sand. The building was perched on a cliff which 'overlooks practically the whole of the Hoggar [part of the Sahara] and stands amid wild looking mountains beyond which the seemingly limitless horizons make one think of the infinitude of God'. What impressed my father was 'the harmonious unity of life and thought'. Ideals were to be expressed in every part of your daily life: where and how you lived, what you wore and ate.

These were the ideas my father adopted enthusiastically in the fifties and he recruited my mother, a fellow art student, as his eager accomplice. Their life in Yorkshire, he ordained, was to emulate the self-sufficiency of Gill and de Foucauld's communities. Like Gill, my father left almost all the domestic chores to his wife. He used to stand in the garden of a summer evening, shaved and tidy after his day of spiritually enriching labour in his studio, on his way out to the pub. My mother had spent her day looking after children, cooking, making jam and cakes, cleaning, mending and dressmaking, but her chores were still far from over. While she was bent digging the vegetable patch, he would point out what she needed to be doing next: the trees that needed pruning, the berries that needed picking, the flowerbeds that needed weeding, the walls that needed repairing. It seemed his belief in the dignity of physical labour meant that my mother's should never end. After giving her the guidance he believed she required, he would then head off to share a pint with friends, leaving my mother to put us all to bed.

Like Gill, my father was to be a sculptor; he earned his living from commissions for churches, hospitals and schools and supplemented it with the regular income of some art-teaching at Ampleforth. It was a life of using his hands to make things. Carving was as instinctive to him as breathing. He carved whatever he had at hand: on family summer holidays at Runswick Bay on the Yorkshire coast he picked up the rounded sandstone rocks and carved them into heads. On another occasion it was a piece of walnut driftwood. A friend remembers how, when her house was being renovated, he picked up an old wooden chair seat from a pile of rubbish. He returned later the same day, having carved into a meat dish, with runnels for the juices and a cavity where they could pool. The resourcefulness with material and lack of pretension were characteristics he learned from Thompson; it was the can-do, make-do approach – or, as Dad would say, 'Just get on with it.' It was how, without any experience of construction work, he built the Chapel on the Plot. He didn't approve of hesitation. One of his pupils remembers him hacking into a huge lump of wood with a chainsaw, and shouting out over the machine's roar, 'Come and have a go.' Another friend recalled the gift of a sculpture, and how Dad brought out his chisel to carve his initials on the piece with a speed and dexterity that others might have with a pen. He applied the same fascination with form and material to every commission, from the simplest gravestone to the biggest composition. At seventy-five he was still carving, and as he was dying a huge block of stone was delivered for a new commission.

He had big hands, with square palms and thick, short fingers. It is the hands that people often remember; they were 'strangely charismatic', commented one friend. I don't remember holding them, but I was glad to see my children do so. They were powerful, fearsomely strong, and often coated in stone dust. His studio was in one half of a converted garage at the gate, and we could hear the chip, chip, chip of chisel on stone from the house. When we were sent with his coffee and biscuits for elevenses, he would stand back – dressed in his patched smock and dust-covered beret – rubbing his hand along the curve of what he had carved and leaning forward to blow the dust away. He never explained what he was doing or why; his art was kept separate from his family. He stood there in his studio, paddling in the fine stone dust or sweet-smelling wood chips, regardless of winter cold in the unheated building or summer heat under the Perspex ceiling. His studio was full of carvings, as was the house: projects not yet finished, work waiting to be collected, new pieces of stone and wood roughly scored out. Our home was his gallery and we lived – and played – among the life-size nudes that crowded around us. Intermittently the deliveries would arrive from the quarry near Rotherham; blocks of York stone were brought in by crane and forklift truck. After my mother left him, a giant stone megalith, fourteen feet high, appeared by the kitchen door; it had to be carved from scaffolding it was so tall. It evolved into a heavy, giant naked male reaching into the sky, its limbs thick with bulging muscle that seemed to express all my father's frustration and pent-up fury.

The focus of Dad's sculpture was mass, its solidity and weight and how it expressed force. Antony Gormley remembers that my father would refer with delight to the weight of Thompson's heavy oak tables at Ampleforth, and of Michelangelo's mallet. Dad carved bodies which were great, rounded curves and voluptuous folds of usually naked flesh and powerful muscle. They echoed the rolling contours and monumentality of the Yorkshire moors. One critic reviewing an exhibition of his in Paris in 1965 commented on how 'his style combines the twists of Zadkine and the curves of Moore with a powerful feeling for physical mass.' The *Guardian* described the figures as 'tormented and brutish, short, stocky, muscular, ape-like' and likened them to work done by Epstein.

Thompson taught Dad to carve wood, and he continued to carve it all his life, but he preferred York stone. Wood was too frail a material, and prone to splitting, worm and rot. He wanted his work to last like that of the medieval craftsmen of Byland and Rievaulx. He admired longevity, and the monks' superb craftsmanship had survived wear, destruction and neglect over centuries. The workings of stone were all around us children in Yorkshire; in the crumbling stone mullion of my bedroom window, which I could rub to the sand it once had been, smelling the dankness of millions of years in its making. The Hambleton Hills are pocked with a long history of digging and cutting stone which stretches from prehistoric times to the abandoned industrial workings above Boltby. We frequently passed abandoned quarries and spoil heaps. Near our home, there was a quarry at Stonegrave, and I used to visit someone at the quarry cottages, fascinated by a world drained of colour in the thick layer of stone dust.

We could never completely forget the ancient solidity of layered rock just under the thin skin of moor and turf, nor ignore the evidence of the skills used to cut, carve and shape stone over thousands of years. It was a language of stone dug from under our feet which was evident in tiny details on and around the Plot: the carefully laid drystone walling along the track and across the moors, the masonry of the old farm-houses with their distinctive herringbone scoring in the toffee-coloured stone, the curved head of a gatepost some fragments of which were now in the Plot's low boundary wall, the arduously worked cattle trough, carved from a single block. Up on the moors, stone crosses were used to guide travellers, and with good luck you could chance on a carved flint arrow-head. Dad would jab his finger at a fine piece of farmhouse masonry as we passed in the car, and run his hand over the rounded stone gatepost on his way through; a man who spent so much time working with stone drew inspiration from seeing so much of it around him. It was these connections between material, skill and place that he discovered in North Yorkshire, and that held strong all his life. As the inscription he asked for his gravestone made clear, his life could be summed up by his art and his sense of place and they were always interlinked.

He used the Plot as a prophetic cry, a manifesto in stone, glass and wood, using the materials and skills of its place. Every part was hand-made, requiring the learning of new skills and the demonstration of old ones to show how human beings could still make things in an age of the mass-produced and the machine-manufactured.

His ambition went even further. He wrote that a chapel was 'capable of doing for us what the chapels of St Francis did for the Gothic Age or the chapel of St Joseph's at Avila did for the Counter Reformation'. A building, he believed, could act as a radical challenge to its times. Such chapels were not just places of private devotional worship; his Chapel was a rallying call to return to a life of craft, faith and relationship with place. The modesty of the architecture was an expression of truth to the local materials he worked with, informed by simplicity and humility. His hope was that everyone who found their way down the track to the Plot in the middle of the forest would leave invigorated by some fragment of this vision, which brought together ideals of faith and art in a commitment to a geographical point. It asserted that the honouring of place could be, above all, redemptive.

For much of his life, my father knew where his ashes would be scattered and where his gravestone would lie – and he recognized that as a rare privilege. He knew where he belonged, and he took great satisfaction from knowing that he had contributed monuments that could last long beyond his lifetime, albeit on a far more modest scale than that of the great Cistercians. Dotted amongst the villages in the neighbourhood of the Plot are the crosses, gravestones and sculptures he carved. Among them are a relief of the mechanic on the wall of an old garage in Norton; a humble cross on the village green at Fadmoor; a thirty-foot-long wooden relief of the Stations of the Cross in Oswaldkirk; the Holy Family at Ampleforth College, as well as those carvings in Byland Inn. He served his community as he understood how, furnishing a district with monuments of memorial and commemoration. And on the Plot he built his dreams.

13

'Pity the land'

My father was not the only one who inherited the legacy of the Cistercians' promised land. He well understood how his was a very brief chapter – an incomer's intrusion even – in a much older story of those who worked the land as the monks had done many centuries before them. He felt a camaraderie with the farmers among whom he lived: like him, they used their hands and their muscle in physical labour. Like him, they prided themselves on a privilege rare in the twentieth century, of being their own men, not beholden to anyone. He shared with the farmers around him a passion for place and the integration of where one lived with how one lived, and he admired how that commitment had shaped character: bred pragmatic stoicism and dogged steadiness of purpose. Dad sought out and enjoyed farmers' company, whether peering over hedges to watch the beagling or standing over a pint at the bar in the pub. But while he appreciated the prosaic, taciturn comments on the state of the harvest or grain prices, he was well aware that many of these neighbours regarded his work with bemused respect at best, and more often as bloody daft.

Dad would have seen the connection between their labour and his: they were both working the land, fashioning its materials, patterning its surface. The sculptor Andy Goldsworthy, who was a farm labourer as a young man in West Yorkshire, draws parallels between sculpture and farming, and his comment comes back to me when I walk along the Hambleton Hills and look at the sweep of the ploughed field, scarified by furrows, or look down from the escarpment on the Vale of York where the dark lines of hedgerows criss-cross the contours of the land. The taxman also recognizes a similarity, since farmers and artists are categorized together on the grounds of their erratic, unpredictable income. Both artist and farmer live on their wits.

The more I dug into the history of the Plot and walked the land, watching the fields being ploughed, planted and harvested through different seasons, seeing the livestock fed, sheared and dipped, the more I wanted to understand the others who worked this land. I particularly wanted to hear the stories of those men of my father's generation who had farmed the land while he had carved, and piece together something of how their sense of place had shaped their lives and labour. I needed the plots of his neighbours to provide a wider context that would throw into relief that of my father. I stumbled on just the right man to help me: Fred Banks.

It was at the end of the long day's walking in hot summer sunshine and we had finally arrived back at Oldstead. I had already read Fred's history of Oldstead, commissioned for the millennium by the village and published on a photocopier, and was curious to meet the writer. When I had asked where I might find him, I had been told to look for the man doing the stone-walling at Oldstead pub. Sure enough, there

he was, and he stood with his trowel in his hand as I
explained how much I had liked his history. But it was only
when I said I was John Bunting's daughter that his face split
into a wide smile of delight, and his eyes crinkled up with
laughter. He launched into an anecdote of how my father's
car had once broken down – many decades ago – and how he
had enlisted Fred to help him harness an old plough horse to
the useless car in a bid to tow it home. It could have been the
old jalopy Dad used to ferry the building materials up the hill
from Oldstead for the Chapel. To Fred, the memory was
nearly as fresh as yesterday as he recalled the two young men
struggling with harness, recalcitrant horse and broken-down
car. He'd seen Dad a few times in the following years, but it
was that initial introduction that had made the biggest
impression and engendered great warmth for anyone associated with him.

Over tea – flowered china and shortbread – back at the
farm he had worked all his life, Oldstead Grange, I explained
how I was writing about the Plot, and he explained how he
had been writing about his plot for much of the previous two
decades. As the printer rattled off copies of his writings for
me, he talked over some of the histories that had fascinated
him. Just over his fields rose the steep, wooded escarpment
where the Chapel stood, a mile away. A mile in the other
direction lay Byland; his sixteenth-century farmhouse was
built on the ruins of one of Byland's granges, and he had
grown up on his father's farm near Kilburn on another of the
Byland granges, at Scencliff. Right from the time he was a
child following his father's farmhand around, his life had
been about the land, and more specifically the agricultural
legacy of the Cistercians. The way he talked and wrote about
his farming revealed an extraordinary dialogue with his

medieval forebears: a sense of shared experience with his predecessors who had worked with the same challenges of soil, drainage and contour. Like any farmer, he knew every bump and indentation, the texture and composition of the soil in every part of his land, and he had become fascinated by understanding how they had come about. An encounter with a medieval archaeologist as a boy had sparked his interest, but he left school at sixteen in 1942, eager to join his father on the farm, and it was only when his own son took over the running of the farm that he finally had the time to devote to studying his land. After years of ploughing – which began as a boy with horses in the thirties – he developed theories on medieval ploughing patterns, the reverse S of ridge and furrow, to explain the shallow undulations of his fields, and corresponded with Cambridge agricultural historians in a bid to enlighten them on aspects he felt they had not properly grasped.

But perhaps his biggest project was to map how the Byland monks had diverted five streams and built a network of irrigation channels, dams and ponds that covered a total of sixteen square miles, the biggest water-engineering project of any English Cistercian monastery and reputedly the biggest of medieval England. The remains had left their mark on many of his fields. He traced some of these channels, sluices and reservoirs by dowsing, and he told me how he had arrived at a great respect for the skill and knowledge of the monks in using the land. Banks concluded that Byland ended up with no less than twenty-five and possibly as many as thirty-four mills, fed by conduits from reservoirs (the early Cistercian prohibition on mills soon gave way to hard-headed pragmatism: water was a significant form of power). He could see how the monks had understood every contour, and had

designed the diversion of streams and the siting of reservoirs
to use them to best advantage. Similarly they used the contours to ensure effective drainage, a layout which had
survived in part until he dug up the hedgerows with government grants in the sixties.

Fred knew every inch of the few square miles around
Oldstead. It was he who told me that the hillock in the field
beside the track leading up to the Plot was an old lime-kiln, he
who told me that if I went up into the woods in Cockerdale
near the Plot, and rummaged under the pheasant pen by
the track I might find the pottery remains of the Roman kiln
there. He told farmer Peter Turnbull that the old mounting
block in his farmyard was a lump of Lake District granite
brought down by the rush of glacial ice in the last ice age. No
detail of his neighbourhood's history seemed to have eluded
him. He wrote up all of his painstaking research in pamphlets, and devised walks in the area which took in some of
the places that had interested him. He gave talks to local
groups about his work, and served as chairman of the White
Horse Association, responsible for the horse's upkeep, for
three decades. He had performed an extraordinary role in
maintaining local memory at a time when such a task could
not be left to chance, given the rate of change as newcomers
moved in.

Fred's work struck me powerfully because it offered so
many parallels with my father. Both appreciated memory,
how it mapped on to place, and both had invested great effort
in communicating that. Both would readily acknowledge how
the legacy of the medieval monastery of Byland had influenced their lives and imaginations centuries after it had been
dissolved. But Fred's story also offered sharp contrasts; his
memory map had been rooted in his community – when I

met people in the neighbourhood, it seemed that everyone
had a fond word to say of Fred – whilst my father's had been
an intensely personal, private project. And there was another,
more important difference, which I discovered when Fred,
almost apologetically, offered the private family history he
had written as something I might want to read. It revealed a
dramatically different story from the one my father believed
he had found in Kilburn in the forties.

Dad and Fred were close in age, and it's not entirely fanciful to imagine that Fred might have been one of the young
men working in the fields as my father pedalled down the
lanes to visit Robert Thompson in Kilburn. If Dad had
stopped to talk to him, he might have learned that, contrary
to his romantic illusions, these Yorkshire farmers had suffered chronic insecurity for decades, with desperate struggles
to pay the rent and avoid crippling debt. Fred had gone back
over his father's and grandfather's bank books, and compiled
a remarkable story of farming fortunes in the area in the first
half of the twentieth century. For the Banks family, farming
had been desperately insecure since agricultural depression
first hit in the 1870s, when cheap grain and meat imports
were brought from the American Midwest by the new rail-
roads and steamships. The First World War brought some
relief, and for the first time in two generations farmers'
incomes rose, but it was a short-lived reprieve and they fell
again sharply in the early twenties when the government
withdrew support and another depression returned which
lasted until the Second World War. Fred's father struggled
throughout these decades with overdrafts and loans from
family members; his income did not cover the rent on the
farm despite sidelines selling butter, rabbits and eggs in
Thirsk Market, and there were hard years when the bank

refused to extend the overdraft. The situation improved slightly in the mid-thirties as concern about another war began to loom and the government took steps to stimulate the country's neglected agricultural sector. But it was only the arrival of the war in 1939 and government-guaranteed prices that made farming economically viable again. It brought to an end a sixty-year period in England in which an area of agricultural land the size of Wales went out of production; thousands of farms had been closed whilst others – like that of Fred's family – had clung on with the aid of those family members who had moved out of farming.

I suddenly understood that the contentment that my father had seen in Kilburn in the forties was a product of a wartime boom, a community thriving at last on the catastrophe of a country at war and in desperate need of food. This was something which my father either never knew or chose to ignore. Yet it was what had made his own Plot possible. That long period of desperate struggle from 1875 to 1939 saw a retreat from many of the areas that were hardest to farm. The farms had to be abandoned, because there were no buyers for what had always been a hard way of life and had now become impossible. Scotch Corner was deserted in the 1890s, and was still a disused ruin fifty years later when my father first found it. He rented the land for twenty-five years for 10s. (50p) a year in 1957. Almost as cheap were the stone cottages that my parents' generation were able to buy on meagre incomes. It was the rural depression's long shadow that ensured my parents could afford their dream of a promised land of craft, children and countryside. What makes my father's idealization and lack of interest in this social history all the more striking is that even as a child I had grasped something of this poignant past, and Fred's explanations immediately brought back memories of a tumbledown farm labourer's cottage in our village, where I used to trespass with a friend to gather apples from the neglected garden.

I was also reminded of an abandoned farmhouse we found on a walk on the moors when I was a child. It was perhaps thirty or forty years after the last inhabitant had locked up and left. The cowsheds were collapsing, nettles and briars had grown up in the walled garden and the odd piece of machinery was rusting as it disintegrated into the long weeds. My sister and I pushed through the half-open door and tiptoed across the rotting wooden floor, layers of newspapers spilling out of the cracked linoleum. Mattresses gushed with stuffing on the rusting iron bedstead, and flowered wallpaper was peeling off the wall. It felt alive with the mould, the fungi and the rot that were slowly dismantling the place. What could not rot was the kitchen range, still full of ash, with its heavy door and catches; rub the dust a little and a proud brand name became visible again. It was testimony to a moment of huge family investment and Britain's industrial heritage when this piece of technology arrived in the remote valley, bringing to an end a long history of cooking over an open fire. We found an old medicine cupboard built into the alcove beside the fireplace; the door was ajar, the shelves loaded with a cornucopia of medicine bottles of every kind of green and blue glass. Some were still half full of their chalky liquids. Each one was different, in the detail of the fluting and the irregularity of the old glass. I wanted to take some home, but maternal intervention insisted that they remain. Even the dead had rights of ownership, and that added to the eerie sense that these farms' occupants had only just left and could return at any moment in some form, dead or alive.

This abandonment was a brief interlude, a mere half-century of neglect. By the late seventies, the derelict farmhouses we had rummaged through as children were being renovated for holiday homes and weekend cottages. The brass carriage lamps appeared, the terracotta pots sprouted by the front door, ruched curtains hung heavy over small windows: it was the decade when Britain discovered history could be turned to a handsome profit. The second-hand furniture shops where my parents had bought old pine farmhouse furniture and bits of china cheap in the sixties could now push their prices high. 'Old' and 'traditional' were transformed from terms of farmwives' complaint to dealers' delight, commanding premium prices. The provincialism of the villages of Ryedale and Hambleton was recast as a new aesthetic of cottage quaint. This ideal was typified by the huge success of textile designer Laura Ashley, with her romanticized designs of flower-sprigged cottons, and a fashion for country-maid flounces and frills that would not have looked out of place in the youth of Fred's aunts in Kilburn at the turn of the twentieth century. In 1977 *The Country Diary of an Edwardian Lady*, with its delicate watercolours of English flora and fauna, was published and became a brand phenomenon, reproduced on everything from stationery to tea cosies. The countryside was back in fashion and my parents' decision to live in remote North Yorkshire was no longer regarded as quixotic but as enviable by some of their southern acquaintances. New roads brought the cultural myth of the rural idyll within reach of city dwellers; day-trips and weekend cottages reached even the remotest corners of North Yorkshire. My father had looked to the countryside as a place to find the past, to escape the twentieth century, but from the seventies onwards an increasing

number of newcomers arrived to share his dream of the picturesque and unchanging face of 'real' England.

   Needless to say, he was horrified to find himself in company. He complained bitterly about these new arrivals and
how they destroyed village life. North Yorkshire was getting
too crowded for him, and he insisted that family holidays
were taken another 450 miles further north, in the empty
wilds of Ross and Cromarty, safe from sightseers. My father's
dislike of this new fashion for rural nostalgia may have been
hypocritical but it was intense, and it obscured for him the
even more threatening changes in the landscape he so loved:
the degradation of the environment. The tourists seemed
equally oblivious, and as the heritage industry geared up to
entertain these visitors with the past, 'retrospective regret
threatened to replace contemporary observation', as sociolo-
gist Howard Newby argued in his 1975 study of the English
countryside, *Green and Pleasant Land?*

   The very year that *The Country Diary of an Edwardian Lady*
was published, the Nature Conservancy Council warned in a
crucial report that wildlife-rich habitats in the intensively
farmed parts of Britain were declining in size and quality at
an unprecedented rate. These habitats were now islands in
'an agricultural sea', it concluded ominously, fearing that
many species would decline in number, and some would
become extinct. The English landscape was being reordered
more aggressively than perhaps at any other time in its
history. But it was a warning that went unheeded, and the
industrialization of agriculture continued largely unchecked
through the eighties. Hedgerows continued to be ripped out,
and populations of farmland birds have declined by 75 per
cent since 1975. As the very butterflies and wild flowers that
had inspired the Edwardian Lady and Laura Ashley were

disappearing, the tills were ringing with the sales of their images on every kind of consumer good from fabric, books and furniture to placemats and pictures. By 2000, 97 per cent of British meadows had been ploughed up, artificially fertilized or planted with higher-value perennial ryegrass. The grasslands of England were once a reserve for dozens of species of plants and flowers, and the creatures that fed on them and in turn became food for others; ryegrass crowded them out, especially when treated with nitrogen fertilizer. Between the sixties and eighties, the application of nitrogen went up by 380 per cent; now 85 per cent of all English grassland is treated with the stuff. Much of this Fred ruefully acknowledges in his history of his farm, as he describes his enthusiastic adoption of the new herbicides and the decision to plough up the old meadows for arable land.

The Hambleton Hills offer the perfect vantage point to reflect on this history. At many points along the Drover's Road, the wide verges have survived without interference from herbicides, fertilizer or ploughing; this is why the Plot is so rich in the moth species that Patrick Wildgust found, as they feed off vegetation that has been left undisturbed for centuries. About four miles north of the Chapel at Sneck Yate, the verge is particularly rich with knapweed, ox-eye daisies, harebells, buttercups, vetch and birdsfoot trefoil scattered amongst the clumps of sorrel and tussocks of false oat-grass and coxfoot. It is a forgotten scrap of land, a postcard from an earlier age when such vegetation was commonplace. But beyond the stone walls that border the Drovers' Road, the land reverts to its even monoculture of crops in minutely measured rows without a weed in sight. Further up the Road, at the trig point on the top of the Black Hambleton hill, it is possible to see in the distance, over the

saddle of the High Moors, the smoking chimneys of the chemical plant at Wilton once owned by ICI alongside the steelworks
on Teesside; these played a key role in the elimination of the
flowers and grasses from many millions of English acres.
ICI built its fortune on the production of nitrate; it was a
substance much used for killing, initially as the explosive in
bombs and then for fertilizer in fields. Turn your back to the
chimneys and face west from the same spot, and you see the
legacy of the nitrate amongst the seductive emerald greens
of the Vales of York and Mowbray. William Blake's 'pleasant
pastures green' are no longer the idyllic contrast to his 'dark
Satanic mills' but are now the product of those mills' con-
coctions. These 'pleasant pastures' are now the subject of
research to determine the levels of nitrates leaching into
England's rivers, why they are rising, how they can be
reduced and how farmers are to be inspected to ensure they
are doing so.

By 1994, a total of 21,000 tons of raw chemical compounds
including nitrates, were poured on to British crops every year;
flowers and weeds were killed off and with them collapsed
populations of invertebrates, farmland birds, voles, mice,
shrews, owls and kestrels. When the *Daily Express* used its
photo of the White Horse of Kilburn with a foreground of a
cornfield rich in red poppies as an image of an English
Arcadia in 2006, it missed the point. Poppies are one of the
most robust survivors of the cornfield flowers virtually obliterated by the chemicals drenching the English countryside;
but poppies only manage to flower, an old farming hand told
me, when a bout of rain prevented spraying at the right
time – or the farmer forgot. This symbol of remembrance of
the killing fields of Flanders now appears in English fields
only if the farmer has not managed to kill it off. The news-

paper photograph was an image, not of eternal, unchanging England and the flower that is one of its most powerful symbols of patriotism, but of the fragile defiance of an exhausted ecosystem.

Pockets of countryside like that around the Plot became places of too much history and too little present. They were deliberately marketed as such in a *Country Living* idyll of escape from an aggressively competitive, time-pressed world. Dad's dreams of sanctuary found new echoes in an age which seemed to be catching up with him. But only the comfortably-off could afford this kind of history; it required expensive modernizing of old houses and long commutes in comfortable cars to places where there was work. The property prices in the villages along the foot of the Hambleton Hills soared because they were within commuting distance of Leeds, York and Teesside, while tight planning restrictions ensured there was very little new building. The day-trippers were also kept at bay by an insistence that they did not belong, they were not 'country'. Imaginative access to the land had been so circumscribed that a novelist like Martin Amis could reach the conclusion that 'our countryside is just bollocks – cute and fake'. Of course, it was not that simple: it was a place as intense with conflict – over ideals, dreams, power, wealth and the past – as it had ever been.

This rural revival was a catastrophe for farmers like Fred. At one of our meetings he told me he had cancer and he wasn't sure of how much longer he had to live; he hoped I could use his writings to pass on the histories he had assembled. But what was really troubling him was how his family could continue on the land they had farmed for generations, because the point of Fred's plot was how it was handed down from one generation to the next. His son, Tom, had run the farm since Fred's retirement and Fred continued to help until his death. He fretted for the future of the farm and what it offered his son and his grandsons, and he was horrified at the enormous wealth farming families had had thrust on them by a property boom that had done them no favours. It had brought a paper wealth which they could not live off, and which could jeopardize a family's chance of passing on the farm to the next generation. Around Kilburn and Oldstead, the charming farmhouses and their handsomely constructed stone barns now command huge prices because of their easy access to the A19 for commuting. It is the latest curse on farming in the area after a century of steady contraction.

In 1890, there were ten farmers and five smallholders in Oldstead; just over a century later two farms – of which Scotch Corner was one – have disappeared completely, planted with coniferous trees, and five smallholdings have become purely residential. Only five of the original farms are still working, and three of them augment their income with bed-and-breakfast. As agriculture in this land designated as marginal has retreated, the population of the village has dropped by 50 per cent over the century. The land was always of the lowest agricultural grade; the complex contours that make it so picturesque for the estate agents also make it near-impossible to farm economically. Fields are small and steep to plough, the land is too wet or too rocky, and the soil had never been good, as the Cistercians quickly discovered after they first cleared the land. Fred and Tom sensed the possibility that nearly 800 years of farming on this land could be drawing to a close. The family had taken a momentous decision and bought the local pub; Fred's stone-walling on the day I first met him was part of the renovations. Tom had no experience of running a pub, let alone a gastro-pub, but he felt that the family's 160 acres could no longer provide a living for himself, let alone for his two sons, even with a successful sideline in bed-and-breakfast. The demand for his contractual work on other people's land was also in decline as neighbours turned their arable land over to grass. But nothing is certain and Tom has kept his hand in in case there's a turn-up and he can get a good enough price to put some of the land now lying fallow back into crops.

When I meet him, he has the harassed air of a man juggling several responsibilities, and either his mobile or landline phone goes repeatedly during our short meeting. 'I've gone from fothering cattle to fothering people, and it is much more enjoyable. I like to lean over the gate and admire other people's cattle but I'm glad I don't have to deal with them. I don't have much livestock now. The farms I knew as a boy have all gone, but farming is still in my blood and we still have some arable. We go back generations in this area. It's my love. I've always encouraged my sons to take an interest in other things, not just farming. I didn't want them to be stuck with no future, but they don't want to go and live in a city, they feel they have roots here. They are keen on a sense of place – but not on the farming.

'I could leave farming but I couldn't leave this place,' he says, looking out of the kitchen window to a stand of magnificent trees that surrounds his barns and up at the wooded escarpment beyond. 'Some farmers have a need to farm, but I have a need to stay here – that's more important to me than farming. It's very difficult to describe a sense of place. I think it should be fundamental to everyone. I've lived here all my life.'

Tom's struggle to stay put has thrown him, as much as any City banker, into gambling on a global market. In 2008, the pub was relaunched and doing well, offering expensive meals to tourists, but farming requires him to keep track of huge price swings. 'It is volatility like nobody's business. I've never seen anything like this – the closest parallel is the potato harvest of 1976 after the drought when some people made a fortune in a year. Now, some farmers are spending like there is no tomorrow on the back of the wheat prices; they're buying the new tractor they've dreamed of for ten years while others are looking at their books and trying to see how to manage. Everyone is in a different situation: some farmers bought fertilizer forward [in advance] and have done well, but those who sold their wheat forward have done very badly.'

The price of oilseed rape has doubled and the price of wheat has more than doubled but there have also been steep increases in the price of inputs such as ferilizer and fuel. Advice from the experts at the grain co-op is no help, says Tom: they can only guess the future like everyone else – anything could happen. China is gobbling up fertilizer, Australia's grain harvest failed, the US is using grain for biofuels: all he can do is watch the Chicago wheat futures market on the internet. His father used to watch the weather.

How typical was the Bankses' story? I asked Fred, and he suggested neighbours to talk to. Start with Howard Metcalfe, who's just sold his dairy herd, the last in Oldstead, he added. Dairy farming was once a staple along the foothills of the Hambleton escarpment, but in recent years one after another has sold up. From the age of sixteen when he began helping his father on the family farm Howard was 'tied to the cow's

tail', with milking twice a day, seven days a week. By the end
he found it lonely and demoralizing as he watched bank loans
nibble into his earnings and the piles of paperwork mount.

'I don't mind hard work, but I didn't like the hassle of the
banks,' he explained, sitting in his office still full of the files
he was required to keep on his herd. 'Hard work never killed
anyone, my dad used to say, and I agreed. But the overdraft
was going up at the rate of £100 a day. People are still romantic about farming, but the reality is not nice.'

He explained how dairy farming had become a matter of
bureaucracy as much as animal husbandry, with minute
calculations on feed and yield, exacting hygiene regulations,
record-keeping and high-tech gadgetry. His cows had elec-
tronic collars to measure the amount they were eating to
a tenth of a kilogram; the collars transmitted the information
to a machine in the office which adjusted the feed to their
yield.

'We had to keep a record of when the vet visited. They
were making us look like imbeciles – there was no trust. I
know there are people who bend the rules but if you don't
look after livestock properly you don't get the best out of
them. They clubbed us all under the same umbrella – we
were all being treated like crooks.'

So Metcalfe decided to sell the herd and joined a gardening 'rescue' company. He loves it: 'I wish we'd stopped
farming sooner. Through the gardening I meet all kinds; I
thought I might mind about being told what to do, I felt I
might be looked down on for cutting grass, but I'm getting a
good name for myself. I absolutely love it.'

He's got the time now for the kind of life he has long cov-
eted – time to take his kids to the occasional football match
and time 'to do what builders do and go for a pint on a Friday

evening before tea'. His wife, also from a farming background, will miss the livestock, he thinks, when they sell the
last of their small flock of sheep, but she is now looking after
the dogs of villagers who commute to Newcastle for work.

Howard's herd went in 2005, and he expected his old barns
to be converted, but when I returned in 2008 the land was
being farmed again. I asked someone in the pub about the
new crop of maize growing on Metcalfe's land. Someone's
bought the farm, I was told. 'She called the evening before
the auction. She didn't even see it. She said she wanted to
buy her husband a hill. It was a hill, so it would do. Half a
million for a hill! Now they've got a young tenant farmer in to
farm it.'

Within the span of a few decades, the area has gone from a
modest backwater where a living was hard-earned to a place
of whim and fantasy in which prices affordable to millionaires
swamp older measures of value such as the capacity of land
to provide a fair living or the emotional commitments to
place. Those farmers who stubbornly hold on are a particular
group; the incompetent or less dedicated have long since
been winnowed out by the tough competitiveness of farming.
Equally, the ambitious have either left to work as managers
for huge farming conglomerates or have moved out of farming altogether. Those who remain are the ones who are most
faithful to place, their whole way of life and being shaped by
the exigencies of a particular geographical space, so that the
idea of giving up and moving is inconceivable.

Since the poor-quality land around Oldstead and Kilburn
makes farming particularly difficult, I followed a suggestion to
visit Peter Turnbull, who farms a few miles to the west, where
the land opens out in a broad vale known as the Coxwold-Gilling
Gap. Perhaps this gentle, undulating countryside, which makes

up part of the famous view from the Hambleton Hills, could tell a happier tale. Peter Turnbull is still farming despite having passed his seventieth birthday. He should be enjoying a comfortable retirement rather than an anxious future. He's a tenant farmer, and he and his son are now doing the work his father had twice the men to do fifty years ago, yet he is still watching his profit margins narrow to the point where he is borrowing money every year just to do the same job. Several neighbouring tenant farmers have retired and the estate makes more money renting the farmhouses than from farming the land. The government tells small farmers to diversify, but Turnbull has tried everything. He and his wife do bed-and-breakfast but he is well aware that it is often cheaper for a family to go to Spain than to stay at his farm. He sells his prime beef on the internet, but competition keeps the price down. He has one of the biggest flocks of lapwings in northern England coming to nest in his fields, two miles off the road and several miles from any village, so he has been able to get some subsidies for environmental improvements such as restoring hay meadows and digging scrapes to attract wading birds, but it doesn't amount to a living.

He's lived on the same farm since he was fourteen, and there were two generations of the family farming in the area before him, but as tenants they could never buy. If he retires, he has nowhere to go. 'It's been a wonderful way of living – I've enjoyed every minute of it; our only mistake was not to get a property when we could,' he says, sitting in the cheerful kitchen which gives on to the back yard where the cows are jostling at the gate for a better view of us.

A year later, food prices were soaring so I returned to see how Turnbull was faring: 'The price of beef has gone up but so have the inputs – electricity, feed, fertilizer. There's more money coming in now than eighteen months ago, but there's also more money going out. The overdraft is bigger this year than last.'

All around the Plot there are people clinging on to a way of life that can no longer generate a living. Peter Turnbull's predicament is echoed by tenant sheep farmers on the moors. Here, flocks were disappearing at the rate of an average of five a year early in the 2000s, although the introduction of an agri-environmental scheme has recently eased the rate of decline. But the end of sheep-farming is the biggest concern at the North York Moors National Park's headquarters, because without the sheep the moors revert to scrubland, which tourists in surveys and focus groups say they do not want. In 1998 there were 125 sheep farmers, and the figure was down to 101 by 2005. As each flock is sold off, it makes the job of the neighbouring farmer that much harder, as the flocks effectively keep each other within their hefted boundaries. Without a neighbour, a flock will wander and the sheep farmer will find himself tracking it for miles across the moor. Farmers' incomes are dropping sharply. Sheep farmers on the North York moors were losing £7.76 gross per ewe in 2006, their margins squeezed as the cost of feed, fuel and medicines rose. In 2007, livestock farm incomes were the lowest in the agricultural sector, averaging £9,300, and with further shifts in the subsidy regime expected, the income from sheep-farming could continue to drop, hitting small hill farmers particularly hard.

Wool exacts such a low price that it only just covers the cost of shearing; Peter Houlston, who has a small flock on the land just below the Plot, was getting £1.80 per clip in 2007, but out of that he has to pay the shearer £1.20 per sheep.

Shearing is now more about sheep welfare and waste management than producing a valuable commodity: it would be cheaper (but devastating to the environment) to burn the stuff. Wool has so little value that the EU has categorized it as industrial waste, and as such it cannot, by law, be buried or burned. The only reason England's fields are not disappearing under a mountain of rotting wool is because one of the last remaining national co-operatives, the British Wool Marketing Board based in Bradford, has a statutory duty to collect the clip from every sheep farmer in the country, from the smallest lifestyle farmer with a herd of five to a big farmer running thousands of sheep – all 60 million kilos of wool per year.

The average age of a sheep farmer is well over fifty, and even the most dedicated upland farmer finds it hard to see a future for his heirs; it requires long hours at well below the minimum wage. Could the eight centuries of sheep-rearing on the North York moors launched by the Cistercians be drawing to a close?

Peter and Audrey Houlston count themselves lucky; they used to have a tenant farm near Peter Turnbull but they moved out in 2001 and had enough money to buy a small-holding – a cottage and twenty-five acres – in Oldstead. They are one of the Plot's nearest neighbours. Houlston breaks in horses and feeds up store cattle and has a small flock of breeding ewes. He supplements his farming income with droving and penning of cattle and sheep at market and working as a beater during the shooting season. It is Audrey, a teacher also from a farming background, who feels the decline of local farming most acutely: 'A farmer used to be valuable and important, now they're often blamed. There is contempt for farming people and their way of life as if we're all cruel and living on subsidies. It's a despicable way to treat independent-minded people. We are told that we kill the countryside, that we're cruel to animals and have destroyed the hedges. This government hates farmers. In France and Germany, farmers are still valued and admired for providing food and keeping the countryside for town people to enjoy. In the eighties you could make money and you could feel independent and a sense of pride. But my father was getting more for feed barley in 1976 than we got in 2003.'

Houlston agrees as he reflects on his own family's history of farming: 'It was hard work but you had a pride in it, the whole community was involved. You didn't know any difference. You felt you had a place in the national scheme of things. You felt you were providing something for the country.'

Now the fields around Oldstead are a sea of golden buttercups in the spring. It looks pretty, but to a farmer this is wasteland: buttercups are poisonous to livestock. Patches of reeds, thistles and nettles grow up thick every summer and the hedgerows are unkempt. Sometimes a contractor is brought in to get the land back into good enough condition to warrant the government subsidies, but on the smaller, less accessible fields even that minimal effort is uneconomic. There has been some growth in 'lifestyle farming', with newcomers buying up a few acres on which to keep some livestock as a hobby alongside their work elsewhere. The bigger farms are still profitable, but only with considerable investment in scale and mechanization such as robotic milking parlours and cheap East European labour; sometimes even these big farms become a hobby which the wealthy buy for the shooting, renting out the farming to local contractors. There has been a steady enough demand from both types of buyers over the last two decades to keep land prices high, though that might slacken as recession deepens. But the way of life which generated the picturesque landscape so prized by these buyers will continue to be increasingly precarious.

This has always been an intensively laboured land, and each field, as Fred told me, had its own name. They are an accurate record of the sweat of generations – 'Dear Bought', 'High Thorns', 'Middle Thorns', 'Low Thorns', 'Fourteen Days' Work' – and it is that regiment of heavy boots and strong arms that has steadily dwindled through the twentieth century. Now the ditching, hedging and uprooting of weeds are done by machines or not at all. A boom in biofuels could bring new prosperity to the arable farms, but only where it is possible to use the massive equipment designed for the American prairies. It is of no use in those fields only accessible through narrow gates, along twisting old English lanes. This area is part of the National Park and adjoins an Area of Outstanding Natural Beauty, and with such nomenclature come tough planning restrictions. Exasperated residents report battles over planning permission on details as seemingly trivial as cutting verges to widen entrances. This English landscape is romanticized in tourist brochures, is fantasized about by city dwellers, but those images require a ruthless mental editing, to omit the deep sense of grievance of the heirs of those who produced that landscape.

The editing is equally apparent on the moors, where the tourists flock to delight in the exquisite flush of purple across the heather moor every August. What might be seen as a symbol of England's enduring age is, in fact, desperately fragile. Three-quarters of the world's heather moorland is in the UK

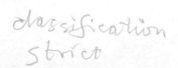

but, contrary to popular understanding, this unique ecosystem is not a natural wilderness but the product of a particular combination of human interventions over several millennia – deforestation, sheep-farming and grouse-shooting – whose continued practice now threatens immense destruction.

As the Drovers' Road runs north above the Chapel over the great expanse of Arden Great Moor, signs bristle on every gate warning of the risk of fire. The August colours of Arden's patchwork of ling and heather – rust, pale apricot, bright pink and bleached mauve – offer rare pleasures to the eye, but the moor is delicate. The North Yorkshire moors have always been drier than other English moors such as the Dales or the Peak District. That tendency was reinforced by the widespread drainage ditches dug to improve the grazing for sheep and the growth of heather for grouse over the last century. Now, changes in weather patterns are leading to drier summers and less snowfall in the warmer winters, which make the moors even more vulnerable to accidental fires. The damage that uncontrolled summer fires can do to a moor is enormous because the fierce intensity of the heat burns peat to a considerable depth – it is, after all, a form of fuel. It is very hard to regenerate the heather, and there are some areas of the moor still bare from the fires of the 1976 heatwave – I remember the sinister grey clouds ballooning into the sky. When peat is bare it dries out quickly in the sun and crumbles like dust.

Some drains have already been blocked on Arden, which is particularly vulnerable because it is a 'thin' moor as opposed to the 'thick' moors of the Cleveland Hills. On Arden, the skinny layer of peat is easily worn away to bare rock on tracks. Water retention is partly inhibited by insufficient sphagnum moss, which absorbs up to eight times its own weight in water and can stay wet long after the surrounding soil has dried out; it is this absorbency that soaks up rain and holds it in the moor long after rainfall, acting as a fire retardant. These modest species, which have created the moor over thousands of years, are sensitive to pollution; the North York moors now have some of the highest rates of acidification in the country. This is usually attributed to low rainfall and their position, sandwiched between the industrial belts of Teesside, the Humber and South Yorkshire.

Sphagnum has another vital role: it can reduce the threat of floods because of its extraordinary capacity to absorb water and protect the peat beneath. Without it, the moors are even more vulnerable to heavy rains, which can cause huge damage by cutting through and washing away peat. Three-quarters of Britain's rain falls in the uplands, and the moss of the moors acts as a reservoir. Climate change is predicted to increase rainfall, and the danger of flash floods like the one in Ryedale in 2005 which cut six feet through peat, washing the dirt and debris down the valley into Helmsley and beyond. It is sphagnum that ensures the stability of this fragile ecosystem, moderating the impact of heat and rain on these uplands, which are particularly exposed to both.

Fire and water can both easily destroy the peat, thus revealing remarkable histories: the Ryedale flash floods cut such sharp swathes through the peat that palaeobotanists found tree stumps which were 3–7,000 years old; a fire on Fylingdale Moor in 2003 exposed twenty-six prehistoric carvings, some dating from as far back as 5000 BCE. The moors are repositories of history, enfolding in the blanket bog human artefacts, plant and animal life; they have recorded, in the layers of compressed spaghnum moss and cotton grass that create the peat, the vicissitudes of rainfall and sunshine for millennia.

It has been a slow accumulation, at the rate of about four inches a century, and at its deepest, it reaches at least twenty feet. Three feet every thousand years.

'Waste' is how the moors were once described; they were unproductive, and it took back-breaking labour to exact a modest living from them. They were inhospitable and offered little shelter from the scouring wind, biting cold and driving rain. But the last few decades have prompted a dramatic revision in our perception of this derided land-scape as we learn that it is crucially important in sustaining our well-being. This is not just a land for a leisured society to play in – shooting grouse, walking, driving – but one of England's biggest reserves of carbon. Centuries of the stuff are captured in the peat bogs of British moors, account-ing for more carbon than is found in all the forests of Britain and France. If fire burns a peat moor, or a flood cuts a deep channel out of it, that releases carbon.

The danger is that as the moors get drier, they are more vulnerable to fires and release more carbon; as climate change leads to more intense rainfall, floods wash away peat and carbon is released. The two trends could interact as drier peat crumbles to dust, which is more vulnerable to being washed away by intermittent intense rainfall. At every stage, the risk is of an increased rate of carbon escape. There is an urgent need to slow the water flow from the moors by block-ing drainage ditches and erosion gullies. Vegetation needs to be sustained to enable it to protect the peat; some argue that the moors should be allowed to revert to the scrub forest they were many thousands of years ago, but that proposal has run into fierce opposition from the shooting lobby as well as criti-cism from some conservation groups who argue that trees would only further deplete water resources. It would also spoil the view; our aesthetic enjoyment of the moors is coming into conflict with environmental imperatives to reduce the release of carbon.

Only now do we discover that, like the back and shoulders of the human body that the moors echo so compellingly in their contours, they have been taking the strain, shouldering the burden of England's industrialization in their own delicate ecosystem, as acid rain impacts on the smallest cells of moss and chokes its life. Instead of a place to fear or to hold in awe, the moors have become a landscape to pity; once they were described in terms of powerfulness, now it is in terms of fragility. 'Pity the land', wrote Bertolt Brecht, 'that needs heroes'. He intended no prescience of ecological crisis, but his words fit our time; pity the land indeed.

This is a situation that presages a dark ages that not even my father's gloomy imagination could have envisaged. I never heard him talking about ecological crisis, and he didn't show much interest in the environmental impact of industrial agriculture. He clocked the loss of hedgerows, of scythes, horse-drawn ploughs and hand milking and saw them as the slow steps of tragic change, but it was the loss of human skills and the measure of self-sufficiency and independence they entailed that he mourned, rather than the impact on the land. He shared that dangerous twentieth-century romanticism that holds that as long as things *look* broadly the same, there is no undue cause for alarm: the tyranny of the view. His only political involvement I can remember was that he went along to some parish-council meetings to stop street-lights being installed in the village. He had too much respect for farmers to ever be tempted by environmentalism; he was awed by the rough pragmatism of farming and country life, the routine killing of every kind. He did not get involved in the great local campaign of the seventies to save nearby Farndale and its banks of wild daffodils (reputedly planted by the Cistercians) from the planners' proposed reservoir. He left the flyers and bumper stickers to the outraged weekenders. His anger was more diffuse, more pervasive and too fatalistic ever to be focused on taking action to fight the changes he hated.

All his life he would stumble across the vestiges of the world that had so inspired him as a boy in Kilburn: an old farmer who had never been to York, twenty miles away, or a man who had lived all his life in the same house, and he cherished what was left of a much less mobile world. In his romanticization of North Yorkshire, there was no recognition of how the living standards of farmers and their labourers had improved over the fifty years he lived there. He disliked the picture windows, wall-to-wall carpets and televisions in prosperous farmhouses that followed the Commmon Agricultural Policy and its golden age of rising farm incomes in the seventies and eighties. Some farmers discovered holidays – and foreign holidays at that – for the first time, and their burden of punishing work was reduced, but this would not have counted in Dad's mind as progress. He always looked at the countryside much as Stanley Baldwin had done, with the aesthetic idealization of someone who has never directly been involved in agriculture.

There was a curious feature of my father's conversation in his last decades: nothing thrilled him more than coincidence. He loved bumping into someone who happened to know someone whom he knew. It was the delight of suddenly spotting a fragment of order; it was the consolation for having long since found the world an utterly disordered, baffling place which became only more random and absent of meaning as he got older. In the quiet villages of Ryedale this disorder was kept at bay, and that earned my father's devotion. It was a world where history was not so ruthlessly disregarded, where the pace of life was slower even if the rate of social change was not.

The escape to the country was part of a cultural rebellion for my twenty-nine-year-old father, one that has become a cliché in subsequent generations looking for the rural good life. Howard Newby called it a 'despairing search for authenticity in a modern meretricious world'. The authenticity Dad craved was that which the Cistercians had also sought 800 years before. Not the kind that clever marketing executives could sell you, but an integration of how one lived and where one lived, so that the one became an expression of the other. This is what he sought in his promised land, and with a stubborn determination he persisted in what became a very lonely dream. Disorientated by the huge shifts and dramatic social revolutions of his lifetime, the continuity of place – and his carving – offered powerful solace, points of reference in a world that offered few others.

There was no worse condemnation from my father, always expressed with sharp bitterness, than to say a place had changed (friends who changed simply ceased to be mentioned). Needless to say, as he grew older fewer and fewer places could avoid such condemnation. That was part of the appeal of his Plot. After the coniferous forests were planted in the fifties, it did not change; the cherry trees grew taller, the moles came and went, the gorse bloomed, but the Chapel remained as it was when he finished building it in 1958. His only addition was the carved oak doors for its thirtieth anniversary. There was the same damp smell of stone; the lichen growing infinitesimally slowly on the old drystone walls. For forty-four years he stolidly cut the grass and pulled the weeds. It felt like a chore and as he aged it became a burden, but it was a regular act of remembrance to the men to whom he had dedicated it, and also to the ideals on which he had built a life that had brought neither money nor fame; he was keeping faith with his younger self, and it gave him a sense of purpose and a fulfilment that elude many more successful people.

What made that achievement poignant in his last decade was that the social changes from which he had spent a life-time escaping caught up with him and the Plot. The angels he carved to top the exterior buttresses were stolen. Whoever took them would have needed a sizeable vehicle to carry them away, and a decent ladder and tools to break the mortar holding them in place. This was no random theft, but carefully planned. Nowhere and nothing was sacred any more. The Hut was broken into and the old pine chest of drawers and chairs were stolen. Then it was broken into again, and again, even though there was nothing left to steal. Just the fact that there was a door there with a padlock was sufficient to stir curiosity. My father found the stumps of old candles inside; he worried about strange gatherings, witchcraft and black Masses.

When my father was in hospital towards the end of his life, I visited the Chapel and found the grass lush and long. Weeds were breaking through cracks in the paving stones and swamping the low dry-stone walls. Over the doorway of the Hut hung the rose that had been planted by my mother. She had protected it from the deer and rabbits for two decades, and now, like the lilac tree on the track by the entrance to the Plot, it promised to stay on, a powerful souvenir of one person's passing commitment to this acre. Cherry saplings had sprouted up and crowded thickly on the hillside behind the chapel and no one was disturbing the moles any longer. The site could be swallowed up by the forest. My father's plot seemed to be in the process of being reclaimed, just as he had once reclaimed it from the moor.

14

Common ground

It was September 2002 and a bright Italian sun was streaming onto the central square of Lucca. My father sat in the café in a winter overcoat and a thick hand-knitted Scottish woollen jumper, his face drawn and pale. He was out of hospital but the doctors had given him only a few more weeks to live. But the favourite child, his youngest son Joseph, was getting married and nothing was going to prevent him flying to Italy to be there. So we ordered him wheelchairs to get through the airports, and taxis to manoeuvre him around Lucca, and the rest of the time he sat, uncharacteristically quiet, though still capable of his sharp jibes – he complained about my hair – surrounded by grandchildren.

We had a few hours free. Dad had never travelled much in Italy and it was perhaps his first visit to the town, but he knew exactly what he wanted to see. He had drawn inspiration all his life from the great sculptors of the Italian Renaissance – Ghiberti, Donatello and Michelangelo – albeit largely via black and white photos until the few visits he made in the last ten years of his life to see my sister, who had moved to Italy. Yet he seemed to have an extraordinarily accurate catalogue in his head

of Italian Renaissance sculpture. He didn't need to look at the
guidebooks to know that he wanted to see the sarcophagus
of Ilaria del Carretto by Jacopo della Quercia in a side chapel of
the cathedral. He could forget the names and ages of his
children, but not of sculptures.

No taxi could drive him across the square, so his eldest grandson took one arm and I the other, and slowly we made our way
on foot, stopping for him to catch his breath. Several times I
suggested we turn back, but he wasn't having any of it. He
continued, this frail shell of a man who had once been so strong.
He knew exactly where to go in the cathedral, as if he had
been many times before. And beside the effigy of the young
Ilaria, he seemed to find something of his old self again. He
walked – alone – around the tomb with animation and engage-
ment, his eyes lit up with appreciation. He didn't talk – he was
not a father who believed it was his job to educate his children
or grandchildren; his enjoyment was private. He was as
entranced as ever by the superb skill of this great sculptor: the
fluid folds of fabric and how they accentuated the solidity of the
woman's curved form, the repose of those eyes as if they had
only closed for a moment. My father was paying his final tribute
as a sculptor to an art that had provided him with joy as well as
inspiring the purpose and determination of his life. This was
Dad at his most admirable. I have a photo of him on that day on
my bookcase.

A month later he was deteriorating rapidly and we brought
him back to London to die. He left Yorkshire meekly, almost
like a child in his desire to be cared for by his children, and each
took a turn. In a curious twist of family history, he arrived finally
at an East End Catholic hospice that his forebears had contributed to founding at the end of the nineteenth century. But
alongside this uncharacteristic meekness his anger remained.

My sister and I took him out for lunch to a Hackney pub which sold his favourite strong Belgian beer. But he could not drink it. He had no appetite left and complained that the crusty bread hurt his tongue, and then he put on a last defiant display of the childish bully he could be. Smiling, he told us that he had left his house and all its contents to his favourite child. He knew it was not true – he wanted to provoke us – but we were both too emotionally weary to respond with more than exasperated exclamations of 'So what?' Money and chattels seemed at that point a very trivial part of his complex legacy. Perhaps he felt remorseful, because as I drove him back to the hospice he made the extraordinary comment that in the end it had all been about family – his children, that was what had mattered. It was so utterly out of character that I have never been able to decide if it was a moment of revelation or just sentimentality prompted by his approaching death.

When I returned the next day, he was very ill. He lay in bed, fretful and in need of constant attention from the nurses. We were warned he was slipping out of consciousness, and just before he did so for the last time he whispered to me, 'Astonishing, astonishing, you've stuck it out to the end.' I knew this to be a benediction: there was no higher praise to be had from a man who had defined himself by his capacity to stick things out. He had not expected it of me, perhaps of anyone; his surprise was painfully poignant. Yet in different ways, all five of us had stuck it out to the end. He lay in a coma for two weeks, shrinking before our eyes into a man so delicate and frail as the fluid drained from his body that I barely recognized him. Bringing another strand of his story to an unexpected conclusion, it was on the watch of my mother, separated from him for twenty-three years, that he finally loosed his grip on life. He would have enjoyed his funeral: a sung High

Mass in Latin plainchant by the Ampleforth monks in their abbey church back in Yorkshire on a freezing November day. A year later we scattered his ashes over the Plot.

By the measure my father set himself as a young man, his life could be judged a failure. His work did not get the recognition he craved, and Catholic churches continued to prefer their plaster saints, or veered off into a clumsy modernism that appalled him. After 1972 and the humiliating catastrophe of an exhibition in the unprepossessing venue of Billingham, in the industrial heart of Teesside, he never put on another. He was haunted by the opening night in Billingham, when he stood with my mother in front of the rows of empty glasses waiting all evening for guests to arrive. Work came in a steady flow, and in 1985 he was awarded the prestigious Sir Otto Beit medal (Bronze) by the Royal British Society of Sculptors, but it was rarely on the scale or with the acclamation for which he had once yearned. One day I was driving with him along a country road and he suddenly veered off down a track; we arrived in a muddy farmyard cluttered with machinery, and there was one of my father's largest stone carvings. It had been abandoned after being removed from the church for which it had been commissioned, and Dad had spotted it by chance years later. He wanted to check it was still there, and he talked of buying it back. With angry resentment, he would tell us that his work would be valuable after he had died and it would be us who would reap the benefits. This was the time when he was angry about everything – one of his former pupils, now middle-aged, still remembers how angry his footsteps sounded.

To a small but steady succession of talented pupils, over his four decades of teaching at Ampleforth, my father was a great inspiration. He found some emotional fulfilment in his students, and a pleasure in communicating his enthusiasm about art which he did not seem to find with his own children. To the sons of comfortable middle-class Catholic families, he offered the challenge of his own radically different life. They came to tea on Sundays, nervous young boys who ate too many chocolate biscuits and took Dad's books away, and some of them have never forgotten the impact it made on them: the art, the home-made home, my beautiful mother, the large quantities of small children, the austerity and above all, the dedication to art.

The sculptor Antony Gormley was a pupil: 'I can see the art room now, the dust motes in the sunlight. It wasn't what we were drawing, but that sense of two hours devoted to this activity. Nothing was said, you could just hear the pencil on the paper. Your father was insistent that we draw from the shoulder, and that our pencils were always sharp. He was a brilliant draughtsman.' Another former pupil and artist, John Dewe Matthews, instantly remembered my father when I called him out of the blue decades after he had last seen his former art teacher: 'He was very exacting. It was as if he could read the body inside out, like he had X-ray eyes so that he could see how muscles linked up and where the body expressed tension and compression'.

But the fulfilment which teaching provided could not compensate for the bitter disillusionment: he had built his life on intense idealism and framed it around figures he cast as heroes, and they foundered. Hugh Dormer was revealed in a less than flattering light by his old comrade Charlie Birch, whilst official recognition eluded the French desert mystic Charles de Foucauld, who has still not been canonized. Then, even worse, Fiona McCarthy published a biography of Eric Gill that revealed a man who, while he played the role of respected Catholic paterfamilias, indulged predatory sexual appetites with women, including his teenage daughters, friends' wives, even animals. My father was deeply shocked.   *me too*

At the same time, the ideals of which the Chapel was to be a standard bearer were increasingly questioned; it was not the precursor of some new counter-reformation. Even the Catholic Church, that 'rock of the ages', failed to hold steady, shaken by Vatican Council II and the controversies that followed. My father lost his Latin Mass, and the social changes of the sixties reached even North Yorkshire. He was bewildered by a younger generation's indifference to God, its taste for long hair, magic mushrooms and rock music. Finally, my mother rebelled and left Yorkshire, exhausted by a surfeit of ideals and meagre love. I followed her, and only my younger brother Joseph remained with our father. None of us children has settled in Yorkshire; three of us returning to the city from which my parents had escaped, London. It hurt him that not only had we left him but that we all ended up leaving the promised land that he thought would be his most valuable legacy to us. Things were not supposed to have turned out like this.

My father was a man of enormous self-belief in his youth, and in his writings he sketched out his vast and many ambitions. The regeneration of faith, of art and of humanity itself: these were the huge themes that preoccupied him, and no modesty or self-questioning seemed to make him hesitate over the role he believed he could play. He pontificated with the *élan* of someone who assumes his audience will be hanging on his every word. Towards the end of his life, no longer certain of biographers, he set himself the task of chronicling his life in small print-runs of pamphlets which he circulated to friends and family; they are eccentric and repetitive, but there are also, finally, traces of modesty and acceptance as the angry bitterness faded. Admirably, during his later years he counted himself as having had a good life, and he appreciated the many riches he had enjoyed. He had lived in a place he loved, doing what he loved, and in the last decade of his life he was confident that that was enough. I can see that my father's ideals about place were deeply and wilfully romantic, but I can also see that they included many insights into the nature of belonging and place which have been too ruthlessly discarded. They gave him a sense of purpose and a fulfilment that elude many.

For nearly three years now I have been walking, reading, listening and talking to people about a place and a landscape. The picture has kept shifting like a kaleidoscope into new patterns. 'Wisdom sits in places,' I kept repeating to myself: a strong sense of place built up in a thousand familiar details can be a way to develop a deeper understanding of relationship and identity. 'Places acquire the stamp of human events', Keith Basso writes of the Western Apache, 'or memorable times, and people wrap these into stories that can be myths, historical tales, sagas or just gossip. Every story begins and ends with the phrase "it happened at . . ."' It was what my father understood about the Plot: he had spun a web of connections, historical and personal, centred on this acre of land which spanned centuries and continents, and he found within that a place for himself and his work. It became clear to me that I was doing much the same, and that the Plot had been a place in which to explore questions of belonging and home. I have used the wisdom that sits in places to come to know and understand a father.

It proved much more difficult than I had imagined. A chance piece of research helped explain it to me. While researching Byland, I discovered an account of twelve encounters with ghosts in the neighbourhood, written in notes in the back of a book from the Abbey on another subject, dating from around 1400. It was the focus of an earnest historical essay in the 1920s, and then appears to have been ignored for nearly ninety years before being taken up with enthusiasm by an American historian. These fifteenth-century ghosts seemed an everyday business, and the accounts are matter-of-fact. Most of the incidents are pinned to specific places such as Hodgebeck, Byland Bank, Kilburn churchyard, Gormire and Gilling. But the stories are shot through with lurid detail: a woman plunged her hands into the ghost's flesh; the ghosts changed shape; a raven that shot sparks from its wings became a dog; a rearing horse became a 'whirling heap of hay with a light in the middle of it'. These apparitions shift form from human to animal, from vegetable to object – one even became a revolving vat. They are restless creatures, usually found to be haunting places of movement such as roads and tracks, and often lurking behind hedgerows. They are portrayed, almost prosaically, as commonplace inhabitants of the night, but they were not at peace and they provoked great fear in their neighbours. One used to linger at night at cottage windows in Kilburn, another walked continually along the road from Ampleforth, causing terror amongst the villagers. All these unhappy beings needed help, and here was the moral of the tales: the dead required absolution and it was the task of the living to get it for them, using bribes if necessary, from a priest. The accounts were used to buttress the authority of the Church and its representatives, but beyond this self-serving purpose they expressed a deep medieval anxiety as to the fate of the dead. Above all, these Byland ghosts begged to be 'conjured'; this medieval term meant a combination of acknowledgement, naming and questioning these spirits on their fate. It was lack of recognition that trapped them in their restless wanderings. After being conjured, the ghosts asked for only modest favours, such as an errand to the priest or the odd coin; they were never aggressive or threatening.

The Byland ghosts are enthralling because they offer a glimpse into a medieval way of seeing the Plot and the surrounding land that finds resonance as late as the nineteenth century, in Canon Atkinson's accounts of the beliefs in spirits and other creatures in his moorland parish. Portrayed in both is a land teeming with the unresolved: anxieties, troubled consciences, disputes and grievances. This land, to which the Cistercians retreated to create the Promised Land, was also a place that harboured unquiet spirits for whom not even death had proved a release. These ghosts restlessly paced the neighbourhood, with no option but to wait. They offered no threat: what they needed was the courage to be faced, to be named, to be recognized. To be known. Perhaps that is all our ghosts ever need from us.

The American nature writer and poet Gary Snyder says that 'the most radical thing you can do is stay home'. In a mobile, impatient culture which promotes 'moving on', the hardest task is to go back, to go home – it is always a very personal reckoning. My father's most painful legacy is a family that cannot share its past, siblings who disagree on their common history. Raised on so much history and such a heavy burden of ideals, it has not been easy for any of us to find our own way into the twenty-first century.

In the course of researching this book, I have found with my own family, my husband and children, new stories of the Plot and its neighbourhood. We have brewed coffee in driving rain in the lee of a barn wall; we have swum in the glassy stillness of Gormire Lake in the chilly damp of an early-August morning; we have fried bacon in the woods as autumn leaves drifted in hazy sunshine; we have played ambushes on the moors and the children have rolled down hillsides of springy heather with screams of delight. We have made new friends. I have refound the childhood associations with the villages of Ryedale and Hambleton, and they no longer centre on the Plot. That is a place so freighted with a painful family history and its compromised ideals that I have said goodbye. My eldest brother has taken over the Plot, and arranges its maintenance; it is now immaculate, with the grass neatly cut and trimmed, the saplings cleared. Once again I do not feel welcome, but I can appreciate how my father would be mightily relieved – and surprised – to see his legacy so meticulously cared for by his eldest son. Just as it was for my father, it is for my brother his own private plot.

It is May 2008, and we arrive in North Yorkshire in brilliant sunshine. I am booked in for a flight the following day, and by now the voice remembers me – 'Oh yes, the writer from London.' We walk from Kilburn to Oldstead, right under the cliffs on which the gliding club perches, and we watch the gawky long-winged planes take off and wheel in the sky over us. There is the intermittent drone of the aerotow as it tugs the gliders up into the air, then returns to collect the next one; it's the sound of the Chapel in summer – that and the skylarks. I feel completely confident that at last my flight is within my grasp. I fail to notice the stiff breeze.

The may is in blossom in the hedgerows, and the air is like the warm milky breath of a contented baby, with sweet suggestions of almond and honey. The cow parsley billows out from the verges, the creamy white heads dancing vivaciously on their delicate green stems. There is an air of celebration, the millions of points of white amongst the vibrant new green like fine champagne bubbles. The holly leaves gleam softly and in their shade the new nettles unfurl mauve heads of pleated leaves.

The lane is a tunnel of this glamorous greenery winding between fields scattered with a rich profusion of brilliant buttercups; their petals are polished to white in the sunlight, but their mock innocence doesn't fool the sharp-eyed cattle, who pick their way past to graze out of their poisonous reach.

This is England at its most seductive. The exhaustion of the chilly spring, so achingly slow to arrive, is finally over. In late May, northern England jumps a season, gives up on spring and plunges headlong into early summer, an intoxicating exuberance of leaves exploding from sticky buds and flowers bursting into bloom. Having watched closely each tentative step of spring – the first brave daffodil – now the pace quickens to a hectic helter-skelter which outstrips one's wintered powers of observation, still attuned to the blasting cold, and one stumbles into this new world hustled and disorientated as if one had landed on Oxford Street in the January sales. There is so much for botanists to miss. during the spring term.

But in all this bustle, there are points of exquisite perfection which still the mind and print themselves into the brain cells. England is rightly famous for its bluebell woods, but in the lanes from Oldstead to Kilburn it is not quantity that makes the impression but the juxtaposition of colour: the soft, pale grey of ash trunks and at their feet the sharp, acidic purple-blue of the flowers.

The next day, the breeze has become a sharp wind. The voice tells me that it's expected to last a couple of days. 'How about Tuesday?' I ask.

'Well, there could be rain then.'

We climb up through the forest below Roulston Scar with a wind in the treetops that sounds like a roaring sea. On the forest floor, with the needles muffling our footsteps, it is almost still – just the shiver of a breeze in the ferns – but all around us this

angry sea grows louder and louder. As we come out on to the top
of Hood Hill, the wind blusters and barges into us; the ridge is
narrow and the hill falls sharply away from the path. Hawthorns
have grown up here, their form twisted and misshapen by
months of these powerful gusts. We are hustled along, and the
trees creak – the small groans of wood on wood, branches heaving, trunks twisted with the strain – and sigh patiently as the
wind pesters them. We can see tiny figures, braced into the
wind, outlined on the cliffs across the valley from us. We halloo
for the children and hear nothing in return but the great
swelling cacophony of the wind wrestling with the thousands
of pine trees on the hillsides around. Perched up here, it feels
like we are in the rigging of a tall ship, tossing from side to
side in a sea of deepest coniferous green.

Back down in the steep-sided valley on the Thief's Highway,
the roar of the sea recedes. It is eerily quiet and warm down
here – so quiet that perhaps one could catch the sound of the
bracken growing, the delicate green stalks shooting absolutely
straight from last year's decaying brown crop. At the stalks' tip,
their heads are bowed, weighed down by their tightly furled
leaves, thick with brown hair; as the fronds slowly unroll, their
tips are beaded with the buds of new leaves which crumble
easily between finger and thumb, yet to develop the leathery
resilience that will last the summer.

Sure enough the next day there is rain, and wind, and thick
mists. I do not bother to phone for weather updates. Even a
week's stay seems unlikely to provide the right conditions for
a single flight; how does anyone ever manage to learn to glide
in Yorkshire?

But Thursday morning is unexpectedly dry and bright. When
I phone I am convinced there will be some freak weather
condition that I have not managed to identify that will rule out

gliding – winds at cloud level or some other meterological phenomenon not visible from Thirsk. But no, all is well. 'Just come over as soon as you can, we'll fit you in.'

An hour later, after a year of cancellations – I've lost count of how many bookings made – I am signing the consent papers at the club. Do I want a woman pilot or a man? I am asked. 'Anyone who will bring me back down in one piece,' I reply, now daunted at the prospect of the flight whose repeated cancellations have always been accompanied by a small sense of relief. I hate flying; I'm the one on the aeroplane who grips the armrests, eyes tight shut and jaw clenched.

My pilot is a tall, broad-shouldered young Viking of a woman called Alex, with flowing auburn hair, an easy smile, an awful tendency to make chilling jokes about crash landings, and a confidence one can only call breezy.

We push the glider along the ground; it feels as light as a lawnmower but sprawls ungainly. Alex hands over a parachute for me to strap myself into but seems rather vague about how it works. 'I've never had to use one,' she explains, and adds helpfully, 'You'll be falling through the sky and you just have to reach over and pull the metal clasp diagonally.'

I finger the metal clasp and try to work out what 'diagonally' means and whether I would have any spatial orientation at all if I were hurtling head over heels through clouds.

'There are tomes on how to read the sky, but what we are looking for all the time are fluffy cumulus clouds vertical on a blue background. What we want to see is how dark their bottoms are. The cumulus are rising air. Our aim is to cruise underneath a cloud and then spiral up with the thermal in the cloud. From there, you identify the next cloud and move towards it, losing height as you go; in the next cloud you spiral up again,' explains Alex.

It sounds like playing three-dimensional hopscotch in the sky. What gliding pilots don't want are cloudless skies, or much wind. What they look for is 'lift', either from the wind as it interacts with the shape of the land or the thermal currents formed by the sun warming the land. The airstrip on the edge of the Hambleton Hills can take advantage of the west winds that blow into the escarpment, 1,000 feet high. Between the lifts, the glider sinks. But the key is 'reading' the sky and its infinite variations of cloud, wind and weather; no two days are ever the same and the nuances of this always-changing text are what draw the gliding pilots' eyes always upwards. To them, clouds are not a shadowy interlude on a summer's day, but fuel. The fascination here is not what is under one's feet but what lies far above one's head in the expanse of air, water and light.

I climb into the glider as if it were a bath and I am leaning back with my feet under the taps – only these are pedals, which Alex instructs me not to touch. I am now belted in – legs and shoulders. I feel ashen but do my best Battle of Britain thumbs-up to the children watching from a picnic table. They smile briefly before returning to their Nintendo games. What a way to say goodbye, I think; not quite those touching moments of maternal love I have sometimes imagined.

But my attention snaps back to Alex, running through emergency procedures. 'I want you to listen to all this and then forget it,' she says.

'Perhaps not forget it but put it out of my mind,' I weakly correct her.

'Here are the paddles to release the cockpit, then shift this knob and the whole control panel will drop away. One twist on the seat belt and you're free.'

Free?

I'm seated in the front of the plane with Alex behind. She tells me to look for other gliders and for clouds – in that order: we need to avoid the former and catch the latter. She's rattling through safety checks, but it doesn't quite dispel that air of relaxed amateurishness. The mechanic who checked the plane that morning is standing beside us, beaming in a floppy sunhat. I crave uniforms, fluorescent jackets and the airport paraphernalia of lights and signs, not this airstrip scattered with daisies.

'It's a terrible day for gliding,' comments Alex cheerily. I'm alarmed.

'Why?' I ask.

'Very little lift,' she responds. I prefer not to ask any more: does that mean we won't get very high or that we will sink like a stone?

The glider is moving. I crane my neck to see the children but they're bowed over their games. I brace myself as the machine bumps over the grass, pulled by a cable attaching us to an aerotow which, to my ignorant eye, could have had a part in a First World War film. The bumping suddenly stops, we're rising. Small thrills of panic run through me as the edge of the cliff rears up. I shrink back in my metal bathtub; every instinct pulls me back in my seat as we shoot out over the wooded ravine that yawns wide below us. The land seems to be falling away from me while I'm stationary, hovering in the air. But that's only a momentary sensation because I am moving. The conical outline of Hood Hill is lost up here as its wooded slopes melt into the haze over the Vale of York. We wheel slowly round, valleys, woods and fields whirling by, an unrecognizable jumble from this unfamiliar vantage point in the sky, and we head back over the airstrip and across the Hambleton Hills. I can see the racing-stables below and the bright fields of oilseed rape chequering the hilltops yellow and green. Sheep are dots of grey-white, like dandruff, scattered across a field. There's the White Horse, and the Drovers' Road wending its way along the escarpment. There are the great slabs of dark green coniferous plantations with their corners and straight lines, familiar from the map and the satellite images. I can see Gormire Lake, a flash of white in the middle of the woods under the cliffs. In the distance the moors are dim lines on the horizon that blend into the grey of the sky – the boundaries between land and air have become indistinct. Above my head through the plastic cover is a marbled cloud-scape of grey and white which has no limits.

There's a sharp rattle of cable on metal and we've lost the aerotow. An extraordinary sensation of gentle calmness settles: an infinite softness. The weight of this metal craft rests on the warmed exhalation of the land – the earth's sigh. It is hard to imagine that this could be dangerous. Alex is looking round for clouds, but I'm looking at this astonishing Lilliputian world into which I've been flung, where cars and farmhouses look like toys. There is Kilburn, and Oldstead. I can see the ribbon of tarmac drive across the field to Fred and Tom Banks' farm; the cottages strung along the villages, and the isolated roof of Peter and Audrey Houlston's farm. The landscape I have experienced all my life and have spent the last few years exploring is strangely distant. No longer full of voices, sounds, smells, movement and shape, the land is reduced to an aetiolated abstraction. The contours I've strained calf muscles walking up and down have been flattened, and the wooded cliffs and valleys have become sinuous shadows twisting across the patterned land. Byland Abbey is the most poignant sight: the ruins, so commanding from ground level, look impossibly fragile from the air, like fragments of crumpled, dusty lace.

When I ask Alex why she glides in her spare time – she's

doing a PhD in Early Modern Drama at York University – she says it's because a mobile phone can't reach you three thousand feet up in the sky. Turning the mobile off might be an easier way to achieve the same end, I think. She tries another tack: 'Because it's a miracle every time that something heavier than air can go up in the sky. And then it's a game. It's like playing chess with the sky. It doesn't feel dangerous any more – at least it feels a lot less dangerous than the roads around here.' With a newly acquired wariness for the impatience of drivers on the twisting roads of North Yorkshire, I see exactly what she means.

'Last February I spent an hour getting up over the clouds and when I finally made it, I was at eleven thousand feet and I watched the sunset from there. It was a beautiful place to be and very peaceful. Up there, you have a fantastic sensation that you can go anywhere you want to.'

I could understand, but it struck me as quite a way to go to find sanctuary – are long journeys always necessary to find refuge, places of peace? Wordsworth enjoyed the sunset from the Hambleton Hills with the solidity of land under his strong walker's legs. That grounding, the contact between body and land, is too satisfying for me (dust to dust, ashes to ashes); this airy floating amongst clouds, pleasurable though it is, could never be more than a novelty.

'We're falling fast,' interjects Alex. 'Do you see?' No, I hadn't seen. Nor had I remembered to look for clouds or gliders.

'Falling fast?' I'm alarmed.

'We can't find lift,' responds Alex calmly, and in the next breath, 'Do you want to take the controls?'

After some insistence from Alex, I cautiously move the stick forward and the nose of the plane dips, and when I move it back the nose rises: delicate little movements to which the plane responds like the finest thoroughbred.

By now, the information has percolated through to even my overloaded brain that the rooftops are closer and we can pick out the parked cars glinting in the sunshine. At this proximity, the land looks strangely still except for an occasional car moving along a lane. We have glided smoothly down to a height only a few hundred feet above the tips of the trees. We have wheeled round to the east to see the Plot and I am still searching for a glimpse of the Chapel as we come in to land; at this altitude, we gain speed and we're racing across the dark green pine trees. Suddenly, the rust-red pantiles of the roof flash into sight, folded into a narrow crack in the trees; there's a splash of green lawn, a line of the wall and then it has all disappeared again, swallowed by the forest.

As we come in to land, the gentleness gives way to brutal speed as we hurtle across the airstrip; then we bump abruptly into the ground, and the plane is rattling like a washing machine on a spin cycle. I can see the edge of the cliff at the end of the airstrip. I shut my eyes, my sweaty hands clutching at the seat belt. Finally, the glider bumps and lurches to a standstill.

I climb out, feeling as if every part of my body has been disconnected. I'm not sure I can straighten my legs, let alone that they will carry my weight. But even in this discombobulated state, I'm exhilarated. I want to go up again: I want to spend more time wrapped up in the sky, wandering from cloud to cloud, with the salty moorland breezes all around me and the land receding into a blur.

In the hours – and indeed, days – that follow, the shakiness and the exhilaration persist. My knees and ankles have lost solidity, but by way of compensation my mind and soul seem to have expanded to contain those scapes of cloud, sky and land. The children are tugging at my sleeves, wanting lunch, so we leave the gliding club and walk through Garbutt Wood to

Gormire Lake for a picnic. The lake, which was a flash of silver from two and half thousand feet up in the sky a couple of hours before, is now an inky, deep stillness across whose surface the insects skitter. In the shallows where the sunlight reaches the golden sand, and tickles the undersides of leaves on overhanging branches, the midges congregate and nibble our hands, feet and necks. The morning's flight has left me with a heightened sense of the blood, muscles and bone joints, their fragility and how the body that hurtled through the air now sits steady on the land.

'Daddy, why is the sky upside-down?' calls a child's voice as he comes down the path to a lake cupped to mirror the clouds I have been flying in.

Jews mark the death of a loved one with the prayer of Kaddish. If it is a child or spouse who has died, the prayer must be said daily for thirty days, but for a parent it has to be every day for eleven months and on every anniversary of the death. It recognizes the centrality of the relationship with the parent: they gave us our life and they shape in us the most basic and central of all human experiences, the capacity to love and be loved. But the Kaddish does not dwell on the individual and their life achievements; its central theme is not about the parent at all but about God. It is a prayer of praise.

The idea of writing a book that was in part about my father arrived in those early days immediately after his death. It was part of the disorientating and exhausting weeks of trying to mourn a father who had been so hard to love, so hard in his loving. But this book of prayer to a landscape that he loved – and that I have come to love again – has been an exhilarating process of knowing him, and knowing again a land reframed as somewhere I can belong.

We live in times when relationship and identity are subjected to increasingly anxious interrogation, but we ignore an equally urgent need to know our place, know where home is and where we belong. This casts questions about the nature of our relationships and identity – who we are and who we belong to – adrift, without an anchoring in a place. The Conservative philosopher Roger Scruton describes what my father believed, that 'belonging is a relationship in history, a relationship which binds both present and absent generations'. But we need to be very careful about our understandings of home at a time when belonging has become one of the most fissile of political issues; if belonging is stripped down to a passport-like starkness as simply the place of your birth, then billions across the globe, the inhabitants of most streets in Britain, are consigned to a limbo of non-belonging. What I now understand is that my father's sense of place was a deliberate (and in some ways quixotic) choice, it was never an inheritance. 'Belonging' became for him a lifelong project, and those 'relationships in history' are not pre-ordained but there to be crafted and recrafted in each generation.

We live on an island so crowded with ghosts that we've become adept at managing their stories, tidying some of them into visitor attractions and 'energetically forgetting' the rest. We put ourselves into a timeless present, with a past designed only to entertain, and with little investment in the future; it makes our present very lonely. What happens to the stories of place that have sustained lives, identities and relationships over generations? Can such stories cling to the fast-changing urban environment where buildings are knocked down and rise up again in cycles outside our knowledge or control? Where will these mobile, urban populations call home? Will they experience its loss as liberation or disorientation – or neither, finding new paths to their own plots?

We don't need to own plots but they need to be our own: each of us needs our acre; we need access – not just physical but also imaginative and emotional – to a land we can honour. An honouring that involves knowledge, observation and familiarity, so that the gnarled bush, the bumpy track, the dip of the hill, the curve of the hedge are relatives; an honouring that listens to the stories that saturate every English acre, so that we walk as comfortably with its ghosts as we would like our descendants to walk with ours.

What I've realized is that belonging is first of all about commitment rather than possession. It is about how one pays attention. What I have learned on the Plot in North Yorkshire has been what a Buddhist might call a practice, a set of habits: the skills of listening, observing, enjoying the many narratives of place and how they collide, compete, echo and repeat each other. My story of the Plot began in my childhood, but the practice of belonging can travel and I use it now on the canals of east London as I urge the kids on, pedalling past the Victorian reservoirs, pylons and vast warehouses. And I use it on the hollow ways over the last fragment of chalk downs in west Berkshire. One can belong in many places. Belonging is where we nurture our capacity for awareness of the myriad histories that constitute a place, and from these rich materials draw inspiration to shape our sense of self and community. These are the insights that helped inspire my father's Chapel as his manifesto in stone, wood and glass half a century ago.

He may be dead, but it's not too late. We have finally found common ground.

An acre's timeline

10000 BCE	Ice Age comes to an end
7000–4000 BCE	Gradual clearing of some patches of forest for agriculture
c. 4000 BCE	A pathway comes into use along the Hambleton Hills
c. 3500 BCE	Kepwick Barrow is constructed
2500–1500 BCE	Bronze Age burial mound on the Plot
c. 1000 BCE	Cleave Dyke
71 CE	Roman occupation of Yorkshire. They use the Hambleton pathway and it becomes known as Hambleton Street
1069–70	William the Conqueror gets lost on the Yorkshire moors as he follows Hambleton Street; it acquires the name Via Regalis in his memory
c. 1100	Hood Castle on Hood Hill is built
1137	The monks first arrive in the area at Hood on a piece of land donated by the de Mowbray family. As part of subsequent donations the Plot is transferred to the Byland Cistercians
1100s	Normans develop the use of parts of the North York moors for hunting
c. 1195	The monks complete the construction of their monastery at Byland; its abbey is the biggest Cistercian monastery church of its time

1200s	Droving begins along Hambleton Street and the Cistercians expand sheep-farming across the moors
1322	The Battle of Byland between Robert the Bruce and Edward II
1536	The dissolution of Byland Abbey; the monastery's former granges continue as independent farms
1689	Sir Charles Duncombe purchases Helmsley Castle and its estate
1750s	Thomas Duncombe has the Rievaulx Terrace constructed
1760s	Laurence Sterne is living at Shandy Hall, Coxwold; he regularly takes walks to Byland
1700s	The toll at Shaw's Gate brings an end to the drovers' trade across the acre. The industrialization of wool-spinning and weaving gathers pace in West Yorkshire
1802	The Benedictine monks establish a monastery at Ampleforth
1802	William and Dorothy Wordsworth walk over the Hambleton Hills; a few months later they return with Mary, William's new wife
1837	Construction of Mount Snever Observatory, Oldstead
1850s	William Greenwell is hard at work barrow-digging in North Yorkshire
1853	The railway station is opened at Coxwold
1857	The construction of the White Horse of Kilburn
1876	Robert Thompson is born
1880s	Grouse-shooting is by now a major sport on the North York moors

1890s	The last resident, Elisabeth Bulmer, abandons Scotch Corner farm
1891	Canon John Atkinson's *Forty Years in a Moorland Parish* is published
1914–18	There is widespread felling of woodland along the Hambleton Hills to meet the demands of the First World War
1919	The Forestry Commission is set up
1927	My father, John Bunting, is born in Whetstone, Friern Barnet, north London
1934	The founding of the Yorkshire Gliding Club at Sutton Bank
1941	Fourteen-year-old John Bunting walks to Kilburn and meets the carpenter Robert Thompson
1944 6	June D-Day; John Bunting finds Scotch Corner
1954–8	Forestry Commission ploughs and plants coniferous forest on the moorland around the Plot
1957	John Bunting signs a fifty-year lease on Scotch Corner and builds his war memorial chapel
1964	Coxwold railway station closes
1969	The Cleveland Way is opened
1987	Bunting carves oak doors for the Chapel to mark its thirtieth anniversary
1995	The plantation along the track is clear-felled and replanted
2002	Bunting dies, and in 2003 his ashes are scattered at the Chapel and a memorial stone is laid, as requested, on the threshold

Bibliography

General

Adams, W. M., *Future Nature: A Vision for Conservation*, London: Earthscan, 2003

Ascherson, Neal, *Stone Voices*, London: Granta, 2002

Atkinson, John C.: *Forty Years in a Moorland Parish*, London: Macmillan, 1891

Banks, F. J., *Oldstead: The History of a Small Rural Community*, Oldstead: Oldstead Millennium Committee, 2000

——*The Monastic Waterworks of Byland and Newburgh*, private paper, n.d.

——*Family and Farming 1820–1970*, private paper, n.d.

——*Kilburn in the Nineteenth Century*, private paper, n.d.

——*Old Ridge and Furrow: A Ploughman's Comments*, private paper, n.d.

Barnett, Anthony, and Roger Scruton, eds., *Town and Country*, London: Jonathan Cape, 1998

Basso, Keith, *Wisdom Sits in Places: Landscape and Language Among the Western Apache*, Albuquerque, NM: University of New Mexico Press, 1996

Burchardt, Jeremy, *Paradise Lost: Rural Idyll and Social Change Since 1800*, London: I. B. Tauris, 2002

Chatwin, Bruce, *The Songlines*, London: Jonathan Cape, 1987

Cowley, Jason, ed., *Granta 102: The New Nature Writing*, 2008

Hoskins, W. G., *The Making of the English Landscape*, London: Hodder & Stoughton, 1955

Howkins, Alun, *The Death of Rural England: A Social History of the English Countryside Since 1900*, London: Routledge, 2003

Jamie, Kathleen, *Findings*, London: Sort of Books, 2005

——'Airds Moss', in *Granta 90: Country Life*, 2005

Mabey, Richard, *Nature Cure*, London: Chatto & Windus, 2005

——*Flora Britannica*, London: Sinclair-Stevenson, 1996

Matless, David, *Landscape and Englishness*, London: Reaktion Books, 1998

Macfarlane, Robert, *The Wild Places*, London: Granta, 2007

McDonnell, J., ed., *A History of Helmsley, Rievaulx and District*, York: Stonegate Press, 1963

Moore, N. W., *The Bird of Time: The Science and Politics of Conservation*, Cambridge: Cambridge University Press, 1987

Naipaul, V. S., *The Enigma of Arrival*, London: Viking, 1987

Newby, Howard, *Green and Pleasant Land? Social Change in Rural England*, London: Hutchinson, 1979

Nicolson, Adam, *The Sea Room*, London: HarperCollins, 2001

O'Hagan, Andrew, *The End of British Farming*, London: Profile Books, 2001

Pretty, Jules, *The Earth Only Endures*, London: Earthscan, 2007

Rackham, Oliver, *The History of the Countryside*, London: J. M. Dent, 1986

Rowley, Trevor, *The English Landscape in the Twentieth Century*, London: Hambledon & London, 2006

Schama, Simon, *Landscape and Memory*, London: HarperCollins, 1995

Scruton, Roger, *England: An Elegy*, London: Continuum, 2006

Scruton, Roger, and Ken Worpole, 'Landscape and Identity in a Globalised World', openDemocracy.net, June 2002

Solnit, Rebecca, *Wanderlust: A History of Walking*, London: Verso, 2001

Spratt, D. A., and B. J. Harrison, eds., *North York Moors: Landscape Heritage*, Newton Abbot, Devon: David & Charles, 1989

Warner, Marina, 'What Are Memory Maps?', www.vam.ac.uk/
activ_events/adult_resources/memory_maps/what/index.html

Worpole, Ken, and Jason Orton, *350 miles: An Essex Journey*, Chelms-
ford, Essex: Essex Development & Regeneration Agency,
2005

Williams, Raymond, *The Country and the City*, Oxford: Oxford
University Press, 1973

Wright, Patrick, 'Deep and True?: Reflections on the Cultural Life of
the English Landscape', lecture broadcast on BBC Radio 3,
2001

Chapter two: Company past and present

Greenwell, William, *British Barrows: A Record of the Examination of
Sepulchral Mounds in Various Parts of England*, Oxford: Oxford
University Press, 1877

Greenwell, William, 'Early Iron Age Burials in Yorkshire',
Archaeologia 60, 251–324

Hayes, R. H., 'The Hambleton Street', *The Transactions of the
Scarborough And District Archaeological Society*, Vol. 1, No. 3,
1960

Marsden, Barry M., *The Early Barrow Diggers*, Park Ridge NJ: Noyes
Press, 1975

Spratt, D. A., *Prehistorica and Roman Archaeology of North East
Yorkshire*, British Archaeological Reports, British series 104,
Oxford: Archaeopress, 1982

——*Yorkshire Archaeological Journal 54* (1982), pp. 32–3

Woodward, Ann, *British Barrows: A Matter of Life and Death*, Stroud,
Glos.: History Press, 2000

Chapter three: Passing through

Bonser, K. J., *The Drovers: Who They Were and How They Went*, London:
Macmillan, 1970

Hayes, Raymond H., *Old Roads and Pannierways in North East Yorkshire*, Helmsley, N. Yorks: North York Moors National Park, 1988

Young, Arthur, *A Six Months' Tour through the North of England*, 1771

Chapter four: A limited kind of company

Backshall, J., Manley, J., and M. Rebane, eds., *The Upland Management Handbook*, Peterborough: English Nature, 2001

British Wool Marketing Board (www.britishwool.org.uk)

British Wool Marketing Board, *Wool in History*, Wakefield, W. Yorks: E. P. Publishing, 1972

Department for Environment, Food & Rural Affairs, *June Agricultural Census 1990–2006*, www.defra.gov.uk/esg/work_htm/publications/cs/farmstats_web

EBLEX (www.eblex.org.uk/MarketPrices)

English Nature, *Sustainable Grazing in the English Uplands*, Sheffield: English Nature, 2004

Farmers Weekly (www.fwi.co.uk/Prices)

Franklin, Sarah, *Dolly Mixtures: The Remaking of Genealogy*, Durham, NC: Duke University Press, 2007

Holderness, B. A., *British Agriculture Since 1945*, Manchester: Manchester University Press, 1985

Institute for European Environmental Policy, *An Assessment of the Impacts of Hill Farming in England*, London: Department for Environment, Food and Rural Affairs, 2004

Kirby, D. K., *An Ecological Economic Approach to Upland Heather Moorland Management*, York: University of York, 2000

Lipson, E., *A Short History of Wool and its Manufacture – Mainly in England*, London: Heinemann, 1953

McVittie, A., Moran, D., Smyth, K., and C. Hall, *Measuring Public Preferences for the Uplands: Final Report to the Centre for the Uplands*, Lancaster: Centre for the Uplands, February 2005

North York Moors National Park Education Service, 'A Profile of the North York Moors National Park: Farming in the North York Moors National Park', *Voice of the Moors*, Winter–Spring 2006

Patterson, G., *The Story of Wool*, London: Scholastic, 1987

Pickering, R., and M. Graham, summarizers, 'The Economics of Hill Sheep Farming on the North York Moors 1995–2000', Helmsley, N. Yorks: North York Moors National Park, 2005

Ryder, M. L., *Sheep and Man*, London: Duckworth, 1983

Chapter six: The view

Bender, Barbara, ed., *Landscape: Politics and Perspectives*, Oxford: Berg, 1993

Daniels, Stephen, and Denis Cosgrove, eds., *The Iconography of Landscape: Essays on the Symbolic Representation, Design and Use of Past Environments*, Cambridge: Cambridge University Press, 1992

Darby, Wendy Joy, *Landscape and Identity*, Oxford: Berg, 2000

Clark, Colette, ed., *Home at Grasmere: Extracts from the Journal of Dorothy Wordsworth (Written Between 1800 and 1803) and from the Poems of William Wordsworth*, London: Pelican, 1960

National Trust, *The Rievaulx Terrace: North Yorkshire*, London: National Trust, 1978

Shoard, Marion, *A Right to Roam*, Oxford: Oxford University Press, 1999

Taylor, Harvey, *A Claim on the Countryside: A History of the British Outdoor Movement*, Keele, Staffs: Keele University Press, 1997

Woodward, Christopher, *In Ruins*, London: Vintage, 2002

Urry, John, *The Tourist Gaze*, London: SAGE, 2002

Chapter seven: Medieval tales

Bates, D., *William the Conqueror*, Mount Pleasant, SC: Arcadia Publishing, 2001

Bell, Graham, *Robert the Bruce's Forgotten Victory: The Battle of Byland 1322*, Stroud, Glos.: History Press, 2005

McNamee, C., *The Wars of the Bruces: Scotland, England and Ireland*, Edinburgh: Tuckwell Press, 1997

Rex, P., *The English Resistance: The Underground War Against the Normans*, Stroud, Glos.: History Press, 2006

Young, A., and M. Stead, *In the Footsteps of Robert Bruce*, Stroud, Glos.: Sutton Publishing, 1999

www.siol-nan-gaidheal.com/byland.htm, 2007

Chapter eight: A land fit for heroes

Bunting, John, *Scullion II: Notes on Hugh Dormer's Diaries*, private publication, n.d.

Dormer, Hugh, *War Diary*, London: Jonathan Cape, 1947

Hynes, Samuel, *A War Imagined: First World War and English Culture*, London: Bodley Head, 1990

Wright, Patrick, *On Living in an Old Country*, London: Verso, 1985

——*The Village That Died for England*, London: Jonathan Cape, 1995

Chapter nine: A weapon of mass destruction

English Nature, *Duncombe Park National Nature Reserve*, http://www.englishnature.org.uk/about/teams/team_photo/DuncombePark.pdf, 2003

Forestry Commission, *A New Focus for England's Woodlands*, http://www.forestry.gov.uk/newsrele.nsf/AllByUNID/6DF4D83A70427A98802566C90044314C (1998)

——*Forestry Statistics 2001*, http://www.forestry.gov.uk/statistics

——*Public Opinion of Forestry Survey: Forestry Facts and Figures*, http://www.forestry.gov.uk/forestry/infd-5zyl9w, 2006

——Forestry Commission, *New Forests for the 21st Century*, 1992

Gledhill, T. D., *A Woodland History of North Yorkshire: A Multi-*

disciplinary Study of Post-glacial Woodland History, Sheffield: University of Sheffield, 1994

Lasdun, Susan, *The English Park: Royal Private and Public*, London: André Deutsch, 1991

MacLean, M., *Farming and Forestry on the Western Front 1915–1919*, Ipswich: Old Pond Publishing, 2004

Martin, S., *Leisure Landscapes*, Edinburgh: Forestry Commission, 2007, http://www.forestresearch.gov.uk/fr/INFD-6XCHWF

North York Moors National Park Authority, *Measuring Change: In the North York Moors National Park*, Helmsley: North York Moors National Park, 1998

Peterken, G. F., 'Native Woodland Development in the North York Moors and Howardian Hills', Wetherby, W. Yorks: Forestry Commission, 2002

Rackham, O., *Trees and Woodland in the British Landscape*, London: Orion Publishing, 1995

Rogers, P., 'The Environmental Costs of War', lecture presented at Lancaster University, 13/07/2002, http://www.preparing forpeace.org/rogers_the_environmental_costs_of_war.htm

Stebbing, E. P., *British Forestry: Its Present Position and Outlook After the War*, London: John Murray, 1916

Willis, Kenneth G., et al, 'The Social and Environmental Benefits of Forests in Great Britain', Edinburgh: Forestry Commission 2003, http://www.forestry.gov.uk

Chapter ten: A killing game

Griffin E., *Blood Sport: Hunting in Britain Since 1066*, London: Yale University Press, 2007

PACEC, *The Economic and Environmental Impact of Sporting Shooting*, 2006, http://www.shootingfacts.co.uk/

Ruffer, Jonathan, *The Big Shots: Edwardian Shooting Parties*, Richmond, Surrey: Debrett's Peerage, 1984

Chapter eleven: Sanctuary

Aelred of Rievaulx, *Spiritual Friendship*, Trappist, KY: Cistercian
    Publications, 1977

Aelred of Rievaulx, *Treatises & The Pastoral Prayer*, Trappist, KY:
    Cistercian Publications, 1961

Beckett, L., *Rievaulx, Fountains, Byland and Jervaulx: The Cistercian
    Abbeys of North Yorkshire*, London: Canterbury Press, 1998

Bunting, John, *Sculptor's Log*, private publication, n.d.

——*Tale of a Tea King*, private publication, n.d.

Burton, J., *The Monastic Order in Yorkshire 1069–1215*, Cambridge:
    Cambridge University Press, 1999

——ed., *The Cartulary of Byland Abbey*, Durham: Surtees Society,
    2004

——*The Foundation History of the Abbeys of Byland and Jervaulx*, York:
    Borthwick Institute Publications, 2006

Carus-Wilson, E. M., 'An Industrial Revolution of the Thirteenth
    Century', *Economic History Review*, 1941

Coppack, Glyn, *The White Monks: The Cistercians in Britain 1128–1540*,
    Stroud, Glos.: History Press, 1998

Daniel, Walter, *Life of Aelred of Rievaulx*, Nashville, TN: Thomas
    Nelson & Sons, 1950

Fergusson, Peter, *Rievaulx Abbey: Community, Architecture and Memory*,
    London: Yale University Press, 1999

Frayling, Christopher, *Strange Landscape: A Journey Through the Middle
    Ages*, London: Penguin, 1995

Harrison, S. A., *Byland Abbey: North Yorkshire*, London: English
    Heritage, 1992

Hill, B. D., *English Cistercian Monasteries and Their Patrons in the 12th
    Century*, Urbana, IL: University of Illinois Press, 1968

Knowles, D., *The Monastic Order in England: A History of its Development
    from the Times of St Dunstan to the Fourth Lateran Council
    940–1216*, Cambridge: Cambridge University Press, 1940

Le Goff, Jacques, *Medieval World: A History of European Society*, London: Parkgate, 1990

Little, Lester K., *Religious Poverty and the Profit Economy in Medieval Europe*, Ithaca, NY: Cornell University Press, 1983

Moore, R. I., *The Formation of a Persecuting Society*, Oxford: Blackwell, 1990

Page, William, ed., *A History of the County of York*, Vol. 3, Woodbridge, Suffolk: Boydell & Brewer, 1974, 'Houses of Benedictine Nuns: Priory of Arden', pp. 112–16

Peers, C., *Rievaulx Abbey*, London: English Heritage, 1986

Robinson, D., and J. Burton, *The Cistercian Abbeys of Britain: Far from the Concourse of Men*, London: Batsford/English Heritage, 1998

Simpson, J., 'Ghosts in Medieval Yorkshire', *Ghosts & Scholars 27*, October 1998

Squire, Aelred, *Aelred of Rievaulx: A Study*, London: SPCK, 1981

Tobin, Stephen, *The Cistercians*, London: Herbert Press, 1995

Waites, B., *Monasteries and Landscape in North East England: The Medieval Colonization of the North York Moors*, Oakham, Leics: Multum in Parvo Press, 1997

www.cistercians.shef.ac.uk

Chapter twelve: A manifesto in stone

Breakell, Bill, *Causeways of the North York Moors*, Hebden Bridge, W. Yorks: Footsteps Books, 1982

Bunting, John, *Sculptor's Critics*, private publication, 1951–5

MacCarthy, Fiona, *Eric Gill*, London: Faber & Faber, 1989

Orwell, George, *Coming Up for Air*, London: Victor Gollancz, 1939

Sharpe, Eric, untitled leaflet of 1930, AHAG AH 2904/93, in Carruthers, Annette, and Mary Greensted, *Good Citizen's Furniture: The Arts and Crafts Collection at Cheltenham*, Farnham, Surrey: Lund Humphries, 1994

Voillaume, R., *Seeds of the Desert: The Legacy of Charles de Foucauld*, London: Burns & Oates, 1955

Williams-Ellis, Clough, *Britain and the Beast*, London: J. M. Dent,1937

Wright, Patrick, *On Living in an Old Country*, London: Verso, 1985

Chapter thirteen: 'Pity the land'

Cumulus Consultants Ltd, 'Assessment of the Impact of CAP Reform and Other Key Policies on Upland Farms', report for the Department for the Environment, Food and Rural Affairs, 2005

Harvey, Graham, *The Killing of the Countryside*, London: Vintage, 1998

Holden, Edith, *The Country Diary of an Edwardian Lady*, London: Michael Joseph, 1977

Lewis, M. R., 'Study of North York Moors Economics of Hill Sheep', Helmsley, N. Yorks: North York Moors National Park, 2000

Chapter fourteen: Common ground

Grant, A. J., 'Twelve Medieval Ghost Stories', *Yorkshire Archaeological Journal 27* (1924), 363–79

Walters Adams, Gwenfair, *Visions in Late Medieval England*, Boston, MA: Brill Academic, 2007

Acknowledgements

There have been many times in the course of writing this book that it has felt like a difficult walk along a precipitous escarpment. Land that I thought was solid crumbled repeatedly beneath me and I could hear it rattling down the rocky cliff face. As on any long walk, what sustained me was the companionship I found along the way. Some set me off in the right direction, others put me back on track, and others simply came and walked alongside for a while. No book on place would ever be complete without acknowledging that place is always about relationship, and that the generosity, patience and encouragement from many people have been far more important than they can ever know in ensuring that this book has seen the light of day.

It was Barbara Bender, whose own understanding of landscape has been built up over decades of study as an archaeologist and anthropologist, who first encouraged the idea of this book, in her kitchen in the steep-sided valley of Branscombe, Devon. She explained to me what I was trying to think about. She has tolerated my magpie tendency to pilfer academic work. With her promptings the journalistic impatience began to subside and I slowly reached an appreciation for the less literal, less linear narratives that landscape prompts.

At times, as I sat at my desk in Hackney with the rooftops, trees and pigeons for company, I could catch another voice pointing the way. Fred Banks was a man I met only a few times before he fell ill, but he generously filled my arms with books and papers. It was all his own work, the fruit of his decades spent trying to understand the many questions he had about the land he had lived in and worked all his life. He was self-deprecating to a fault, despite his considerable skill as a writer; he was a man of his place who knew his place – in a way which our time has little understanding of – and that knowledge has sat in my study with me. I was very lucky and grateful to have met him. His son, Tom, has also been full of advice and interest in the book.

One of the biggest debts I owe is to John Bell and Mandy Metcalfe. Their wonderful house in Thirsk was a magical place to stay on my research trips, and their hospitality was extraordinarily generous; the enormous kitchen table cluttered with old newspapers, magazines and marmalade jars was always a welcome retreat after rainy walks. John was a fund of good ideas and insights – eighteenth-century maps, Dorothy Wordsworth's journals, land drainage and Gormire Lake myths: all I owe to John's promptings. And he also pointed me towards two artists who have shared my fascination with the Hambleton Hills. I can now lie in bed in London and look at the view from the Hills as seen by Ann Kilvington, and in my sitting room I am confronted by Norman Ackroyd's magnificent portrayal of the Hills in the snow.

Several people in Yorkshire were generous with their time and support. In particular I'm very grateful to Lucy Beckett, who parcelled up precious books to send in the post and offered encouragement at every stage, including a swift and meticulous reading of the manuscript. Likewise Patrick Wildgust provided tea and enthusiasm as well as insights into moths; he braved winter weather on walks up to the Plot to check small details for me. It was he who tracked down

Marion Frith's stunning image of a moth which she kindly let me use.

I much appreciate the help of several staff members of the North York Moors National Park: Michael Graham, Graham Lee and Rona Charles all offered their knowledge generously, checked parts of the manuscript and gave important advice; Caroline Shelly and Andy Wilson also helped at key points. Several farmers in and around Oldstead found time in their busy lives to talk to me, including Colin Furness, Peter and Audrey Houlston, Howard Metcalfe and Peter Turnbull. There was more invaluable advice on a range of issues related to farming, forestry and landscape management from David Sullivan, Ted Sclater, Richard Thomas, David Palmer, George Wynne Darley, Brian Walker, Dr Keith Kirby, Shaun Thomas, Keith Gittens and Patrick James. Shaun Spiers and several other staff of the Campaign for the Protection of Rural England lent books, made suggestions and invited me to several seminars that were helpful in thinking through some issues relating to the future of the countryside. Richard Poole of the British Wool Marketing Board filled in some gaps on wool, and it was Martyn Rawles who introduced me to the Byland ghosts. Thanks to the *Guardian* Picture Editor Roger Tooth for the loan of a decent camera.

Some friends in London were remarkably understanding of the obscure direction home I had taken, and urged me on every step of the way: Adam Curtis (who came up with the book title) and his partner Tessa Hunkin both insisted on detailed updates; Ian Christie kept telling me 'to put everything in' and in so doing uprooted many of my mental enclosures; Brigit Connolly was a wonderful tonic at the school gate in the morning when she reassured me that it was no bad thing to get lost – to each of my bewildered comments, she brought a new insight. And then Caroline Evans and Calum Storrie offered coffee and helped me to see that one could be a *flâneur*, and wander – that getting there was the least important part, that what mattered was what one encountered on the way. Marina Warner, Patrick Wright, Lisa Darnell, John Vidal, Martin Woollacott, Tom and Sue Stuart Smith, Jim Perrin: all had words of encouragement and suggestions of books to read when I was flagging. Cathy Troupp read the manuscript with great empathy and insight.

A number of former pupils offered memories of my father as a teacher, including Jamie Muir, William Dalrymple, John Dewe Mathews and George Trapp. Long conversations with both Antony Gormley and Simon Brett were especially insightful. From Ampleforth, Fr Aidan and Fr Dominic Milroy knew my father for many decades, and offered their thoughts generously. Fiona McCarthy provided advice and helpful articles on Eric Gill's work and how that might have influenced my father. My father's sisters, Paddy Cox and Peggy Barber, have both been kind enough to help, and Betty Bunting, the last surviving child of the Tea King, gave me a warm welcome.

Ken Worpole was the first to suggest that place could be redemptive, and it took me two years to understand how right he was. I'm grateful to Professor Mark Edmonds, whose thoughtful company warmed a cold January walk from Sneck Yate to Sutton Bank, and who found time in a busy schedule of teaching to read and make careful comments on the manuscript.

My editor Sara Holloway has been superb, bringing patience and attentiveness to her task, for which I am hugely grateful; Vicki Harris's copy-editing has been sympathetic. As ever, my agent Natasha Fairweather offered her judicious editorial judgement and unstinting support, and I was equally fortunate in my editor at the *Guardian*, Alan Rusbridger, for his tolerance of my commitment to writing books. The indefatigable Harriet Hunter was a terrific researcher, giving invaluable help on certain sections.

Lastly, I come to the company closer to home. It was my mother Romola who helped me to enjoy the stories that places provide; she talked as we walked, for example describing Napoleon's long trek into Russia in 1812, on a particularly bleak winter moorland walk when I was still very young. She was also my first listener as I began, aged seven, to tell her stories on the daily walks we took across the valley in Oswaldkirk, so that each farmland track took on its own memories of our shared tales. My parents brought us up in an extraordinary place and taught us how to love it; that has proved a rich resource for my life and I'm deeply grateful to them both.

I think some of my siblings have been nonplussed as to why I wanted to understand the Plot, but they left me alone to write my story – they, of course, have their own. My sister Emily accompanied me on some magnificent walks, and my husband Simon and three children shared many more. I dedicate this book to my dearest children, Eleanor, Luke and Matthias, all of whom understand so much about plots already. It has been the greatest gift to nurture their appetite for adventure, place and story. And my thanks to Simon, whose appreciation of place is where we began, where there is no need for any explanation and where we have continued to find our deepest connection.

Index